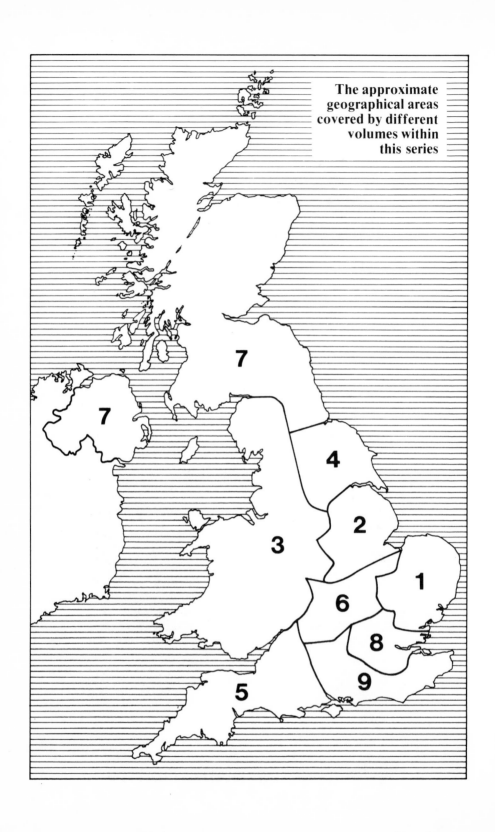

The approximate
geographical areas
covered by different
volumes within
this series

ACTION STATIONS

3. Military airfields of Wales and the North-West

David J. Smith

PSL **Patrick Stephens, Cambridge**

Title page *Pupils and Spitfire at Rednal, circa 1942 (IWM).*

First published August 1981
Reprinted March 1984

British Library Cataloguing in Publication Data

Action stations
   3: Military airfields of Wales and the North-west.
   1. World War, 1939-1945—Aerial operations,
British
   2. Air bases—England—History
   3. Air bases—Wales—History
   I. Smith, David, *b. 1931*
940.54'43'427

ISBN 0-85059-485-5

Photoset in 9 pt and 10 on 11 pt Times by Manuset Limited, Baldock, Herts. Printed in Great Britain on 100 gsm Fineblade coated cartridge, and bound, by The Garden City Press, Letchworth, Herts, for the publishers Patrick Stephens Limited, Bar Hill, Cambridge, CB3 8EL, England.

Contents

Introduction   5

Glossary   7

Origins   9

Wales and the North-West at war   12

Airfield architecture   17

Flying control and airfield aids   26

Map of the airfields
for Wales and the North-West   30

The airfields   32

Index of units referred to in the text   215

Introduction

Aeroplanes were never common in the skies of Wales and North-West England until the late 1930s but things altered as soon as the war started. Shropshire rapidly rivalled East Anglia in the density of its airfields but in the other counties they were generally sited much farther apart, notable exceptions being the clusters around Carlisle and certain parts of Lancashire and South-West Wales.

The area covered by this book is generally dismissed as merely a rearward training zone but there was a fair amount of operational flying nevertheless. Fighter squadrons found a reduced level of action compared with the South-East but it was often far from the rest they had expected when they were withdrawn here. The Wellington OTUs at Lichfield and Pershore joined their counterparts in the South Midlands to swell the numbers for the first Thousand-Bomber Raid on Cologne in May 1942. They flew other bombing operations too, plus many leaflet-dropping sorties over enemy occupied territory.

Training units were based here in force and it is often difficult to follow the 'musical chairs' situation caused by changes of policy to meet the shifting demands of the war. The target-towing flights were 'Cinderella' units doing a valuable job but often moved from one airfield to another as the need arose. Units had a quota of trained pupils expected from them within a specified time and the instructors moved heaven and earth to meet it. The result was round-the-clock flying in all weathers and the accident rate was high.

There remains tangible evidence of almost all the airfields described, apart from one or two which have vanished under houses and some of the bases in South-West Wales which have been cleared as the derelict buildings were considered an eyesore. This is, of course, a matter of opinion and if one knows an airfield's history one tends to see things in a different light.

Please always ask before investigating a disused airfield as it is bound to be owned by someone. The only time you are likely to be refused permission is if some particularly disease-prone livestock like chickens or pigs are reared on the airfield. Some sites are used for storage, often of high value goods, so if you want to take a closer look write for permission first. In these security-conscious days it is unwise to show too much interest in military airfields which are still active and the same applies to major airports and contractors' airfields.

Opposite *The last Wellington to be delivered, T 10 RP590, flies over the Squires Gate factory on October 25 1945* (Charles E. Brown).

Much of the material within these pages comes from official documents held by the Public Record Office. I am grateful also for the help of the RAF and FAA Museums and the MoD (Air Historical Branch). I have talked to many ex-aircrew and their accounts breathe life into the often dull facts in the official records.

I am particularly indebted to Aldon P. Ferguson whose own books on the histories of Sealand, Shawbury and Woodvale are definitive, for his excellent plans of representative airfields. He also generously put his extensive archives at my disposal. John Huggon provided invaluable assistance with airfields in his native Cumbria. Andrew Ayers of the Airfield Research Group did the same with South Wales and helped with photographs where my own were lacking.

To Alec S.C. Lumsden MMPA goes the credit for much of the photographic processing and the tracking down of relevant photos.

Thanks go to many others who helped in various ways but particularly: Barry Abraham, Chris Ashworth, Roy Bonser, Joe Collier, Neville Doyle, Paul Francis, Walter Gibbs, Mike Hollick, Harry Holmes, Brian Martin, David Stansfield, Mike Stimson and Frank Wright.

Having no personal memories of wartime airfields when they were active, I have picked the brains and log books of John Teasdale of Stafford, Doug Darroch of Birkenhead and, of course, Mike Bowyer.

I hope that exploring these sites will give you as much enjoyment in discovering the past as I have experienced in researching this book.

David J. Smith
Bebington,
August 1980.

Glossary

AA Anti-Aircraft.
AACS Air & Airways Communications Service.
AACU Anti-Aircraft Co-operation Unit.
AAP Aircraft Acceptance Park.
AAU Aircraft Assembly Unit.
ACHU Aircrew Holding Unit.
AEF Air Experience Flight.
AFS Advanced Flying School.
AFSC Air Force Service Command (USAAF).
AFEE Airborne Forces Experimental Establishment.
AGS Air Gunnery School.
AI Airborne Interception (radar).
AMWD Air Ministry Works Department.
ANS Air Navigation School.
AONS Air Observer Navigation School.
AOS Air Observer School.
APC Armament Practice Camp.
ARDU Aircraft Receipt & Dispatch Unit.
ASR Air/Sea Rescue.
ASU Aircraft Storage Unit.
ASV Air-to-Surface Vessel (radar).
ATA Air Transport Auxiliary.
ATS Armament Training Station.
Baedecker raid German reprisal raid delivered upon historic city.
BAT Flight Blind Approach Training Flight.
BFTS Basic Flying Training School.
BG Bomb Group (USAAF).
B & GS Bombing & Gunnery School.
CAACU Civilian Anti-Aircraft Co-operation Unit.
CATCS Central Air Traffic Control School.
CCDU Coastal Command Development Unit.
CCGP Coastal Command Group Pool.
CFS Central Flying School.

CLE Central Landing Establishment.
CNCS Central Navigation and Control School
CO Commanding Officer.
COT Flight Czech Operational Training Flight.
CPF Coastal Patrol Flight.
Drem lighting System of outer circle lights leading into flare-path installed at many wartime airfields.
EATS Empire Air Training Scheme.
EFTS Elementary Flying Training School.
E & RFTS Elementary & Reserve Flying Training School.
FIS Flying Instructors' School.
FP Ferry Pool.
FPP Ferry Pilots' Pool.
FPU Flying Practice Unit.
FRU Fleet Requirements Unit.
FTS Flying Training School.
FTU Ferry Training Unit.
FU Ferry Unit.
GCA Ground Controlled Approach.
HCU Heavy Conversion Unit.
HGCU Heavy Glider Conversion Unit.
Highball Bouncing bomb designed to fit the Mosquito.
IFF Identification Friend or Foe.
ITW Initial Training Wing.
MAP Ministry of Aircraft Production.
MATS Military Air Transport Service.
MRU Mountain Rescue Unit.
MSFU Merchant Ship Fighter Unit.
MTCA Ministry of Transport & Civil Aviation.
MU Maintenance Unit.
Nickel Leaflet-dropping operation.
OCTU Officer Cadet Training Unit.
OADU Overseas Aircraft Dispatch Unit.
(O) AFU (Observers) Advanced Flying Unit.

OAPU   Overseas Aircraft Preparation Unit.

OTU   Operational Training Unit.

(P) AFU   (Pilots) Advanced Flying Unit.

PSP   Pierced Steel Planking (runway).

PTS   Parachute Training School.

RAE   Royal Aircraft Establishment.

Ramrod   Bomber raid escorted by fighters and aimed at destruction of a specific target in daylight.

RAT Flight   Radio Aids Training Flight.

RDF   Radio Direction Finding.

RFS   Reserve Flying School.

Rhubarb   Low-level strike operation mounted in cloudy conditions against enemy fringe targets in occupied countries.

RLG   Relief Landing Ground.

RNAS   Royal Naval Air Station.

ROC   Royal Observer Corps.

RRE   Royal Radar Establishment.

r/t   Radio telephone.

SAC   Strategic Air Command.

SAN   School of Air Navigation.

Scatter Scheme   Temporary withdrawal of operational squadrons to rearward bases on outbreak of war.

SFTS   Service Flying Training School.

SLG   Satellite Landing Ground.

SMT   Square Mesh Track.

SPTU   Staff Pilot Training Unit.

RAFVR   Royal Air Force Volunteer Reserve.

TDS   Training Depot Station.

TEU   Tactical Exercise Unit.

TFU   Telecommunications Flying Unit.

THUM Flight   Temperature & Humidity Flight.

TRE   Telecommunications Research Establishment.

TSCU   Transport Support Conversion Unit.

UAS   University Air Squadron.

USAAF   United States Army Air Force (designated thus from June 20 1941, although the term Army Air Corps remained in common use long after that date).

USAF   Post-war formation from the USAAF, the United States Air Force.

Origins

Aviation in North-West England dates back to the 18th century when the early balloonists made several demonstration flights before an incredulous population. One of the earliest was in 1785, from a site in Manchester which is still known as Balloon Street. In 1795 an ascent was made from Chester with a landing near what was to become Burtonwood Airfield well over a century later. The early 19th century saw ballooning become much more common but Wales and Cumbria remained virtually untouched by the phenomenon.

It was some six years after the Wright brothers made the first sustained powered flight in 1903 that aeroplanes came to the north. The Air Pageant held at Blackpool in October 1909 and sponsored by the *Daily Mail* attracted many of the famous airmen of the day. Several flying records were broken by the French pilots who dominated European aviation at that time. A.V. Roe in his triplane was unsuccessful and who would have thought that he would one day found one of Britain's most important aircraft companies? During the meeting a Farman biplane made a record sea crossing of 63 miles, landing near Llandudno and thereby becoming the first aeroplane to touch down in North Wales.

Lake Windermere, later to be the scene of Sunderland test-flying, witnessed many such flights by early seaplanes. The first truly successful flight by a seaplane in England took place on November 25 1911 when H.S. Adams took off from the Lake in an Avro-Curtiss biplane. By December 1915 so much expertise had been gained in flying from Windermere that a local firm, the Northern Aircraft Co Ltd, was contracted to train pilots for the Royal Naval Air Service. In May 1916 the latter took over the school entirely.

Although the Great War resulted in a tremendous upsurge in aerial activity in the south of England, it had little effect at first in the north. Aircraft had so little operating range in those days that it would have been pointless to establish airfields so far away from the Channel coast. Avro were now building 504s in Manchester and as these and other aeroplanes became more efficient so they were ordered in greater quantities. National Aircraft Factory 2 was built at Heaton Chapel, Manchester, in 1918 and here almost 400 DH 9s and a few of the twin-engined DH 10s were built. The Armistice caused production to be terminated abruptly and the same fate befell the assembly of American-built HP 0/400s at the Oldham Aircraft Factory. Although 100 incomplete sets of components had been received not one aircraft was delivered from here. Alexandra Park aerodrome had been established as No 15 (Manchester)

Aircraft Acceptance Park to test fly and store the output of the local factories. At Aintree on the outskirts of Liverpool National Aircraft Factory 3 built many Bristol Fighters which were tested from the racecourse.

A name which was to become famous was the English Electric Co formed in 1918 by the amalgamation of four companies from Preston and Bradford which separately had been the main contractors for production of the Felixstowe F 3 flying boat. This had been produced in prototype form by the RNAS Experimental Station at Felixstowe. English Electric went on to build two flying boats of their own design, the Kingston and Ayr, neither of which went into production. They were flown from the Ribble Estuary off Lytham. On the other side of the Ribble there was an Aircraft Acceptance Park at Hesketh Park, Southport, the adjacent beach being used as a landing ground. It was still in use in the Second World War as an aircraft dispatch unit but all the aircraft appear to have arrived by road.

Military aviation in the North-West and Wales during World War 1 comprised four basic types: training, AAPs, coastal patrol and Home Defence against the Zeppelins which by the end of 1916 were ranging far and wide across the country. Landing grounds for the defence squadrons were established in many areas, consisting of little more than large fields cleared of obstructions and supported by small ground parties who could light flares and refuel the aeroplanes which had probably taken off from bases in the eastern counties. Airships were mainly used for coastal patrol and stations were set up at Barrow, Ramsey in the Isle of Man, Llangefni in Anglesey and Pembroke. Some of these airship stations and landing grounds were destined to become airfields in the next war. Scale Hall near Lancaster was unusual in that it appears to have been sited as a refuelling point for aircraft travelling north or south in an area otherwise devoid of airfields.

Until late in the war most pilot training was done in southern England but in 1917 several airfields in the North-West were laid out for Training Squadrons, soon to be renamed Training Depot Stations. Tern Hill, Shawbury, Shotwick and Hooton Park were all founded to house TDSs but only Shotwick survived the defence cuts of the early 1920s, although the others were revived at a later date.

Civilian flying was allowed to resume on May 1 1919 and the first scheduled domestic air service in Britain was started on May 26. Using Avro 504s, it connected Manchester and Blackpool via Southport and ran for nearly five months without a single forced landing, although bad weather occasionally caused cancellations. Pleasure flying suddenly became a growth industry because almost everybody had become familiar with aeroplanes during the recent war but few had had an opportunity to fly in one. Almost every town and resort in England and Wales had a visit by one or more of the many small companies operating surplus Avro 504s. This led directly to Sir Alan Cobham's Air Circuses which did so much in the 1920s and '30s to make the country air-minded.

There were still very few airfields but this was of little consequence as a good flat field or, better still, a stretch of firm sand would suffice. Airports in the sense that passengers and freight would be picked up and set down were unknown in the Provinces, London's Croydon being the only one in operation. Manchester determined to be the first to have an airport and opened one in

1928. Others followed rapidly until most cities had one, few of which could really aspire to the grandiose title of 'airport'.

The expansion of the RAF resulted in several former World War 1 aerodromes being reopened and in the late 1930s construction of new ones at Llandow, Silloth and High Ercall was started. As the war approached more modern types of aircraft appeared in the sky, such as the Harvards of Tern Hill whose characteristic noise soon became the scourge of the local inhabitants. Low flying in those days really was low and it was not uncommon to see a Harvard rounding an oak tree with its pilot returning a wave (or shaken fist) from the ground!

On a Saturday morning in August 1939 Tern Hill was covered with yellow Harvards and newly-delivered Henleys in glistening yellow with burnished metal cowlings. Silver Bombays were lined up outside the MU hangars and the whole impression was one of smartness, or 'bull' as it was known then. A month later the bright colours were gone, replaced with a coat of camouflage paint. The free and easy days were over.

Wales and the North-West at war

At the start of World War 2 there were 27 airfields in the area covered by this book. By 1945 the total stood at 115. Outlying districts which had rarely seen an aircraft flying over before the war now found themselves surrounded by airfields.

The industrial areas on the West Coast, hitherto considered out of range of enemy attack, suddenly became vulnerable when a German bomber force was established in occupied France. A number of new airfields were planned and built in Lancashire, Cheshire and Shropshire to house the fighters of the newly-formed 9 Group which was intended for the defence of the North-West. The Isle of Man, too, acquired a fighter station at Andreas which was ideally placed for squadrons protecting the convoys to and from Liverpool.

Early in 1940 the Luftwaffe began to make daily appearances over the Irish Sea with a Ju 88 reconnaissance flight up St Georges Channel and round the north of Scotland. The AA defences were forbidden to fire on these aircraft so as not to give away their positions. When the ban was lifted my father had the honour of firing the first shell by Merseyside's defences and this fact was verified by his CO. The 4.5-in shell missed, but not by very much! Soon Condors and He 111s roamed the Irish Sea looking for ships to attack, a practice which became almost suicidal later in the war when fighter squadrons could be spared from the Home Counties to protect the Western Approaches.

South Wales, virtually untouched by aviation until now, found itself in the front line of the Battle of the Atlantic. There were only the Sunderlands from Pembroke Dock at first but airfields like Dale and Talbenny were built for Coastal Command anti-submarine aircraft. This coastline and ports such as Milford Haven and Swansea needed fighter protection and Angle and Fairwood Common were built specifically for this purpose and controlled by 10 Group.

Before the war the Air Ministry had planned 12 airfields for use as Aircraft Storage Units, all of them in the safer western half of the country. Silloth and Kirkbride in Cumberland were the most northerly in England, then Burtonwood in Lancashire, Hawarden, Sealand, St Athan and Llandow in Wales and Shawbury, Tern Hill and High Ercall in the Midlands, the remainder being in the South-West Midlands.

A spin-off from this, although they didn't call it that in those days, was the Satellite Landing Ground, one or more of which were allocated to each ASU for the dispersal of precious aircraft. These should be differentiated from satellite stations which were full airfields (although not necessarily possessing concrete runways) supporting a main airfield and usually in the same vicinity. Sites for the SLGs were selected by Sir Alan Cobham who, with his pre-war Air Circuses, was well versed in finding suitable landing grounds. Helped by a small group of RAF pilots on rest tours he located several hundred sites which were shortlisted to 50, all identified by a number. They were not marked on aeronautical charts to preserve secrecy and were heavily camouflaged.

Proper airfields were also well camouflaged but this usually took the form of netting, the planting of trees and painting all the buildings in green and brown 'shadow shading'. Runways, too, were painted to enable them to blend into the landscape, chippings of pinewood being embedded into the tarmac to help the effect and also to reduce tyre wear and skidding. Creosote lines were painted on the grass to simulate hedges and differential mowing of the grass helped break up the outline.

Decoy airfields drew the enemy's attention away from the real thing, the 'K' Sites often being highly elaborate with dummy buildings, time-expired or dummy aircraft and derelict cars in cinder car parks. The night decoys, known as 'Q' Sites, were merely lights on poles in open country simulating a Drem system. After several of our own aircraft came to grief trying to land, red warning lights were placed across the lead-in funnels hooded so that they were only visible from aircraft making an approach. All the decoys were abandoned by the end of 1943 but in the meantime some, like Tatenhill, had ironically been found suitable sites for real airfields.

The North-West was also dotted with training airfields, some of them grass Relief Landing Grounds, others quite sophisticated stations built for operational squadrons but no longer required when the tide of war moved elsewhere. As one progressed from East Anglia into the East Midlands there was a noticeable change in air activity. Gone were the operational types, instead the skies were full of Wellingtons from the bomber OTUs. Further west the Oxfords and Masters of the FTSs in Shropshire dominated the scene but there was a mixture of other types as well, many of them operational as the following reminiscences from a Shropshire ROC member recalls:

'Locally, any day could be described as an air display, with aircraft involved in circuits and bumps, navigational flying, fighter affiliation exercises and so on. There would always be a Beaufighter in the area, and no day would be complete without the Lancaster, Halifax, Spitfire and Hurricane. Often a Mosquito would suddenly appear flying fast and low and Lightnings, Thunderbolts and Mustangs would zoom around. Occasionally we saw less common types like the Barracuda and Whirlwind.'

The West Coast all the way from Barrow around North Wales and down to Milford Haven supported a string of training schools for ground gunners and never a day passed over Morecambe and Cardigan Bays without a Henley, Lysander or, later in the war, a Martinet dragging its sleeve target across the sky.

Royal Navy aircraft were quite rare in the eastern counties but over Lancashire and Cheshire it was a different story. Naval training units in this area produced a constant stream of Swordfish, Fulmars, Avengers and Barracudas. The Admiralty had its own airfield construction programme entirely separate from that of the Air Ministry and to which the Isle of Man owes the basis of its fine airport at Ronaldsway. Royal Naval Air Stations at Rhyl in North Wales and Helsby in Cheshire were planned but never built, however, and there was a certain amount of 'wheeling and dealing' between the RAF and RN. For example, in exchange for accommodation reserved at RNAS Macrihanish for an RAF squadron the Navy was given the use of the former RAF airfield at Stretton. The Navy also sought the use of Jurby, Andreas and Barrow, amongst others, for operational training in 1942 but the RAF refused to give up these stations.

The Americans operated only three airfields exclusively in the North-West and none in Wales, apart from a detachment at Valley. These were Burtonwood and Warton, both providing vital back-up to the bombers in the East, and Atcham which gave operational training to Thunderbolt and, to a lesser extent, Lightning pilots before they were sent to combat units. The US Army had a number of airstrips for light aircraft, few of which are documented apart from those at Swanwick in Derbyshire, Kington in Herefordshire and Porthcawl in South Wales. Piper Cubs could operate from almost any large field and they are known to have flown from such diverse locations as Enville cricket ground in Worcestershire and Arrowe Park in Birkenhead.

If the North-West could not field its own bomber squadrons it was able to hit back through its aircraft factories which produced a goodly proportion of all the aircraft committed to combat. The West was often a haven for the returning bombers when their bases were fogged-in and even the smallest airfield could boast that it had once acted as host to a lost heavy bomber. Training was severely disrupted at the bigger stations by mass diversions which often happened at short notice.

Going back to the beginning of the war, only one airfield in the whole area had concrete runways and that was High Ercall in Shropshire. The operational bomber stations had priority for runway construction but it was soon realised that flooded grass fields could neither deliver new aircraft nor train replacement pilots and crews. From late in 1940 all new airfields, apart from RLGs, were built with concrete runways and existing airfields were provided with them retrospectively as time and labour allowed. Training programmes suffered as a result and new airfields were often pressed into service as temporary RLGs as soon as they opened.

As most of North-West England and Wales is mountainous many of the new airfields were built on the coast from Carlisle all the way south to Cardiff. Inland, Shropshire and Staffordshire had the most suitable terrain for airfields but certain apparently suitable areas such as mid-Cheshire remained almost devoid of them. There is evidence that many suggested sites were turned down because the loss of food production was considered unacceptable.

Although the most common aircraft on the western side of the country were trainers, combat aircraft were seen as well. Most were on training flights but as the war progressed the massed formations of the VIIIth Air Force were seen over the North Midlands forming up for a flight over France before turning east over the battle front. On August 24 1944 348 B-17s were seen over Stafford between 05.30 and 07.30 hours circling ever higher until the contrails streamed in the blue sky. The same day over 180 other aircraft of 23 different types were logged over the same district, mostly Oxfords and Wellingtons but also P-47s, P-51s, B-26s, Stirlings and Lancasters. The following day 375 B-17s were noted on the way to attack a number of targets in Germany.

In those days aircraft were rarely seen flying above 2,000 ft and most were much lower than this. On October 10 1942 51 Lancasters and six Hurricanes were seen thundering over Stafford at rooftop height (practising for the low-level attack on the Le Creusot Armament Works) and on April 9 1943 my informant noted in his diary that the pilot of Lancaster AJ-B was wearing white overalls! What he did not know at the time was that this was a 617 Squadron aircraft which would be shot down over Holland during the Dambuster operation a month later.

On May 27 1943 ten B-26s were noted in formation, among the first to be seen over the Midlands. Other highlights were a Beaufighter with USAAF markings taking off from nearby Hixon on June 14, a Dominie on August 5 with 'US Army' painted on its yellow wing undersurfaces and a USAAF Spitfire with a 'star and bar' under *both* wings on December 20 1943. On April 14 1944 40 C-47s came over towing 28 Hadrians and 12 Horsas and four days later another 36 were seen towing 20 Hadrians and 16 Horsas. Other unusual American aircraft recorded were an all-black Liberator from Harrington and a US Navy PB4Y-1.

RAF highlights of wartime spotting over Stafford included an Airacobra on July 1 1942, the first local Typhoon on August 5 1942 and a pressurised Wellington with bubble hood for the pilot on December 29 1942. A Hampden flew over low on October 21 1942, so low in fact that the pilot was plainly visible. Tomahawks with sharks' teeth markings on their noses were common in 1944 'attacking' the Hixon Wellingtons and giving the gunners practice in tracking the incoming fighter. Wheaton Aston's Oxfords were overhead frequently, the code letters and serials clearly readable, for example AA-HM618, FP-LX139, FZ-V3241 and GJ-AT661.

Merseyside, too, saw a wide variety of aircraft in the later war years; earlier on they had tended to keep well clear because of the balloons. A few sample loggings from 1945 illustrate what flew over. On January 12 an Albemarle towing a Horsa, on February 12 three Whitleys in formation and two days later two Mitchells. March 17 saw 17 C-47s towing Hadrian gliders southwards. They were probably from Warton as part of the build-up for the Rhine Crossing due to start on March 24. A rare Black Widow was seen on April 21 and on April 27 22 B-17s flew over. Contrast was provided the same day by a formation of 12 Tiger Moths.

Michael Bowyer spent several holiday weeks near Morecambe Bay during the war years, the first being in September 1942. The contrast with the intense activity over his home at Cambridge was amazing but there were some redeeming features. From the train at Crewe he saw his first Hurricane with long-range tanks. Target-towing aircraft were continuously over the bay, comprising Lysanders, Battles, Master IIIs, Henleys, Skuas and even an Audax complete with yellow and black stripes. On September 2 'Experimental Aircraft 100' appeared, alias the Barracuda, and on the 6th a tropicalised Spitfire Vb with two cannon.

A year later, on September 5 1943, he recorded such oddities as a Beaufort I, a Tiger Moth in old-style US markings without the bars, a Warwick with Sky undersides, and a Coastal Command Hampden flying low in company with Whitley V KG-E of 3 OTU. The real prize, however, was a Cleveland with yellow undersides flying north-west in the early evening. A second Cleveland with different markings appeared later going the opposite way.

On August 15 1944 from the train passing Burtonwood an estimated 300 B-17s were seen on the airfield. The Lancashire coast was now busy with American types from Warton, such unusual sights as a two-seat P-51 and many C-47s,

B-26s, B-24s, A-20s and P-47s being logged. The RN airfields, Inskip and Burscough, were responsible for the many Swordfish, Hurricanes, Fireflies and less common types like the Corsair, Helldiver and Stinson Reliant. If you could tear your eyes away from the sky there were sights to be seen on the road too such as the seven all-silver T-6 Texans in a convoy on the A6 between Carnforth and Lancaster. Crated CG-4A gliders were also noted, each with its serial conveniently marked on the outside.

Mike's next trip north was in August 1946 to Llandudno but very few aircraft were seen until the journey home. Passing Hawarden hundreds of Halifaxes and Wellingtons were lined up waiting to be scrapped. This was to be the beginning of the end for one of the largest air forces the world has ever seen. The North-West had built many of its aircraft and was now claiming them back for its industry. From Kirkbride and Silloth in the north to Llandow in the south thousands of unwanted aircraft waited to be melted down. Some of the airfields from which they flew have followed down the road to limbo but happily bricks and concrete are more durable.

Never again will Tilstock reverberate to the thunder of a Stirling towing a Horsa off the long runway, the juggernaut lorries on the A41 make all the noise nowadays. The flare-path at Cranage which once guided the tired fighter pilots back to earth is dimmed for ever. Apart from the rusting hangars, the broken concrete and the windowless huts full of hay, the only memorials are the neat rows of airmen's graves in the country churchyards, an everlasting reminder of the price which was paid for a fragile peace.

Airfield architecture

Airfields within the area under review fall into six categories:
i) built by 1918;
ii) municipal airports taken over and usually improved by the RAF;
iii) erected on both old and new sites as a result of the 1934 Expansion Scheme, some not being completed until after the war started;
iv) hastily built airfields to a dispersed pattern intended for the 'duration' but in a few cases retained and developed for post-war use; these can be further sub-divided into grass-surfaced RLGs, grass airfields to which runways were added later and airfields built with runways from the start;
v) Royal Naval Air Stations;
vi) satellite landing grounds for the camouflaged dispersal of aircraft.

The hangars give an instant clue to the origins of a particular airfield. Hooton Park and Sealand still have the Belfast Truss hangars of 1917 which are sufficiently ancient to come under a preservation order. The civic airports of the 1930s reveal no common style of hangar and range from small side-opening sheds like those at Meir to the massive buildings at Liverpool Airport. The classic style of the Expansion airfield has already been well covered by Michael Bowyer in volume 1 of this series. Suffice it to say that Silloth, Tern Hill, Cosford and Burtonwood possess examples of the large 'C' Type and the first three also have 'D' Types for storage. An innovation peculiar to the ASU airfield was the large blister hangar originally known by its commercial name, Lamella. The advantage of its shape was that it cast a smaller shadow than the conventional style and was therefore less noticeable from the air. It could also be covered with earth and grass as protection against incendiary bombs, apart from the camouflage effect. The RAF referred to it as the 'E' or 'L' Type and many can be seen today, the 'E' being of reinforced concrete construction and the 'L' of steel.

The stations nearing completion in 1939 were often equipped with 'J' and 'K' Types (outwardly indistinguishable) designed to be the same internal dimensions as the 'C' Type but built more quickly with less materials. Some airfields thus acquired a mixture of buildings, Burtonwood for example having 'C' Types and 'J' and 'K' Types on two separate sites.

The fighter stations built in the North-West in 1940/41 were usually provided with easily erected sheet steel hangars of the 'T1', Callender-Hamilton or Bellman types. Three excellent examples of 'T1's can be seen at Calveley looking exactly like a scaled-down 'T2'. The Callender-Hamilton was a low-

Opposite page top to bottom *'D'-type at Tern Hill; Lamella at Tern Hill; 'J'-type at High Ercall.* **This page top to bottom** *'T1' at Calveley; Callender-Hamilton at Atcham; 'T2' (left) and 'B1' at Seighford.*

roofed building identifiable by its unusual door runners which project on each side. Atcham and Madley both have them. The latter also has some Hinaidis, a 1927 design with a 100-ft door opening. Perhaps they were dismantled and brought in from elsewhere. The Bellmans came in two basic sizes, one with a 26 ft door height, the other much lower, but both had the same length and breadth. Both types can be seen at Cosford.

The familiar 'T2' was the hallmark of most bomber OTU bases but a single 'B1' was often available for major overhaul work, its greater roof clearance easing the use of overhead hoists for engine changes. The 'B1' has distinctive supports to the door runners and a steeper-pitched roof than the 'T2'. It was designed by the Ministry of Aircraft Production who had already produced the 'A1', a type which survives in many parts of the country. Liverpool Airport has one near the main entrance and another can be seen at the old Fairey site at Stretton. The 'A1's roof slopes down to within about 7 ft of ground level. The 'B2' was identical to the 'B1' apart from the door height which was reduced by 6 ft 6 in.

Blister hangars were built in a bewildering variety of styles and local modifications. The standard pattern was the Over Type (Steel) with an opening of 65 ft but also common was the Enlarged Over Type with a span of 69 ft. Some were placed end to end to produce a double blister. They were not only used for housing aircraft because at Calveley two were joined together to form the station cinema. At RLGs they were the only shelter available for the aircraft in the event of a gale warning. They were usually left with open ends but canvas curtains could be provided. Few Blisters are left today on the airfields but one or two can be seen on farms serving as barns. Also in this temporary category was a throwback to World War 1, the canvas Besonneau which was used quite extensively as a stopgap if labour could not be spared to build something more substantial.

Royal Navy airfields had their own hangar types. Aircraft were usually kept in Admiralty Type 'S' Sheds, sometimes referred to as Squadron hangars, a 60 ft by 70 ft building eminently suitable for aircraft with folding wings. Earth blast walls were placed on each side. Major servicing was done in Pentads, a hangar about the size of a 'T1' but possessing sloping sidewalls.

Buildings at SLGs were deliberately kept to a minimum but one or two Robin hangars were normally put up for maintenance work. The Robin, which had doors at one end only, was another creation of MAP and was designed to resemble a private building and house two aircraft of about Spitfire size. Cleverly painted with doors and windows it would certainly be inconspicuous from the air. A slightly larger version, the Super Robin, was produced later in the war and both types can be seen at Penkridge. Some were erected at RLGs and others as extra accommodation at aircraft component factories well away from airfields. (It should be noted that some official documents refer to them as Robins hangars but the majority use the singular.)

The watch office or flying control tower, as it became known from around 1944, was the nerve centre of every airfield. Prior to the Expansion Scheme it was merely a wooden hut based conveniently near the parking apron where

Opposite page top to bottom *'A1's at old Fairey Aviation site at Stretton* (B.H. Abraham); *Admiralty 'S' Shed at Burscough (note blast walls of earth); Navy Pentad at Hinstock; Super Robin (left) and Standard Robin at Penkridge.*

pilots could book in or out. The new airfields built after 1934 were honoured with a purpose-built brick building to pattern 1959/34, having a small tower on top. The pattern was improved slightly at stations like Shawbury but it was still not a control tower in the true sense as radio was not in general use. The building was employed mainly for weather forecasting staff, briefing and other administrative jobs.

Wartime airfields appear to have been equipped with one of seven basic types of watch office although some had local modifications and there are a few one-off types which defy explanation. In the area covered by this book most of the main OTU stations had the 518/40 type which had a stairwell built out on the back of it. The building was about 40 ft square and the roof was reached via an internal stairway. After 1941 the familiar squat box-shaped building, to pattern 12779/41, began to appear. It was even more austere than its predecessor, the roof on which a small observation box was often built being reached by an external stairway, although there was an internal stairway to the first floor. The entrance door was to the rear and the front windows varied in size, often being small to facilitate blacking-out.

There were three types of tower at satellite stations. The first two were a small oblong affair, 17658/40 with an external ladder to reach the first floor, a good example being at Montford Bridge, and a smaller version of the 12779/41 pattern known as the 13726/41. This has four windows at the front rather than the six of the bigger tower and a typical example can be seen at Tatenhill. Some of the bomber satellites such as Seighford had a two-storey type to pattern 13079/41 with an external concrete stairway.

Several airfields had more than one type as a result of changes in requirements during their operational life. Bobbington (Halfpenny Green) was merely given a bungalow with bay window as a watch office in the style of those at SLGs but an extension to one of the runways resulted in part of the airfield being out of view. A 12779/41 type was then built in a more sensible position. Calveley had a satellite building like that at Montford Bridge but as the station expanded, a 12779/41 type replaced it. The original building was used for filling met balloons but it has now been demolished.

The last version to be designed during the war was a three-storey building, the only one left in this area being at Pershore. It is interesting to note that London

Left *Early 'Fort-type' watch office to pattern 1959/34 at Cosford* (R. Bonser).

Top right *518/40 pattern watch office at Silloth, common to most OTU parent stations* (J. Huggon).

Above right *The classic austerity tower to pattern 12779/41. Windows varied in size. This example is at Hixon.*

(Heathrow) Airport's old tower on the north side was of this variety. It perhaps stemmed from the example of the Royal Navy's wartime tower which also consisted of three storeys and was standardised from the beginning. Particularly good examples exist at Hinstock and Burscough and they are a rabbit warren of stairs and connecting rooms surmounted by a roof observation post.

Technical accommodation on airfields had originally been incorporated into the sides of the pre-war hangars but the widespread use of sheet metal hangars made this impracticable. The accommodation formerly annexed to hangars was now provided as detached but adjacent huts, their functions varying according to the differing needs of each station. They consisted basically of minor workshops, battery charging rooms, instrument rooms, Squadron and Flight offices and other similar facilities. Maintenance blocks housing armouries, aircraft equipment stores, etc, were also provided. Workshops and stores were built in composite blocks of hutting of normal spans, but on the larger stations two or more Romney or Iris huts would be included. General purpose huts were provided at aircraft dispersal points for ground crew shelters and minor workshops, but few of these have escaped demolition.

Above *Satellite station tower to pattern 17658/40 at Montford Bridge.* **Below** *Tower at Tatenhill to pattern 13726/41. Note small windows to facilitate blacking-out.* **Bottom** *13079/41 pattern provided at many bomber OTU satellite stations. This example is at Seighford.*

Training airfields generally had an instructional site placed between the technical and domestic building groups. Depending upon the function of the station it contained such buildings as Link Trainer, Turret Instruction Block and navigation and armament lecture rooms. Numerous other buildings were developed to meet the progress made in synthetic training. Standard huts were modified to house celestial navigation trainers, dummy operations rooms, Fisher Front-gun trainers, free gunnery trainers, Hunt range, night visual trainer, r/t trainer, Silloth and Hawarden trainers (early forms of flight simulator), and torpedo-attack teacher. A close study of the airfield plans available from the RAF Museum reveals just how many different ones there were.

Other ancilliary structures specially designed and still to be seen include machine-gun test butts, pigeon lofts, parachute stores and drying rooms, and motor transport sheds. Several types of air-raid shelter were provided and together with gun posts and pill boxes have mostly survived the bulldozer because of their great strength.

Domestic buildings normally followed a standard pattern but were affected by the successive reduction in accommodation during the war period. In 1939 planning of quarters was based on 120 square feet per officer, 70 square feet per sergeant and 45 square feet per corporal or airman but, as station 'strengths' crept over the establishment for which they were planned, so the scale was reduced. In July 1943 officers were down to 90 square feet and corporals and airmen only 32 square feet! Economy prevented the erection of other than the bare minimum of sanitary facilities on dispersed sleeping sites, so that such buildings as bath houses were only provided on messing sites and the resultant inconvenience had to be accepted.

Communal buildings such as dining rooms, NAAFIs, officers' and sergeants' messes remained unchanged throughout the war and, broadly, involved a 25 per cent reduction of the pre-war size of the main rooms. However, considerable economies were effected in planning by the omission of certain ancilliary rooms and the deletion of all unessential space in halls and corridors. Further austerity measures were taken in 1943 by the reduction of seating capacity in dining rooms to 50 per cent of establishment, necessitating two sittings for meals. In the initial provision made for WAAF personnel early in 1940 separate dining rooms, institutes and messes were provided. It became policy, however, in 1942 that the WAAF should share RAF buildings of these types and thereafter WAAF communal buildings were omitted.

To service its aircraft and house its staff, the average airfield would possess over 500 separate buildings dispersed over several miles of countryside. Looking at the tumble-down huts today it is hard to imagine how neat and tidy they and their surroundings once were, with neatly trimmed grass, flower beds and even vegetable gardens for which competitions were held. It is all very different now; the smell of manure assails the nostrils where once it was high octane aviation fuel, the stuttering tractor replaces the sweetly-tuned aero engines of long ago. The old saying about turning swords into ploughshares was never so apt.

Flying control and airfield aids

Before the war there were no formal attempts to control the movement of aircraft on or around aerodromes, apart from a watch office at which pilots reported on arrival or before departure. The huge increase in wartime flying soon revealed this deficiency and attempts were made to improve the situation.

A total of 1,451 aircraft were either written off or damaged as a result of airfield accidents during the latter half of 1941 and concern was expressed that standardisation of Flying Control was necessary before the Americans arrived with thousands more aircraft. At that time it was not even standardised within the Commands, each Group having its own system. Training aircraft were not generally fitted with radio equipment and a solution to the large number of runway collisions was to place a caravan alongside the touch-down area. It was occupied by the Aerodrome Control Pilot (ACP) who was armed with an Aldis signalling lamp and Very Pistol to warn pilots to overshoot and go round again if they were approaching with another aircraft in a blind spot or with undercarriage retracted. RAF Woodvale claimed the credit for this idea in the summer of 1942 but it seems to have evolved simultaneously at other locations.

No 27 OTU formed at Lichfield in April 1941 for night bomber training but it was over a year before some form of control was exercised over its flying. Even then, the first Flying Control Officer posted in was housed in the Duty Pilot's room on the ground floor of the watch office, the control room proper being used as the Chief Instructor's office. It was some time before the latter was persuaded to move elsewhere. Inevitably there was friction until the aircrews' traditional mistrust of non-flying personnel began to be broken down by the realisation that they could be of much practical help. Lichfield was a proving ground for many procedures which became standard throughout the RAF. Early developments here were the regulation of vehicle movements, clearance of airfield obstructions and control of taxiing. Standard taxi routes were devised and, to assist aircraft taxiing at night, white lines one foot wide were painted on all perimeter track bends.

The runway-in-use at an airfield obviously depended upon wind direction and was differentiated by a number from one to six, beginning with the one nearest north and continuing in a clockwise direction. The correct runway could be passed to an aircraft by radio but if it was not so equipped a landing 'Tee' displayed in the signals square in front of the tower would indicate the direction. Another 'Tee' placed at the downwind end of the runway would confirm. In addition, a large board would be hung on the side of the tower with the runway number on it and at certain aerodromes, Atcham for instance, a colour-coded flag would also delineate the active runway. If the wind direction necessitated a runway change a smoke candle would be lit to warn pilots in the circuit to hold off until the caravan and 'Tee' were moved. From March 5 1944 runways were referred to by their magnetic heading; for example, '23' for 230 degrees. (235 degrees and above would be rounded up to '24' and so on.)

For security reasons, airfield names were not employed on the r/t, codes being allocated instead. These were changed frequently at first but by 1944 those for training stations at least were fairly static. Wheaton Aston, for example, was 'Banet White', Pershore was 'Sideslip'. The identification letters in the signals square gave a clue to the airfield's location as they were usually based upon its name. They included 'DV' for Condover, 'SD' for St David's, 'OK' for Tilstock and 'TY' for Towyn. The codes were also flashed in Morse by a beacon at night.

For an aircraft in an emergency there were a variety of aids which could lead it to a safe landing. The basic life-saver was the Darkie System in which an aircraft could call for a homing using the call-sign 'Darkie'. Most RAF stations operated a permanent Darkie watch on a common frequency and by taking bearings and comparing them by telephone were rapidly able to fix an aircraft's position. In areas where RAF coverage was poor Royal Observer Corps posts were also equipped with radio. Apart from this, all ROC posts plotted aircraft movements both visually and by sound and passed the information to their regional control centre where a complete picture was built up on an operations table. On a clear night searchlight beams would point towards the nearest airfield. Three searchlights on the airfield, known as Sandra Lights, were directed upwards to form a cone overhead and, if there was a low cloud base, the glow on it could be seen from above. As a last resort a night fighter could be vectored on to a lost aircraft by radar and lead it to an airfield. Other visual aids were rockets, Very lights and a mortar which fired a brilliant pyrotechnic high into the sky.

The 'ZZ' Approach was an early form of 'talk-down' but the later QGH or Controlled Descent Through Cloud was a more satisfactory method using D/F to place the aircraft in a safety lane down to the runway. Standard Beam Approach or Lorenz was a pilot-interpreted aid using audible dots and dashes and 'nulls' to position the aircraft on the runway centre line. With practice it could be very accurate and in a wartime environment a successful landing could usually be made in poor visibility.

A complex system of lighting developed during the war, having its origins in unofficial experiments conducted at RAF Drem in Scotland. The basic system was officially named Airfield Lighting Mk 1 but was colloquially known as Drem Mk I. It consisted of an outer circle of lights with lead-in funnels and hooded runway and taxiway fittings, replacing the earlier contact lights which shone upwards to the heavens—and enemy aircraft. Electric lighting could be extinguished immediately in the event of an air-raid, something which could never be done with the pre-war style paraffin flare, known as the goose-neck after its shape. At Sealand in 1941, for instance, enemy raiders were approaching and there was a rush to douse the flarepath. In the excitement one of the airmen spilled burning paraffin on his trousers. The officer-in-charge actually shouted 'put that man out!' and he was rolled on the grass before the flames penetrated the material.

Warning of enemy intruders was given by a hooded red light on the roof of the control building visible from all parts of the aerodrome. Aircraft in the air were warned on r/t by the phrase 'Hun about' and given suitable instructions. For those without radio a triangle of red lights was lit beside the identity beacon (or 'Pundit') which itself was placed about a mile from the aerodrome on a mobile trailer. The aircraft would then circle until the red lights were switched off or fly a pre-arranged route. At Lichfield, for example, it was Base-Tatenhill-Base.

Rapid changes in aircraft design resulting in increased speeds and weights soon rendered the Mk I system obsolete and a completely revised layout, known as Airfield Lighting Mk II, was introduced. It allowed for larger diameter outer circles of lights, improved and repositioned approach-funnel lighting and greater brilliance. The outer circle was laid out with an approximate diameter of 3¾ miles based on the geometrical centre of the airfield. The 52 light fittings were spaced some 400 yards apart, pole-mounted to avoid being screened by trees and other obstructions. Overhead lines were used to supply power outside the airfield boundary, except on runway approaches where they were diverted underground.

Mk II approach lighting was divided into four sections, namely the Lead-in String, Outer Funnel, Intermediate Funnel and Inner Funnel. The purpose of the Lead-in String was to give visual indication of the point at which an aircraft turned in from the outer circle towards the correct runway for landing and the curvature of turn required to ensure a smooth turn-on to the centre of the approach path. The three funnel sections were arranged to give continuous visual cues to a pilot to enable him to keep his aircraft right on the longitudinal centre-line of the runway whilst approaching to land.

The runway was marked by lights down each side spaced about 100 yards apart longitudinally. If required the pilot could call 'Floods' on the radio and a trailer-mounted floodlight, often known as the Chance Light after its manufacturer, would be switched on to illuminate the touch-down zone. Taxi-track lighting, after much experimentation, was standardised with amber lights on the outside edge and blue on the inside.

In many cases airfields were located so close to one another that their outer circle lights were very close or even overlapped. To overcome the danger a 1,000 yard light bar of six flashing lights 200 yards apart marked the extent of the safe flying distance beyond the outer circle. At a coastal site like Talbenny the outer circle lights might be continued on buoys but more often they were doubled at the coast and a small searchlight indicated the correct direction to fly to stay on the circle. Flying-boat bases such as Pembroke Dock were equipped with a 3,000 yard-long flarepath of battery-fed lights on anchored steel buoys. They were white except for the end lights which were red. The outer circle and approach lighting were a simplified form of the land-based Mk II system. Priority in the installation of lighting obviously went to the operational stations but by 1943 most of the OTU airfields in North-West England were equipped with the Mk II system.

Control of circuit traffic differed in detail between RAF Groups but generally the traffic zone was considered to extend 3,000 yards outside the airfield perimeter and up to 2,000 ft overhead. In visual conditions at training stations radio was rarely used, although a listening watch was kept on the common frequency of 6,440 kcs, all instructions being given by Aldis lamp from the

ACP. At night when downwind in the circuit a pilot would flash his code letter in Morse on the downward identification lamp. A green light from the ACP flashing the aircraft call letter meant 'you may land', a similar flashing red meant 'wait and try again' and a steady white 'you may not land here, go away'. On receipt of a green the pilot would switch the identity light to 'steady' and keep it on until after landing. An aircraft in emergency and requiring a priority landing had three alternatives, namely to call the watch tower on r/t, make a series of short flashes on navigation lights or Aldis lamp, or fire a white Very light. After landing the standard procedure was to leave the runway with a left turn at an intersection or when reaching the perimeter track. On grass airfields the pilot was to turn left and taxi by the shortest route to the perimeter provided he was certain that other landing aircraft would not be obstructed by this course of action.

Control was non-existent on cross-country flights but the ROC plotted aircraft movements and D/F stations at Sealand, Wigtown and Aldergrove provided coverage over the Irish Sea and the North-West. The bomber OTU Groups required their crews on cross-countries to listen out for five minutes on their station frequency on the hour and half hour for possible broadcasts of diversion, recall, weather deterioration, etc. In 1942 all aircraft flying above 5,000 ft at night were to burn navigation lights continuously whilst flying over Great Britain. Aircraft intercepted above 5,000 ft without lights, unless recognised as friendly, would be regarded as hostile. In addition, the IFF (Identification, Friend or Foe) set was switched on at all times except when over the sea more than 50 miles from the coast. This transmitted an identification signal when interrogated by a radar pulse from the ground and confirmed the aircraft as 'one of ours'.

Immediately after the war Flying Control was renamed Air Traffic Control and gradually developed into today's complex system. The basics, however, remain the same; the light signals to non-radio aircraft, the standard circuit joining procedures. Some of the control towers which once passed messages to Beaufighters, B-17s, Wellingtons and the like now control BAC 111s, DC-10s and other sleek modern aircraft.

The Military Airfields of Wales and the North-West

Airfields with runways

1	Andreas	25	High Ercall	49	Ronaldsway
2	Angle	26	Hixon	50	Samlesbury
3	Anthorn	27	Hooton Park	51	St Athan
4	Ashbourne	28	Inskip	52	St Davids
5	Atcham	29	Jurby	53	Sealand
6	Barrow	30	Kirkbride	54	Seighford
7	Brawdy	31	Lichfield	55	Shawbury
8	Burscough	32	Llanbedr	56	Shobdon
9	Burtonwood	33	Llandow	57	Silloth
10	Calveley	34	Llandwrog	58	Sleap
11	Carew Cheriton	35	Longtown	59	Speke
12	Cark	36	Meir	60	Squires Gate
13	Church Broughton	37	Millom	61	Stretton
14	Condover	38	Mona	62	Talbenny
15	Cosford	39	Montford Bridge	63	Tatenhill
16	Crosby-on-Eden	40	Pembrey	64	Templeton
17	Dale	41	Pengam Moors	65	Tern Hill
18	Darley Moor	42	Peplow	66	Tilstock
19	Defford	43	Pershore	67	Valley
20	Fairwood Common	44	Perton	68	Warton
21	Great Orton	45	Poulton	69	Wheaton Aston
22	Halfpenny Green	46	Rednal	70	Woodford
23	Haverfordwest	47	Rhoose	71	Woodvale
24	Hawarden	48	Ringway	72	Wrexham

Establishments without runways or with grass landing strips

73	Abbots Bromley	86	Chetwynd	99	Manorbier
74	Aberporth	87	Cranage	100	Penkridge
75	Barton	88	Hardwick Hall	101	Penrhos
76	Battlestead Hill	89	Hells Mouth	102	Rudbaxton
77	Berrow	90	Hinstock	103	St Brides
78	Bodorgan	91	Hoar Cross	104	Stormy Down
79	Bratton	92	Hodnet	105	Tatton Park
80	Brayton	93	Hornby Hall	106	Teddesley Park
81	Bridleway Gate	94	Hutton	107	Towyn
82	Brockton	95	Kingstown	108	Wath Head
83	Burnaston	96	Knowsley Park	109	Weston Park
84	Burnfoot	97	Little Sutton	110	Wolverhampton
85	Chepstow	98	Madley	111	Worcester

Sea-plane bases

112	Beaumaris	114	Pembroke Dock
113	Lawrenny Ferry	115	Windermere

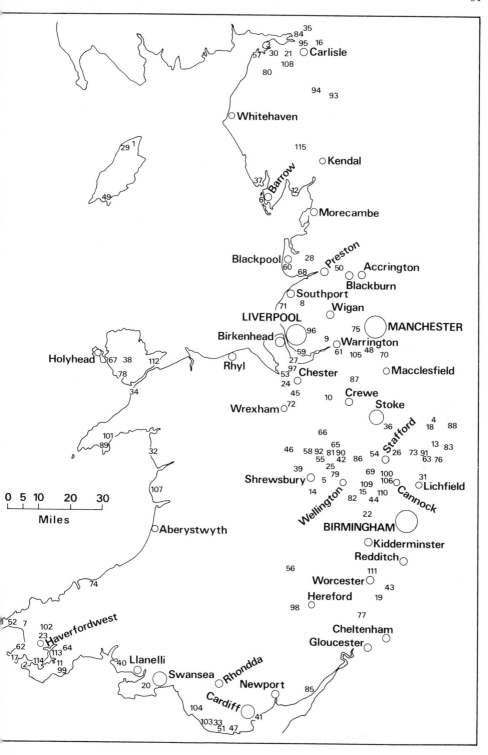

35
84
95 16
3
57 30 21 ○ Carlisle
108
80

94 93

○ Whitehaven

29 ¹
49

115

○ Kendal

37
Barrow
12
6
○ Morecambe

Blackpool ○ 28
60
68

Preston
50 Accrington
Blackburn

○ Southport
71 8 Wigan
LIVERPOOL
96 75 ● MANCHESTER
Birkenhead
9 Warrington
Holyhead ○ 67 38 112
59 61 105 48 70
Rhyl
27 ○ Macclesfield
53 97 Chester 87
24 45 Crewe
10 Stoke
78
34
Wrexham ○ 72 36 Stafford 4
18 88

66
65 13 83
101 46 58 92 81 90 54 26 73 91
89 55 42 86 63 76
32 39 25
Shrewsbury ○ 5 79 69 100 31
107 14 109 106 ○ Lichfield
Wellington 15 110 Cannock
82 44
22
Aberystwyth ○ BIRMINGHAM ●

○ Kidderminster
Redditch ○
56 111
Worcester ○
43
74 Hereford 19
98 ○
77
52 7 Cheltenham
102 Cleltenham ○
23 Gloucester ○
62 Haverfordwest
113 64
17 11
2 114 99
40 Llanelli
20 Swansea Rhondda
○ Newport
104 Cardiff 85
103 33
51 47 41

0 5 10 20 30
|_|_|___|___|
Miles

The airfields

Abbots Bromley, Staffordshire

SK075255. Beside B5014, ½ mile NW of Abbots Bromley

Just outside the village of Abbots Bromley is a small military guard-hut which stands at the entrance to one of Staffordshire's lesser-known flying sites. A narrow concrete road leads up a slight incline to a cluster of chicken houses, a few wartime buildings and a solitary Robin hangar, flanked by the concrete floors of other dismantled Robins. The airfield, once humming with Magisters and Tiger Moths, is now rich pasture divided by wire fences. It owed its existence to the need to reduce congestion at the parent aerodrome at Burnaston where 16 EFTS had its base and was brought into use later in 1941.

In the early post-war years it was employed as an Air Ministry Works Depot and a sign at the entrance still proclaims the fact in almost indecipherable lettering. It served also as one of several sub-sites for 21 MU at Fauld before reverting to agriculture. Alphabetically the first airfield in this book, it is alas one of the least interesting!

Aberporth, Dyfed

SN255495. On A487 5 miles NE of Cardigan

On the headland just to the south of the seaside village of Aberporth is a cluster of low buildings which forms the Rocket Research Establishment. The wartime airfield nearby has been kept open for liaison flights and has been provided with a single runway, something which it never had during the war. It opened in December 1940 as an AA co-operation base for the many gunnery ranges in Cardigan Bay and was occupied by the Henleys and Westland Wallaces of 'L' Flight, 1 AACU. 'Q' Flight of 1 AACU joined the other Flight on July 1 1941. 'X' Flight with Queen Bees was also here for a while. In a paper re-shuffle of the AACUs on October 1 1942 'B' Flight, which had been here for a year, became 1607 Flight, 'L' Flight became 1608 Flight and 'Q' Flight became 1609 Flight.

From mid-1942 Ansons of 6 AOS were detached here from the unit's base at Staverton. Training continued until January 1943 when the aircraft returned to Gloucestershire. On December 1 1943 Nos 1607, 1608 and 1609 AAC Flights were amalgamated to form 595 Squadron at Aberporth. They were still to provide co-operation for the 1st AA Practice Camp based locally and the 13th Light AA Practice Camp at Aberayron and Manorbier, aircraft for the latter to be detached to Carew Cheriton. Most of the aircraft were Miles Martinets although the first Vengeance arrived on November 29 1944, being delivered by a lady ATA pilot. They were not popular aircraft, however, and the squadron was glad to see the back of them in July 1945.

Being one of the few airfields in this part of Wales, Aberporth attracted many aircraft lost or in distress. The short grass field was even used successfully on February 22 1944 by a USAAF Liberator flying from North Africa to Valley. One wonders how it was flown out! The same day a C-47 from Gibraltar landed and five days earlier three American C-47s had landed with troops from the Middle East. Two Halifaxes came to grief on the small field, the first being W1097 of 405 Squadron which put down with engine failure on July 12 1942 and overshot. The other was LK643 of 1664 HCU which ran through the hedge on February 29 1944.

The HQ of 595 Squadron was transferred to Fairwood Common on April 26 1946, 24 aircraft flying there in groups of six. The level of serviceability was such that a formation of six Martinets was considered remarkable! On May 15 1946 the RAF ensign was lowered and the station placed on a care and maintenance basis. This state of affairs was not to last long, however, the airfield soon being revived. Ansons, Devons and Pembrokes have been regular visitors over the years and a grounded Hawker Hunter is kept here by the local ATC. There are two Bellman hangars but the two wartime Blisters have gone. The control tower is a box-like structure.

Andreas, Isle of Man

NX425000. On A17 between Andreas and Bride

The northern end of the Isle of Man consists of flat, fertile farmland, ideal for the building of airfields. On Ballaghue Farm were some level sandy fields of about 20 acres each. In 1940 they were recognised as possible landing places for enemy aircraft so they were obstructed with old buses and lorries. Their suitability had not escaped the notice of the Air Ministry either, as it appeared that the conduct of the war would require a fighter airfield on the island to supplement nearby Jurby. A local firm called Moss and Co was appointed as contractor and a dozen vehicles were hired from the local bus company to bring in labourers from all parts. The concrete runways were slightly longer than the contemporary norm for a fighter station so use by larger and heavier aircraft was possibly envisaged. This is what did, in fact, happen when it became an emergency landing ground for the Atlantic Ferry Route in 1944, although only a few Fortresses and Liberators were diverted. One B-24 with brake problems made a spectacular arrival with parachutes trailing from the waist gun positions as an impromptu air brake, an emergency technique pioneered by the XVth Air Force in Italy.

From the outset, the flying field was made secure with several rows of concertina wire entirely surrounding it, apart from the single main gate and a few crash exits. This contrasted with the layout of nearby Jurby where there was little or no fencing and roads remained open to the public. Three Bellman hangars

were joined later in the war by eight Enlarged Over Blisters, none of which is left today. The aircraft were protected by a total of 24 blast pens, 12 for single-engined fighters and 12 for medium bombers. All in all, the defence of the aerodrome was taken very seriously indeed and its first fighter aircraft, in the form of Spitfires of 457 Squadron detached from Jurby, arrived early in October 1941. Many shipping patrols were flown but the only scrambles were after what turned out to be friendly aircraft. The squadron moved to the south of England in March 1942 and was replaced by another Australian squadron, 452, this time wholly based at Andreas now that the airfield was fully operational. No 452 Squadron had seen a lot of action at Kenley and the Isle of Man posting provided a rest period before the pilots were shipped out to Australia in June 1942 to fight the Japanese.

The third and last squadron to be based here was No 93 which reformed with Spitfires on June 1 1942 and spent most of its time on convoy escort before being withdrawn to the mainland for overseas service the following October. On the day it left, three Handley Page Harrows, two of them named *Augusta* and *Boadicea,* were to be seen on the field, together with three Lysanders, three Defiants, 16 Spitfires, a Whitley and a Chesapeake. The latter probably belonged to a detachment of No 772 Squadron which was at Andreas for most of its life. Another

Andreas 518/40-type tower with small observation post on top.

unusual aircraft, an AW Ensign with yellow undersides, had been seen on November 2 1941.

The war was now remote and Andreas was quiet for about six months, only a detachment of No 275 Air Sea Rescue Squadron being present with Lysanders and a couple of Walrus amphibians on stand-by. They had been here since October 1941 and there was plenty of trade with all the aerial activity around, and particularly *in,* the Irish Sea. A visit on June 14 1943 met a surprise; there were now 15 Ansons and 15 Martinets to be seen, the vanguard of No 11 Air Gunnery School which had been here since May 6. The school followed a monotonous routine of airborne firing on towed targets so that gunners could learn their craft. Accidents were rare but those which did happen were usually fatal as they involved mid-air collisions. On June 8 1944, for example, two Martinets collided with the loss of three men whilst 'attacking' an Anson to relieve the boredom.

Visiting aircraft of note during 1944 were a Barracuda on January 13, a USAAF Lightning with engine trouble on January 24 which amazed the RAF pilots with its size and complexity, a Martlet on March 17, a Marauder on August 4 and two Corsairs in November. No 772B Squadron formed in May 1945 with an unusual collection of aircraft, namely Boston IIIs, Corsairs and Mosquitoes, but disbanded in September of the same year. The airfield was open to the public for Battle of Britain Day in 1946 but five days later No 11 AGS left for Jurby and Andreas was reduced to care and maintenance.

Today, the airfield presents a dismal picture of desolation, dominated by the control tower with its locally modified roof observation post. All the dispersed living sites have been cleared and ploughed over and some of the technical site buildings have been adapted for pig farming. The rasp of go-cart engines on the cracked concrete is a faint echo of the Merlins of long ago.

Angle, Dyfed

SM860015. On B4320, 7 miles W of Pembroke

The scene of the first Sunderland *airfield* landing in Britain, base of a rare twin-engined fighter and built on a peninsula, Angle was never a popular posting because of its remoteness. Sailing and

bathing were an off-duty occupation in the summer months but in winter it could be as bleak as Iceland.

Its career began on December 1 1941 as a forward station in the Fairwood Common Sector under 10 Group. From April 18 1942 it was home for 263 Squadron, one of the two which operated the Westland Whirlwind. The squadron had experienced an endless succession of engine failures since re-equipping with the Whirlwind but by the time it moved to Angle the problems with the Rolls-Royce Peregrine seemed to have been solved. The move itself was not without incident because the railway truck containing the entire stock of 'A' Flight's armoury caught fire whilst passing through Llanelli. The truck was isolated and moved to a siding where the exploding Very cartridges made a spectacular display. Fortunately the local fire brigade managed to extinguish the blaze before it reached any of the 20 mm shells.

The squadron's job was the protection of shipping off the Welsh coast, assisted on occasion by a section of No 421, a new squadron under training at Fairwood. Much to their annoyance, it was found that the anti-shipping Ju 88s were extremely evasive and it was thought that their crews listened in to British radio communications as their radar plots were seen to diverge so widely from the vectors given to our fighters. May 22 saw the longest operational flight ever made with Whirlwinds when two aircraft tried to intercept an enemy bomber over the Irish Sea and chased it to the Irish coast near Dublin. At this point they were forced to give up because of rain, low cloud and fuel shortage. Base was now out of range so they headed east and were lucky to make a landfall on the Lleyn Peninsula in North Wales and squeeze in to the small aerodrome at Hell's Mouth.

Since the Ju 88s seemed to be going about their business unmolested it was decided to hit their bases on the Brittany coast and try to destroy some on the ground. The first *Ramrod,* as these operations were called, was organised on April 30 1942 using Predannack in Cornwall as a forward base. Ten Whirlwinds escorted by Spitfires of No 310 Squadron attacked Lannion and Morlaix airfields without loss to themselves. There was a repeat performance on June 5, again via Predannack, but this time escorted by the Spitfires of Nos 130 and 234 Squadrons. At Lannion a Ju 88 being

Part of the domestic site at Angle (A.J. Ayers).

serviced in a hangar was damaged but ammunition was wasted on what turned out to be five dummy aircraft. Morlaix was attacked too but with no observed results and all aircraft returned safely.

Convoy patrols continued but no interceptions were made apart from one near-disaster when two sections of Whirlwinds were vectored on to one another in error and almost opened fire. No 263 Squadron suffered its first casualty since December 1941 when two aircraft were shot down by Me 109s on the way back from a *Rhubarb* over North-West France on July 23. On August 15 1942 the squadron repositioned to Colerne having consistently achieved the highest number of operational flying hours in 10 Group.

Apart from the Whirlwind squadron, Angle was the base of several other fighter units for varying periods. The first was No 32 Squadron from June to November 1941, flying convoy patrols with Hurricanes until moving to Manston. It was replaced by 615 Squadron's Hurricanes which had just spent a hectic two months in Kent. This unit left for Fairwood Common in January 1942 leaving room for No 312 Squadron's Spitfires to fly convoy escort for three months before following 615 to Fairwood. After 263 Squadron left, the Spitfires of 152 Squadron spent a month here before going to Wittering in September. The station was occupied by the Hurricane IVs of No 421 Squadron until January 1943 when they left to replace 412 Squadron in the Kenley Wing. The latter squadron then came to Angle but only stayed for a month before moving to Fairwood.

Angle now had no flying units for a few months until a detachment of Whitleys and Horsa gliders was based for a week in April 1943 for exercises with the 9th Parachute Battalion. Also in April the *Highball* weapon, a variant of the Dambusters' bouncing bomb, was tested by a Mosquito flying from Angle.

The airfield was loaned temporarily to the Royal Navy for No 794 Squadron, an air target towing unit, from May 1943 but was then occupied by Coastal Command Development Unit which exchanged its base at Dale on the other side of Milford Haven with the Royal Navy on September 5 1943. The swop was made so that the control of all flying in Milford Haven could remain in RAF hands. Since Pembroke Dock's dispersed flying boat flare-path in Angle Bay was next to Angle aerodrome it was essential that all night flying in this area be co-ordinated.

CCDU carried out many trials from Angle including tests to measure the audibility of aircraft from submarines on the surface. It was found that a Wellington could not be heard at ranges greater than about three-quarters of a mile, the chief reason for this being that the noise of wind, water and diesel engines swamped the aircraft sound until it was very close. The U-boat crew therefore could not rely on audible detection of the aircraft for their safety. CCDU eventually moved to Thorney Island in January 1945, its small fleet by then consisting of two Beaufighter Xs, two Wellingtons, one Halifax II, one Liberator V and one Proctor for communications work.

On May 29 1943 there occurred the bizarre Sunderland incident mentioned above. T9114 of 461 Squadron had suffered extensive hull damage whilst taking off in a heavy sea. This necessitated a touch-down on dry land which was performed successfully at Angle. When the salvage party from 78 MU inspected the boat they considered that it would have to be written off because any attempt to remove it to the nearest beach for repair would cause much more damage. After further consultation it was decided to risk moving it. The job took several days and covered a distance of two miles. Many fields had to be negotiated and gaps were made in six fences. Civilian contractors then made repairs and it was put back into service, although only as a maintenance training airframe.

Angle in its heyday had only one 'T2' and four Blister hangars. Six fighter dispersal pens were located on the southeast side and the watch tower was in one corner of the airfield facing south-west. Today only a few huts remain and the runways have been ploughed up leaving the meandering perimeter track to trace out the outline of a forgotten airfield now given back to the gulls and rabbits.

Anthorn, Cumbria

NY180580. On unclassified coast road, 3 miles NW of Kirkbride village

The newly appointed Lieutenant Commander (Flying) arrived in Anthorn's circuit for the first time to be greeted by a barrage of red Very lights even though it appeared safe for a landing. No radio being available, he landed his Oxford at RAF Kirkbride nearby. A telephone call established that since no twin-engined aircraft had ever landed there previously it was considered prudent to warn him off!

The airfield had only been commissioned three weeks earlier on September 7 1944 as HMS *Nuthatch* for the use of No

1 Aircraft Receipt and Dispatch Unit. Its first occupants were a few Hellcats which had been delivered by ATA pilots. The contractors, John Laing & Son, had not yet completed all the runways and aircraft were diverted to Kirkbride in the event of a cross-wind, being flown over when conditions were more favourable. Hellcats were the principal aircraft type handled during its first year but one or two others passed through such as the Fireflies which were received for the rectification of armament problems.

Aircraft usually arrived at the ARDU with a bundle of unfitted accessories so that the aircraft could be brought up to the operational standard of the day. These requirements were always being amended or modified which led to frustration and delays. Equipment fitted at Anthorn included guns, gun sights, rocket rails, bomb racks, radar, radio, flotation gear and dinghies. There was often some 'rush order' necessitating technicians working all night, sometimes to find that the whole thing was cancelled the following day.

Because of the amount of liaison necessary a large and varied Station Flight was maintained for destinations as far apart as Lee-on-Solent in the south and Orkney in the north. Pilots visiting Northern Ireland were expected to bring back eggs and those who went to the Isle of Man, kippers, as neither was rationed in these areas. Ansons and Oxfords were the most numerous supported by a very popular Beechcraft Traveller, FT498, a Stinson Reliant and an Avenger, FN769. A couple of Tiger Moths were also on hand so that the test pilots could keep in practice with aerobatics.

Resident test-pilots at Anthorn with Sea-fire in 1945 (W.H.C. Blake).

Anthorn tower in 1945 (W.H.C. Blake).

At the end of the war the ARDU pilots were busily ferrying aircraft from RN air stations which were closing down. Most of them went to the scrap heap and one of the most heartbreaking jobs was flying almost-new Hellcats to Sydenham in Belfast. They were then taxied alongside an aircraft carrier, hoisted aboard and subsequently dumped in deep water, all part of the Lease-Lend agreement. The much-loved Traveller was spared to everyone's relief and went to Abbotsinch for shipment back to the States.

Anthorn's post-war history was relatively uneventful; it retained its wartime job of aircraft preparation until Gannet WN448 flew out on December 2 1957. This was the last of more than five thousand aircraft of 25 different types which had passed through the unit. Several FAA squadrons were based here at intervals, the first being No 772, a fleet requirements unit, which arrived on May 31 1946. No 813 with Firebrands was present in 1948, followed by 801 with Sea Hornets which it later replaced with Sea Furies. Two Dutch Navy Squadrons, 860 and 861, worked up in 1956, the former probably with Sea Hawks, the latter's equipment being unconfirmed.

Anthorn is now covered with the huge aerials necessary for Very Low Frequency radio transmissions. These have the useful property of being able to bend around the earth's curve and in this case are used to relay reports from Fylingdales early-warning radar direct to the American Air Defence HQ in Colorado. Around the perimeter many of the curious Fromson hangars which doubled as gun-butts can be seen.

Ashbourne, Derbyshire

SK195455. On A52, 1 mile SE of Ashbourne

Perched on a hill 600 ft above sea level overlooking the town of Ashbourne, this turned out to be a poor choice for an airfield site. The high ground of the Peak District was close and it was often shrouded with low cloud.

The station's opening-up period was very protracted and the uncompleted airfields at Church Broughton and Darley Moor were intended to be satellites although only the latter was taken over when completed. No 81 OTU formed at Ashbourne on July 10 1942 but did not receive any aircraft until moving to Whitchurch Heath on September 1 1942.

No 42 OTU arrived from Andover on October 26 1942 bringing with it Blenheims, Whitleys, Oxfords and Ansons. Parented by 70 Group, the OTU taught army support but when Army Co-operation Command was disbanded on June 1 1943 Ashbourne came under the control of Fighter Command.

Blenheim training ceased on July 7 1943 and Whitley Vs became the main equipment, the Ansons and Oxfords of 'A' Squadron being detached to the new satellite at Darley Moor. Ashbourne's exposed position caused it to be plagued by hill-fog and the aircraft were often grounded for days at a time. It was, nevertheless, used by aircraft diverting from other stations, for example a Halifax of 102 Squadron returning from operations on August 18 1943. American bombers found it occasionally, like the three Polebrook Fortresses lost returning from operations over Northern France on September 9 1943. A month later 13 more

Fortresses, this time from Snetterton Heath, landed safely.

On September 5 1943 No 42 OTU received its first Albemarle (V1701) and became the main training unit for this rather mediocre aircraft. Its arrival preceded a change of role when Ashbourne was transferred to 38 Group for airborne forces training which soon included glider towing. Four of the Albemarles were detached to Hampstead Norris to take part in operations on D-Day and one was reported missing with its crew.

No 42 OTU disbanded on March 20 1945, the main party going to expand 81 OTU at Tilstock. The airfield was then handed over to 28 MU which used the runways as a store for unfuzed bombs. These were later exploded on the moors and the station was abandoned in 1954.

In 1973 a sky-diving club started using the airfield and various hired Cessnas flew from here. Unfortunately a local lobby succeeded in closing down their activities on the grounds of noise and the effect on the local environment. Several minor accidents culminated in the dramatic crash of a Cessna 172 when a parachutist got tangled up with the tailplane. The aircraft then refused to fly and fell straight to the ground, slowed up by the open parachute. Although the aircraft was written off both pilot and parachutist suffered only minor injuries.

The control tower was a ruined shell until recently when a private company renovated it for use as their offices. Many of the buildings were bulldozed to make way for industrial development. Next to the eastern perimeter track the fire tender and ambulance bays stand stripped of their roofing but behind them the parachute packing shed is still in fair condition. Four 'T2' hangars were built during the war but only their concrete floors remain.

Atcham, Salop

SJ570105. 4 miles SE of Shrewsbury on B4394 which follows course of old 06/24 runway

The first time that many RAF men realised that the Americans were at Atcham was the day in August 1942 when Lightnings 'buzzed' the airfield at Tern Hill and gave them their first look at this curious twin-boomed fighter.

'Atcham Field', as it came to be known, was planned originally as a Sector Station accommodating two day fighter squadrons, with a satellite at Condover. The intitial unit to arrive was 131 Squadron whose Spitfires flew in on September 27 1941. At the same time, 9 Group Sector Operations Room was transferred from Tern Hill to a new building about a mile from Atcham. The Spitfires immediately began a programme of intensive training which included a mock attack on the town of Crewe together with Beaufighters from High Ercall and Defiants from Cranage. A Hotspur glider and its Hector tug were attached for a few days for fighter versus glider exercises.

In January 1942 the Sector Ops Room vectored a Valley Beaufighter on to a Do 217 and the latter was chased all the way from North Wales to Nuneaton before being shot down. The following month, a flight of Masters from 5 SFTS was detached here whilst runways were being laid at their Tern Hill base. At the same time, 131 Squadron left for Llanbedr and was replaced by 350 (Belgian) Squadron which had just formed at Valley and was thirsting for action. The Luftwaffe was rarely seen over the North-West by this time but the Spitfires were scrambled on several occasions although they never made contact owing to poor weather. In April 1942 No 350 Squadron moved to Warmwell on the South Coast and finally got all the air-fighting it wanted. No 74

Collision on a Sommerfeld track taxiway at Atcham (Ray E. Bowers).

Top *Two fighter pilots-in-training pose in front of a P-47 in an Atcham revetment* (R.W. Dean). **Above** *P-47C 41-6237 pranged in a field near Atcham in May 1944* (Ray E. Bowers).

Squadron had shared the Shropshire base for about two months before embarking at Liverpool for the trip to the Middle East.

On April 10 1942 No 232 Squadron re-formed at Atcham with Spitfires and carried out training which included a practice interception on a high-flying Fortress. One month later they moved to Valley. At this point the station entered the second stage of its brief existence when it became one of the first to be occupied by the infant VIIIth Air Force. The airfield was handed over on June 15 1942 for initial use by the 31st Fighter Group. Five days later 35 Spitfires arrived and the whole airfield was packed with Spitfires, Masters, Fairchild UC-61s and Dominies, during which time a Wellington elected to do circuits and bumps. Fifteen more Spitfires were flown in and the American top-brass, including Generals Eaker and Spaatz, made a tour

of inspection, accompanied by the US Ambassador. On June 29 the station witnessed the first pilot fatality of the VIIIth Air Force in Europe when First Lieutenant A.W. Giacomini crashed his Spitfire on final approach.

During August 1942 the Lightnings of the 14th FG were based here for working-up, replacing the 31st FG which had moved to Westhampnett. By an odd coincidence their unit number was the same as that of the Roman XIVth Legion whose HQ had been close to the airfield site centuries before. Becoming operational in October, the Lightnings were detached to Tangmere and Ford, from which they escorted B-17s to Le Havre. They eventually positioned back to Atcham but left for Algeria and assignment to the XIIth Air Force in November. Meanwhile, the 6th Fighter Wing had established a Combat Crew Replacement Center which would be Atcham's function for the next two years. Equipped initially with Spitfires, Masters and a few Airacobras, the unit soon gave these up in favour of the Thunderbolt and a small number of Harvards.

The CCRC was roughly equivalent to an RAF OTU but also gave indoctrination into flying procedures and tactics in Britain. Many of the fighter pilots fresh from the 'States had trained in the cloudless skies of the American South-West and their first taste of English weather came as a shock. In the words of one of them, Lieutenant Sam Lutz:

'I don't remember seeing many clouds during my initial training but on our first flight from Atcham we climbed for 20 minutes through dark grey overcast with only glimpses of our leader. We received more training and experience that day than in months of previous efforts.'

The 6th Fighter Wing disbanded on paper in October 1943 and was re-designated the 2906th Observation Training Group, an inaccurate description as it became the 495th Fighter Training Group a few days later. Many of the VIIIth Air Force's later aces passed through, including Ralph 'Kid' Hofer who became one of the top-scorers with 30½ kills to his credit.

With the build-up of the IXth Air Force in England early in 1944, Atcham also became responsible for the theatre training of pilots destined for its Thunderbolt groups and dive-bombing and ground attack were added to the syllabus. The total number of flying hours in June 1944 was a staggering 9,208, all the more impressive because no satellite field was available. Circuit congestion was severe and only good flying discipline kept the accident rate to an acceptable level, despite the use of war-weary aircraft cast off from front-line combat units. It wasn't all hard work, however, and as the pace eased a little after the Allies became well-established on the Continent the instructors, all veterans of at least one combat tour, amused themselves with little stunts like chock-to-chock races round the Wrekin, a prominent Shropshire landmark.

In August 1944, 18 P-38s were allocated to the 495th so that replacement pilots for the IXth's few remaining Lightning groups could be processed. P-38 training had formerly been done at Goxhill in Lincolnshire but this base was now concentrating on the Mustang. The 495th finally left Atcham for Cheddington in

February 1945 and the airfield was handed back to the RAF on March 14 1945.

It lay idle for several months until becoming a satellite to Tern Hill for No 5 (P) AFU during the rest of the year. A detachment of 577 Squadron was also based here, with the task of providing target-towing and tracking for AA and searchlight units under training. An assortment of Spitfires, Oxfords and Vengeances was used. Flying ceased here on April 8 1946 when the detachment moved to Hawarden and the airfield soon reverted to agriculture although it was used for the storage of surplus AA guns for a while.

The parking pens which once dotted the perimeter were levelled and the tower demolished but fortunately the technical site remains in excellent condition with the three Callender-Hamilton hangars used for storage and the huts for office accommodation. Standing on the road which runs along one of the old runways, it is hard to imagine that this was probably one of the busiest airfields in Shropshire. To this day, one of the most enduring wartime memories of older Shropshire residents is the sight of those massive roaring Thunderbolts skimming low overhead.

Barrow (Walney Island), Cumbria

SD175710. On Isle of Walney 1 mile NW of Barrow-in-Furness

The first aircraft to be based here were four Lysanders of No 3 AGS which landed on October 17 1941 even though the airfield was still not completed. No 3 AGS was sent to Castle Kennedy ten days later and 10 AGS, which had formed at the latter airfield, moved to Barrow on December 1 1941. It brought with it Blenheims, Defiants, Lysanders and Masters plus 108 pupils in the middle of their training. In September 1942 the pupil capacity was increased to 240 and by this time Flight Engineers were being trained here as well.

Ansons were now the main type to be seen but if the Royal Navy had had its way Barrow would have become a fighter training base at this time. The RAF, however, refused to give it up as the AGS was now well established and too important to be uprooted.

When the AGS finally left in June 1946 it had trained many thousands of air gunners, despite the hazards of the nearby

Top *Mayfly naval airship at Barrow in 1911. It broke its back in September 1911* (via J. Huggon).

Above *Barrow in June 1962* (J. Huggon).

Right *Modernised tower at Barrow* (W. Gibbs).

mountains and the balloon barrage at Barrow shipyard. A detachment of 577 Squadron had been here from October 10 1945 to February 11 1946 for army co-operation with Vengeances, Spitfires and Oxfords. After RAF Cark closed its MRU moved here on January 9 1946 until Barrow itself closed later in the year.

The airfield started life with three Callender-Hamilton hangars near the control tower but nine Blisters were later placed in the dispersal area off the north-eastern perimeter track. These have all gone now but the 518/40 Type tower is still used by Vickers who own the airfield and base their executive aircraft here. Glider launching also takes place at times.

Barton, Greater Manchester

SJ745970. 2 miles WSW of Eccles on A57

Barton owes its existence to Manchester's inter-war quest for a municipal airport. The location was selected in 1928 but the Council was anxious for their city to have the first civic aerodrome in Great Britain so a temporary site was opened at Wythenshawe. This breathing space allowed work to proceed on the improve-ment of the ill-drained surface at Barton and the airport finally opened on June 1 1930, the first aircraft to land being Avro Avian G-AADL. In those days the King's Cup Air Race was a lengthy affair and the aerodrome was used as a staging point for the 1930 event. A scheduled air service was started on June 16 1930 between Croydon, Birmingham, Manchester and Liverpool. Operated by Imperial Airways, it was short-lived despite being subsidised.

Railway Air Services and Hillman Airways ran quite successful internal schedules through Barton but an attempt to make the airport international was thwarted when KLM surveyed it for a

possible Amsterdam service but found it unsuitable for the sort of aircraft coming into operation. The Council immediately began to look for a better site and found one at Ringway to the south of the city.

In 1934 the Fairey Aviation Company took over the former First World War aircraft factory at Heaton Chapel to deal with large orders for the Fairey Battle. Before production got under way 14 Hendon bombers were built and test-flown from Barton. The first Battle followed on April 14 1937, 21 being flown from Barton before testing was transferred to the new airfield at Ringway. During October of the same year Airwork Ltd opened 17 E&RFTS to train pilots for the RAFVR, six Moths being used initially. The school closed down when the war started and the airfield was requisitioned for National Air Communications.

Air Taxis Ltd repaired Ansons in the main hangar and the airport was later taken over by the Ministry of Aircraft Production who built four more hangars. One was used by F.H. Hills for the assembly of Percival Proctors, over 700 being delivered to the RAF as radio trainers and communications aircraft. Another was occupied by David Rosen-field Ltd for the repair and modification of Hurricanes, Fulmars and Corsairs.

Civil air transport returned in 1940 with West Coast Air Services Ltd and Aer Lingus operating DH 86B Express air-liners to and from Dublin until the service reverted to Speke. Permanent runways were not considered necessary at Barton but this did not deter such heavy aircraft as the Wellington, Whitley and Dakota

Piper Caribbean and Colt at Barton on November 5 1961 with pre-war tower in background.

Hornet Moth at Barton in 1960.

which visited on occasion. Perhaps the biggest was Lancaster ND920 on April 25 1944 which took off with room to spare, despite the airport staff's grave misgivings.

After the war ended, Barton returned to civil flying alongside the Tiger Moths and then Chipmunks of 2 RFS, the latter disbanding in 1953. The Lancashire Aero Club is still here and despite certain air traffic restrictions owing to the airfield's position in the Manchester Special Rules Zone, continues to thrive. The outlook for private flying was sufficiently bright here in 1976 to justify the construction of a new hangar. The pre-war control tower still dominates the airfield but the four overhanging direction-finding aerials have recently been taken down.

Battlestead Hill, Staffordshire

SK210230. 2 miles NW of Burton-upon-Trent

The only clue that there was ever an active aerodrome here is the name 'Aviation Lane' given to a road which once led to the flight offices and hangar. Almost the entire area is now covered with houses and the Tiger Moths and Magisters have gone for ever. It was referred to also as the Burton-on-Trent RLG and was in use by April 24 1941 when Magister N3789 stalled and crashed on approach. Throughout its career it was controlled by 16 EFTS at Burnaston with occasional employment by 30 EFTS at Wolverhampton. Still in use in June 1945, it probably closed soon afterwards and reverted to agriculture.

Beaumaris, Anglesey

SH610775. On B5109 1 mile N of Beaumaris

Beaumaris came into being because Saunders-Roe's HQ was on the Isle of Wight, right in the forefront of the air war. Since they had been given a contract for the modification of newly delivered Catalinas to bring them up to the required standards for Coastal Command, it was necessary to find a less vulnerable spot to carry out this important work.

The Menai Straits east of the suspension bridge were found to be an

Auster V on floats at Beaumaris in 1944 with Catalina JX598 behind (Leicester City Museums).

Auster V at Beaumaris in 1944 (Leicester City Museums).

ideal alighting area and there was deep water right up to the bridge where the flying boats could be moored in reasonable shelter. A small estate called Friars about a mile away from the town of Beaumaris was selected as a factory site and a slipway was built from it down to the water.

Over 300 Catalinas passed through and work done on them included the installation of armament, radio equipment, ASV radar and Leigh Lights. Some of the Catalinas were ferried to Largs on the Scottish coast before onward transit to Beaumaris but most flew over direct. The first few crews managed to avoid customs inspection but officialdom soon noticed the loophole and a sudden check produced an enormous haul of silk stockings, tobacco and spirits, it is said! Other types of flying-boat such as the Sunderland were occasional visitors as a bad weather diversion.

In 1944 an Auster V floatplane carried out trials from here and in 1955 Auster did further tests with aircraft on floats. Both experiments appeared to be successful but the ideas never went into production. Today the slipway and hangars are very much as they were 35 years ago.

Berrow, Worcester and Hereford

SO805340. Between A438 and M50, 6 miles W of Tewkesbury

As 5 SLG, and sometimes known as Pendock Moor, this site was taken into use in March 1941, originally parented by 5 MU at Kemble then 20 MU at Aston Down. When the SLG was handed over to 38 MU at Llandow in August 1942 the east-west runway was found to be too rough for Spitfires but the other one was

acceptable. In September 1942 No 5 Glider Training School at Shobdon carried out practice glider landings with Master tugs and Hotspurs. One of the gliders was slightly damaged and conveniently repaired on site by the MU.

Berrow looked like becoming an unofficial satellite to Shobdon but the powers-that-be found out that 23 Group had no authority to use it and 5 GTS was forbidden to operate there again. Despite some objections the TRE from Defford, who had an installation adjoining the SLG, occasionally landed aircraft there in connection with radar trials. This practice was allowed to continue with a half-hour limit on parking to minimise the danger of the site's existence being given away to enemy reconnaissance aircraft. It closed on May 31 1945 but one or two buildings survive alongside the road.

Bobbington (Halfpenny Green), West Midlands

See Halfpenny Green

Bodorgan, Anglesey

SH385685. 8 miles W of Menai Bridge

For many years remote-controlled target drones have been launched from Llanbedr over the ranges in Cardigan Bay but it is not generally known that similar flying in North Wales dates back to 1940. The airfield concerned was Bodorgan, a grass field out in the wilds of south-west Anglesey. The aircraft were Queen Bees, a radio-controlled version of the Tiger Moth which had provision for a human pilot if ferrying were required. Control was so unreliable in those pioneering days that a thinly-populated coastal site was desirable, a requirement which Bodorgan met admirably.

The station opened as Aberffraw on September 11 1940 and was occupied by 'Z' Flight of 1 AACU which was to fly Queen Bees for test shoots by AA gunners at the Ty-Croes Range. As there were no aircraft available until November, the airfield was partially obstructed to discourage an enemy landing. The first pilotless flight was made on December 2 1940, P4804 being up for 2½ hours before crashing on landing. Control depended on the degree of skill of the operator and most of the accidents occurred on landing which was obviously the tricky part. One or two simply went out of control and disappeared out to sea. Another turned inland and crashed on Snowdon to the chagrin of the Llandwrog Mountain Rescue Team who searched all night for the presumed survivors of the crash. The owners, unfortunately, omitted to report their loss!

A detachment of Lysanders from 13 Squadron at Hooton Park kept in night flying practice during the full moon period of March 1941, despite a constant stream of enemy aircraft flying towards Liverpool. Other Lysanders appeared when the aerodrome became 15 SLG as a dispersal field for Hawarden's 48 MU. Hurricanes were flown in too, and there were 30 aircraft stored here by the end of May. On May 15 1941, the name was changed to Bodorgan to rectify eight months of postal and rail delays, mispostings of airmen and erroneous consignments of equipment.

Wellingtons and Swordfish joined those types already dispersed from Hawarden and MU test pilots were scornful of squadron pilots on collection duties who had some trouble getting into the small field safely. After several accidents it was decided that it would be a sounder proposition to ferry aircraft back to Hawarden prior to dispatch.

The remainder of 1941 saw varied activity. In July a Dragonfly and a Lysander of 6 AACU were detached to Bodorgan to carry out night-flying from here and Valley. 'J' Flight of 1 AACU was also in residence by then, crammed into one hangar with 'Z' Flight. Some USAAC officers visited in August to study the

operation of the target drones. In October an aerodrome defence flight for 48 MU began training on Lysanders. This included invasion exercises in which two Ansons made a dummy attack on the town of Conway.

'J' and 'Z' Flights became respectively 1606 and 1620 Flight on October 1 1942. No 1606 operated Henleys, Tiger Moths and Magisters and 1620 continued with the Queen Bee. No 2 Maintenance Flight was also here for the repair of the local Henleys and those of flights elsewhere, becoming 3506 Servicing Unit on December 1 1943.

Many Wellingtons were received in 1942 but the total at any one time was maintained at about 30 to prevent them from becoming too tempting a target. The storage fields were surrounded by woodland between the aerodrome and Bodorgan Hall to the east. As an SLG Bodorgan was unusual because it was impossible to camouflage it effectively owing to the day-to-day flying by the AACU. The two Bellman hangars and such give-aways as a wind-sock drew attention to it but luckily it was never attacked. Surface conditions were such that it was closed as an SLG each winter whilst the based units operated when they could, using local runway airfields when the grass got too muddy; for example, in January 1944 two Martinets were detached to Mona.

By the end of 1944 dispersal of aircraft was no longer necessary and in order to consolidate its activities Hawarden took over Hooton Park as a sub-storage site and gave up its SLGs. Bodorgan was clear of 48 MU by December 30 and some of the vacant space was filled by a detachment of 577 Squadron, yet another Army co-operation unit with sub-flights all over the North-West. It joined 650 Squadron whose Martinets had flown in from Cark in November 1944.

The airfield closed for flying on September 30 1945 and soon returned to agriculture. The two Bellmans and one Blister hangar were dismantled and some of the huts are now used for light industry, others being derelict. There was never a control tower but a bungalow-type building was employed as a watch office.

Bratton, Salop

SJ635150. On A442, 2 miles N of Telford

The autumn of 1940 was unusually wet and played havoc with grass airfields all over the country. If the field was not actually flooded it soon became a mess of muddy wheel tracks. Training Command suffered badly from the disruption of flying and was unable to meet its quota of the trained pilots who were so urgently needed. During the previous summer there had been no opportunity to build concrete runways as flying could not be suspended. As a compromise perimeter tracks, or 'taxiing circles' as they were known then, were laid at many aerodromes. Shawbury's grass was in such a poor state that RLGs in the area had to be found. One of them was Bratton, a stretch of level fields just north of the town of Wellington.

Oxfords of 11 SFTS did some flying from here but it too soon succumbed to flooding and had to be abandoned for the winter. From the spring of 1941 the RLG was used when surface conditions permitted but the availability of satellite aerodromes such as Condover and Wheaton Aston lifted the pressure and allowed time for runway construction at Shawbury. The training aircraft were joined occasionally by odd strays like the Spitfire from 57 OTU which force-landed lost in a bad snowstorm on December 7 1941 and skidded through the fence.

The field was transferred to 5 (P) AFU at Tern Hill in January 1944 for use by their Miles Masters and was employed also by Oxfords from the Royal Navy's instrument training squadron based at nearby Hinstock, another overcrowded aerodrome. It was closed during the summer of 1945 and only an area of flat fields bisected by a recently dug drainage ditch shows where the flying field once was. A modern bungalow has been built on the former refuelling apron and the adjacent farm has a few wartime huts amongst its outbuildings.

Brawdy, Dyfed

SM850250. Off A487, 3 miles E of Solva

Brawdy is best known for its wartime association with 517 Squadron which flew meteorological sorties from here with Halifaxes. The crews were proud to say that they flew when the birds were walking and the information they gathered on the weather brewing far out over the Atlantic was invaluable for the planning of bombing operations from the UK. There were no weather ships in those days and accurate flying at different altitudes was called for to check barometric

pressure and temperature so that the meteorologists back at base could plot the approaching fronts. Their forecasts were essential to the success of the Normandy landings.

On D-Day itself one of the squadron's Halifaxes, X9:F-LL144, was in trouble some 800 miles to the west. The constant speed unit on the port outer engine failed and the Canadian captain, Flying Officer Aveling, was unable to feather the propeller which set up severe vibration in the aircraft. This in turn produced oil leaks in the port inner engine which seized and caught fire. The aircraft was ditched but the nose section with the pilot still in it broke off and sank, although the rest of the Halifax remained afloat for about ten minutes. The pilot managed to escape and all the crew got into the dinghy unscathed. After three days adrift they were lucky to be picked up by an American ship and eventually ended up at its destination, New York!

Others were less fortunate. On November 14 1944 LK962 was found wrecked in the sea with no sign of its eight crew. Others were simply never seen again after take-off. Weather and mechanical failure were the biggest hazards and the only enemy aircraft encountered that far out over the ocean were Focke-Wulf Condors on similar duties. Although the squadron records would never admit it there is said to have been a tacit agreement with the German crews that neither would interfere with the other in the event of a chance encounter. Sometimes if the weather were bad at base diversions were made to places as far away as Gibraltar and Port Lyautey in North Africa.

Brawdy did not open until February 2 1944 when 517 Squadron moved in. It had, however, been used prior to this when cross-winds at St David's, its parent airfield, had made full load take-offs impracticable. Although very close to the other airfield Brawdy's runways were differently directioned, longer and more favourable to the prevailing wind in these parts. A decision on the departure airfield was made on the forecasted wind velocity for the probable take-off period of the Halifaxes of 58 and 502 Squadrons based at St David's. If Brawdy was more suitable the aircraft were flown across 1,000 gallons short and refuelling completed here. This obviously complicated the organisation and added to the work of the ground-crews.

Apart from 517 Squadron which, in

Gannet AEW 3 at Brawdy, circa 1972 (via Dr A.A. Duncan).

September 1945, was to leave for Weston Zoyland, a detachment of 595 Squadron was based here for trials with target gliders towed by Spitfires early in 1945 but did not stay very long. The possibility of using the airfield for pilotless aircraft experiments was discussed in July 1945 but was never taken up. Also, 8 OTU at Haverfordwest detached 30 Spitfires and Mosquitoes here for a few months from February 27 1945 for photographic reconnaissance training.

On November 1 1945 the Station HQ was transferred from St David's to Brawdy and with effect from January 1 1946 the airfield was taken over by the Admiralty. Amongst the naval squadrons which flew from here were 898, 806 and 807, all with Sea Hawks, the first aircraft of this type being assigned to 806 Squadron when it reformed here in March 1953.

The RAF regained its old airfield in 1974 for 228 Operational Conversion Unit which was later to be renamed No 1 Tactical Weapons Unit. It is now made up of two Hunter squadrons, 63 and 79, and 234 with Hawks. The function of 63 and 234 Squadrons is to give weapons training to pilots who have graduated from Valley so that they can go on to the Operational Conversion Units which lead to Harriers, Buccaneers, Jaguars and Phantoms. The third training squadron, 79, has a rather special function; it provides refresher courses for pilots who have been on ground tours and the 'students' are frequently senior officers with vast numbers of hours in their log-books. For some years now a US Navy Oceanographic Research Unit has been in residence.

Brawdy today bears little resemblance to its wartime days. One of the three runways has now been closed, the other two have been extended and huge concrete aprons replace the old dispersals. The tower is original but topped by a modern control room with all-round vision.

Brayton, Cumbria

NY172425. On B5299, 1 mile E of Aspatria

Flying Fortresses and Halifaxes landing in what the Americans would describe as a cow pasture and more Wellingtons (over 200) than were ever seen together on an operational airfield, these were some of the sights at 39 SLG, Brayton. Sometimes referred to as Brayton Park, it was prepared with agonising slowness during 1941 because of all sorts of problems including protracted negotiations to close a minor road.

It was May 29 1942 before it was opened and this was only after orders from 41 Group to get it into use as soon as possible. At this time Kirkbride, the parent airfield, had an urgent commitment to prepare Halifax aircraft and Brayton was needed to store Wellingtons displaced by Halifaxes at other SLGs in the area. A pair of Wellington aircraft were the first to be delivered and work got under way to fence the aircraft parking area from grazing livestock. At the same time dummy hedges were painted on the landing strips and more hides were provided to disguise some of the 30 aircraft received during June 1942.

The No 2 runway now being 1,100 yards long, the SLG was more suitable although it was November 30 1942 before a Halifax was landed here. No 12 MU at Kirkbride was also responsible for Fortress aircraft for Coastal Command and the first was put into Brayton on September 2. In August 1942 many Spitfires were readied for operational service, the first one landing at the SLG on the 17th. It was decided to remove the fences at the south-west end of the runway to allow a 350 yard over-run in the event of a brake failure or bad landing. In September a stranger arrived, when a Spitfire from 154 Squadron force-landed in a storm.

The first landing by a Mitchell took place on June 26 1943 and many more were to pass through. As soon as the war ended there was no further need for dispersal so the huge stocks of surplus

Robin hangar at Brayton SLG (J. Huggon).

Wellingtons which built up at Brayton in the summer of 1945 were transferred to Kirkbride. Sixty-three aircraft were flown over in October and another 69 followed in November. Some Vultee Vengeances were similarly transferred and the SLG finally closed towards the end of December 1945. There were a few buildings on the SLG during the war and all have survived, including a Robin hangar.

Bridleway Gate, Salop

SJ545260. On A49, 1 mile N of Preston Brockhurst

This was another of the RLGs created in order to take pressure off Shawbury. Its first recorded movement was on January 16 1941 when an Oxford made a precautionary landing but snow and waterlogging rendered the airfield unserviceable until the following April. Thereafter, Oxfords made countless circuits and bumps when surface conditions allowed, the activity only easing off in 1943 when runway airfields became available. Things had been pretty primitive; for instance, there was, and still is, a cottage perilously near and the family living in it were asked to display a light in an upstairs window to warn pilots of the obstruction during night flying!

The RLG was closed for flying on January 10 1944 and was taken over by 245 MU for the bulk storage of packed fuel in jerrycans and five gallon drums. This was a stockpile for the planned

invasion and 327,502 cans were on the airfield at the end of March. The cottagers wished those nice safe aeroplanes were back! Hadnall railway station was used for the delivery and onward dispatch of the fuel.

In May 1944, Tilstock was given permission to use Bridleway for parachute and container dropping exercises and this took place on an almost daily basis until the end of 1945. On April 13 1945, Wellington NC810 of 81 OTU made a forced landing, was then repaired and departed on April 17, probably the last aircraft to use the field. It was then intended for use by 16 MU Stafford but their CO found it unsuitable and it was reduced to care and maintenance on October 25 1945.

The ten Blister hangars sited around the perimeter were removed and the only sign of its existence now are a few concrete hut bases beside a stretch of flat fields divided by wire fences.

Brockton, Salop

SJ730035. 1 mile N of Sutton Maddock

A German raider flying over this SLG would have seen nothing which betrayed the fact that this was not just another stretch of peaceful Shropshire countryside. The casual visitor on the ground—if he could have got near enough without being challenged—would have been faced with a curious landscape of camouflage nets, hides, small Robin hangars painted to look like farmhouses and, if he looked very hard, aeroplanes. Disguise and deception were the stock-in-trade at an SLG but extra-stringent precautions were

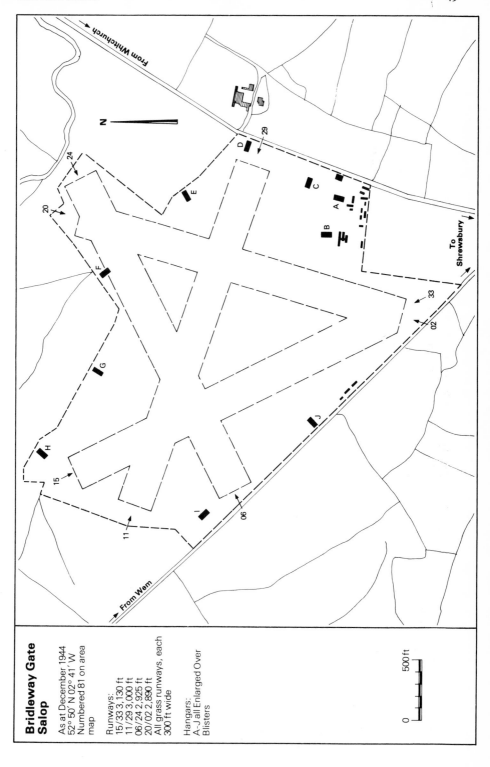

**Bridleway Gate
Salop**

As at December 1944
52° 50' N 02° 41' W
Numbered 81 on area
map

Runways:
15/33 3,130 ft
11/29 3,000 ft
06/24 2,925 ft
20/02 2,890 ft
All grass runways, each
300 ft wide

Hangars:
A–J all Enlarged Over
Blisters

0   500 ft

From Whitchurch

N

To
Shrewsbury

From Wem

29
24
20
F
E
D
C
A
B
33
02
G
H
J
I
15
11
06

taken here to protect the precious Spitfires and Hurricanes which were stored by 9 and 29 MUs. 'Hedges' were painted across the grass runways and cattle were allowed to graze in fenced-off areas to complete the effect.

It opened as 30 SLG on June 30 1941 and, as well as fighters, some Wellingtons were dispersed here during its early career. Later, a mixture of types were handled, including five Beaufighters in November 1942 and Royal Navy aircraft like Wildcat JV722 which was present in July 1944. The common giveaway of an old airfield, SMT in use for fencing, can be seen for some distance around. There were two runways originally, reinforced with Sommerfeld Track but later replaced by the more durable SMT.

A track leads to the bungalow which was once the watch office and continues to the armoury which is identifiable by its barred windows. A stop butt for machine-gun testing, rare at an SLG, is nearby but the sole remaining Robin hangar was dismantled a few years ago. The airfield's secrecy was so instilled into the local people that some of the older inhabitants are reluctant to talk about it even now! There was a section of Horsa glider fuselage at a local farm until recently but this actually originated from Cosford long after the dispersal site had closed.

Burnaston, Derbyshire

SK290305. Beside A38, 4 miles SW of Derby

The little aerodrome beside the Lichfield-Derby road is quiet now after seeing several generations of aeroplanes come and go. First the Hawker Hind and Audax, then the Magister and Tiger Moth, and finally on to the Heron and Herald. Even the four-engined Argonauts

flew from here, amongst the largest aircraft ever to land on its turf.

A site at Burnaston had been surveyed as early as July 1935 for use as a municipal airport and the contract for laying out the landing-ground was won by Messrs Bradshaw Bros of Leicestershire. The official opening ceremony was performed by Sir Kingsley Wood in June 1939 but the airport had been used for flying since at least September 1938 when 30 Elementary and Reserve Flying Training School was formed here. An air display was organised to support the ceremony and featured formation flying by 12 Spitfires, nine Skuas in a dive-bombing and carrier landing demonstration, and many other Service and civilian types.

No 30 E & RFTS was administered by Air Schools Limited and was equipped initially with Hinds and Audaxes for advanced training and Magisters and Tiger Moths for *ab initio*. Air Schools also ran the Derby Aero Club with two Taylorcraft Model Cs and a Leopard Moth.

When the war started the school became 30 EFTS with control passing to 51 Group Flying Training Command. No less than 180 pupils were under training at Burnaston at this time and one of the first changes was a decision to standardise on the Magister. The Tiger Moths were reallocated to 22 EFTS at Cambridge and by January 1 1940 the Magister strength had built up to 54 aircraft, organised in three 18-aircraft Wings. The next major change occurred on May 10 1940 when 30 EFTS was renumbered 16 EFTS. The size of the Magister fleet was soon doubled to a peak of 108 aircraft in six Wings.

After the introduction of the Commonwealth Air Training Scheme in 1941, most pilot training was given away from the

Lancastrian G-AHCC at Burnaston in 1947 (J. Teasdale).

Derelict Anson 1 OY-ADB at Burnaston on July 26 1960.

crowded skies of Britain. However, before the prospective pupils were sent abroad they were given three weeks' basic instruction to determine their suitability. Those deemed to be acceptable were trained until ready to go solo and then sent abroad to complete the course. No 16 EFTS became one of these grading schools and Tiger Moths started to arrive in June 1942 to supplement and eventually replace the Magisters.

No 16 EFTS became 16 Reserve Flying School on March 27 1947 when the RAF's Reserve Command came into being. The EFTS was still run under contract by Air Schools Limited with the instructors and staff reverting to civilian status. Aircraft establishment was now 12 Tiger Moths and two Ansons.

Civil flying had been allowed to resume in 1946 and two brand-new Auster J/1 Autocrats arrived at Burnaston for service with the aero club. Some conversion work was performed on ex-RAF Dominies to turn them into Dragon Rapides and the acquisition of a Miles sales and repair agency brought several Messengers here, some for local use and others for resale. The charter fleet included a Miles Monarch, Aerovan and Rapide and the club aircraft were transferred to Derby Aviation Limited when this company was set up in February 1949. Most of the activity at Burnaston was now controlled by this firm which was later to become British Midland Airways.

No 16 RFS re-equipped with Percival Prentices in 1951 and was joined by 3 Basic Flying Training School on December 5 1951. This unit had 12 Chipmunks and trained National Service entrants so that they could spend part of

their two-year service in a front-line squadron and then revert to the RAFVR. Late in 1952 this policy was reviewed as training of National Servicemen appeared to be wasteful as most of their two years was taken up by flying training. The Government's drastic cut in the reserve forces saw the demise of 16 RFS and 3 BFTS on June 30 1953.

There was now spare hangar capacity and eventually all repair and overhaul facilities were centralised at Burnaston from the subsidiary base at Wolverhampton. Derby Aviation also launched its first airline service with a Rapide between Derby, Wolverhampton and Jersey. The airline side of the business was built up rapidly with the acquisition of some Dakotas and Marathons.

Some unusual aircraft were to be seen here in 1956, in the form of a batch of ex-RAF Mosquito B 35s. One was sold to a Spanish customer and ten others were converted for Spartan Air Services of Ottawa as photo-survey aircraft. Three ex-Royal Navy Ansons also languished here for many years awaiting conversion but were finally scrapped.

Derby Airways became British Midland Airways on July 30 1964 and was by then operating seven Dakotas and three Argonauts. The latter made an appalling mess of the grass airfield even though they only did crew-training and empty positioning flights from here. Standard practice was to align the three wheels in the ruts made by previous movements, open the bellowing Merlins up to full power and release the brakes.

Burnaston was finally killed off by the construction of the East Midland Airport on the site of the wartime Castle Donington airfield. BMA moved its operations to the new airport when it opened on April 1 1965. Since Derby City Council was part of the consortium of city and county councils which had financed the regional airport, Burnaston was closed down soon afterwards. Its buildings remain intact and many continue to be used by BMA for storage. Light aircraft still make occasional visits on company business.

Burnfoot, Cumbria

NY375660. 1 mile SSW of Longtown off A7

One of two RLGs for Kingstown, the other being Kirkpatrick over the border, Burnfoot was first used during the second half of 1940. It was designed to take some of the pressure off 15 EFTS's main base and later in the war became almost self-contained with two of the school's flights based here. The aircraft were initially Magisters but Tiger Moths had taken over completely by the spring of 1942. Due to the proximity of RAF Crosby, special flying areas were allotted to the Burnfoot aircraft so that they would not conflict with the Beaufighters of 9 OTU.

The airfield closed in July 1945 and its five Blister hangars were then dismantled. There were only a few permanent buildings, and the original farmhouse was used as a flight office.

Burscough, Lancashire

SD425110. On A59, 2 miles NE of Ormskirk

A formation of seven Curtiss Helldivers racing low over the Slyne rooftops making a fantastic din: this is Mike Bowyer's most cherished aeronautical memory of wartime holidays by Morecambe Bay. The Royal Navy received only 30 of these dive-bombers which were used so successfully by the Americans in the Pacific. They were operated by 1820 Squadron which

arrived at Burscough (pronounced 'Burscoe') on July 25 1944 and stayed until the beginning of November 1944 when it moved to Hatston. A few weeks later the squadron returned and disbanded at Burscough on December 15 1944, the Helldivers never seeing operational service.

Their airfield amidst the Lancashire potato fields consisted of 650 acres of land acquired by the Admiralty by compulsory purchase on December 12 1942. Four runways were laid down by the time the station was commissioned as HMS *Ringtail* on September 1 1943. It was planned to accommodate day fighter, night fighter and torpedo fighter units, an FRU and a radar school. About 40 squadrons were attached for short periods for working-up, conversion or disembarkation from carriers in the Mersey. The first to appear was 809 Squadron with Seafires on July 27 1943, staying until the end of the year. Other Seafire squadrons here around the same time were 807, 808, 879, 887 and 894.

The 14 Corsairs of 1836 Squadron were based here from January 9 until March 8 1944 when they embarked on HMS *Victorious*. The remainder of the year saw a mixture of Barracudas (810 and 822 Squadrons), Hellcats (888 and 1840 Squadrons), Wildcats (896 Squadron), Avengers (846 Squadron), Swordfish (835 Squadron) and Fireflies (1771 and 1772 Squadrons).

After February 1945 the operational aircraft flying from here were mainly Fireflies but second-line units continued to use Swordfish, Barracudas, Ansons and Avengers. For example 707 Squadron, a radar trials unit, formed at Burscough on February 20 1945 and moved to Gosport on August 14 1945, 735

Below left *Burscough on June 18 1976* (A.P. Ferguson). **Top** *Firefly on dispersal at Burscough in the summer of 1944* (V.M.G. Bennett). **Above** *Aircrew of 1772 Squadron with Firefly Z1946* (V.M.G. Bennett). **Below** *Pranged Firefly Z1960 at Burscough* (V.M.G. Bennett).

The airfield site is still remarkably complete with many 'S' sheds dotted around the perimeter and three Pentads on the north side. The control tower is the usual three-storey naval type with an observation post perched on the top. Unlike the RAF variety, the handrails were of wood and most of the posts still remain. The aerials nearby are an air traffic radio beacon known as 'Ormskirk'. Three of the narrow runways were 1,000 yards long, the fourth being 1,240 yards and all are in fairly good condition.

Burtonwood, Cheshire

SJ565905. 2 miles NW of Warrington

Squadron came from Inskip for ASV training, being disbanded in May 1946, and 737 Squadron was here between May and December 1945, also for ASV training. The inevitable FRU, in this instance 772 Squadron, was in residence between December 1945 and May 3 1946 when it left for Anthorn. Several obsolete types were used including Defiants, Blenheims, Fulmars and Hurricanes and some were detached to stations on the Isle of Man. A detachment from another FRU, 776 Squadron, was also here for a while.

Woodvale became a tender or satellite in April 1945 as HMS *Ringtail II* but Burscough's days were numbered and it closed to flying in May 1946 apart from the occasional communications flight. The numerous hangars continued to be used by RNAS Stretton for the storage of aero engines until about 1957, after which the field was returned to agriculture. The runways were still used by crop-spraying aircraft, a Grumman Ag-Cat in 1968 carrying on the tradition of its wartime brethren.

The unofficial spotters' vantage point was quite close to the runway in 1956 and it was possible to wait at the traffic lights on the taxiway on one's bicycle whilst a C-123 Provider or a C-124 Globemaster lumbered past. The variety of aircraft to be seen at Burtonwood in those days was amazing. To my eternal regret, I was not present when 16 of SAC's giant B-36s flew in for a short visit in 1956. I did, however, see many other interesting aircraft such as Sikorsky H-16s, Albatross amphibians, B-47s, and Constellations and DC-4s of several obscure American airlines on military charters. Seen almost every day here were the WB-50s of the resident 53rd Weather Reconnaissance Squadron, 'The Hurricane Hunters', C-47s, C-118s and C-119 Packets, the latter from the Italian Air Force as well as the USAF.

This vast complex stemmed from small beginnings, No 37 MU opening on April 1 1940. An Oxford which force-landed on April 19 was probably the first aircraft at Burtonwood but the first aircraft for the MU were four Hampdens which arrived on May 26 direct from the manufacturers at Samlesbury. A number of Beauforts, Magisters and Oxfords followed and, in July, 82 aircraft were received, including nine Brewster Buffaloes.

The airfield was now an important target as from the start it had been planned to be the country's largest ASU. However, the only attack came on September 27 1940 and this was probably a chance encounter. Two bombers flew over low and were fired on by the station's machine-gun posts. Several incendiary bombs were dropped near the runways but no damage was caused.

A total of 94 aircraft was received in September, mostly British types but six Martin Marylands were unusual. All these aircraft needed to be kept out of sight if possible, and construction of 20 Robin hangars was started in the surrounding fields. The new hangars were not all ready for use until April 1941, which was not before time as there were now nearly 300 aircraft held on the station, including 64 Lysanders, 45 Beauforts, 21 Buffaloes and 53 Spitfires. Work on Turbinlite Havocs was also undertaken here. Some of the dispersals were only accessible via the Liverpool road and traffic delays were caused when aircraft were on tow.

The first of 20 Fortress Is was delivered here in April 1941 to be fitted out for RAF service. Less than two years later hundreds of the radically improved B-17F and G models of this aircraft were passing through Burtonwood prior to issue to the combat groups of the USAAF.

In late 1941 and early 1942 Burtonwood became the centre for the repair of all American-built airframes and engines. During this period the depot, although owned by the MAP, was operated by a private firm called the Burtonwood Repair Depot Ltd. The actual management was shared equally between the Fairey Aviation Co and the Bristol Aeroplane Co.

Early in 1942 the USAAF had been allocated sites at Langford Lodge in Northern Ireland and Warton, neither of which was complete, to set up Base Air Depots for their anticipated needs. The search was on for a third depot and the choice fell upon Burtonwood as it was already familiar with American aircraft and very much a going concern. The transfer plan required the British technical staff to continue in service until US personnel became available. A policy had already been agreed upon to leave to the USAAF the responsibility for the supply, maintenance and modification of all their aircraft operating from the UK. The urgent need behind this was realised when General Arnold revealed that current plans called for 1,000 aircraft in the UK by August 15 1942 and 3,500 by April 1943.

It was intended to transfer Burtonwood to the Americans' exclusive control following an interval of joint operation which began in June 1942, when the RAF

Old and new towers at Burtonwood (P. Francis).

Top *The flight line at Burtonwood in 1944 with A-20s, B-26s and B-17s in sight* (L. Master via A.P. Ferguson). **Above** *B-36 on approach to Burtonwood in 1957* (S.G. Jones).

aircraft in storage here were sent elsewhere. As construction at Langford Lodge and Warton fell behind schedule the airfield assumed increasing importance and the 2nd, 7th and 21st Air Depot Groups were sent in to furnish the bulk of the trained man-power, coming under the control of the VIIIth Air Force Service Command.

Since this station alone would not meet all the needs of the expanding air force, and was a long way from the bases in East Anglia, advanced depots were set up at Honington and Little Staughton. British rail transport was unable to cope with extra traffic in the autumn of 1942 so a truck transport system was started to link Burtonwood with the forward depots and operational airfields. Trucking operations increased in scope and became an indispensable means of supplying the bomber force.

The winter of 1942/43 saw the XIIth Air Force re-equipping and drawing most of its material and personnel from the

VIIIth Air Force. Burtonwood devoted most of its efforts during this period to supplying the XIIth's requirements and when the latter left for North Africa it was estimated that it had taken 75 per cent of the VIIIth's current stock of supplies.

Burtonwood overhauled engines and propellers, repaired instruments and accessories, performed fourth echelon aircraft repair and gave increasing attention to modification. The joint Anglo-American operations ceased in October 1943 and subsequently the depot was almost completely militarised as American troops replaced both the British and American civilians. The expansion of the three BADs, all of which were now in operation, permitted an increasing specialisation in their work. In December 1943 all radial engines were assigned to Burtonwood for overhaul and all in-line engines were sent to Warton.

The pressing need for long-range escort fighters later in 1943 induced the VIIIth Air Service Command to establish a P-38 production line here for simultaneous assembly and modification of the type. Also from December 1943 all crated aircraft were put together here so that the plants at Speke and Renfrew could concentrate on the cocooned aircraft which came over as deck cargo. In January 1944 Burtonwood assembled 389 aircraft whilst Speke and Renfrew together managed only 219.

The depot was also handling B-26s and C-47s for the expanding IXth Air Force. Detachments of the 310th and 311th Ferry Squadrons were based to help with all the deliveries. The pressure was eased a little when the IXth Air Force began to modify many of its own aircraft at Tactical Air Depots in the south of England.

In December 1944 four Luftwaffe prisoners of war escaped from a camp in Cheshire and tried to steal an aircraft from Burtonwood. An alert sentry spotted a glimmer of light in the nose of a Marauder and arrested the Germans, who had almost figured out how to start the bomber.

When hostilities in Europe ceased the depot began to reduce its activities. After December 1 1945 the installation was retained in a shrunken state as one of the two remaining holding depots for USAAF supplies in the UK. It was re-occupied by the RAF when 276 MU formed here on January 7 1946 as an aircraft and ground equipment depot. It was to stay until September 20 1950 when it moved to RAF Handforth.

The Americans returned in 1948 but contrary to general belief the depot was re-opened not specifically for the Berlin Air Lift but to stockpile material in support of 'Project Skincoat', a plan to supply SAC units on rotation in the UK. The Air Lift, however, needed a maintenance base for its C-54s and Burtonwood seemed ideal. The transports were sent here for inspection and overhaul after each 200 hours of flying and when the work was in full swing the base was turning out about ten aircraft per day.

When the Airlift ended Burtonwood found itself responsible for the maintenance of aircraft and the supply of USAF bases in the UK. It became the Northern Air Materiel Area on September 1 1953 and was now one of the largest US bases in Europe. The MATS Terminal was transferred to Mildenhall in 1958 and Burtonwood was deprived of its aircraft literally overnight, the WB-50s going to Alconbury and the C-47s of the local AACS detachment to Speke for a few months.

The third phase of operational activity at the base began when the US Forces vacated their installations in France. The US Army was offered storage facilities at Burtonwood and started to move in during January 1967, since when many helicopters have been seen here. The only fixed-wing flying was now done by Sedberghs of 633 Gliding School.

Suggestions that the airfield might form the basis for a regional airport to replace those at Liverpool and Manchester had been made for many years but subsidence from the local coal mines ruled against it. The M62 Motorway is aligned along the old main runway, most of the sites have been cleared of their 1,045 Nissen huts and some of the dispersal areas have been returned to civilian ownership. The

Burtonwood apron scene in 1957 with two C-119 Packets in the foreground and a mixture of C-124s, C-54s, C-118s, R4D-8s, WB-50s and C-47s in the background (Dr A.A. Duncan).

Government has agreed that the airfield should one day be released for development as part of a new town scheme for Warrington, leaving only a small part of this once gigantic base under military control.

Calveley, Cheshire

SJ595575. On A51, 4 miles NW of Nantwich

Per ardua ad astra—its days of hardship long over, Calveley now literally looks to the stars because on a concrete slab which was once the floor of a Blister hangar stands a huge radio telescope. Built on farmland in 1941 by contractor Peter Lind Ltd, it was one of those airfields in the North-West planned as fighter stations under 9 Group but found redundant in this role and relegated to training.

It was intended to be an operational satellite to Atcham so the latter's Commanding Officer inspected it in September 1941 and found it well-planned with the communal sites not too widely dispersed. However, 5 (P) AFU at Tern Hill had a more pressing demand while runways were being built at its base and when Calveley opened on March 14 1942 it was as an RLG for Tern Hill's Miles Masters. A whole course of about 50 pupils was promptly sent here to finish their training, one of them being killed in a crash during night flying on April 7.

No 5 (P) AFU gave up Calveley in May 1943 in favour of Tatenhill so that 17 (P) AFU could vacate Watton and Bodney as soon as possible. These two airfields were in Norfolk and, of course, in an operational area which was unsuitable for training. Calveley and its new satellite Wrexham now held a total of 174 Master IIs. As it turned out 17 (P) AFU did not

stay very long, being disbanded on February 1 1944, but not before it had reached its target of producing several hundred fighter pilots for postings to the OTUs.

This was all part of a very complex plan because the Central Navigation School at Cranage was unable to operate large aircraft from the latter airfield and needed to move to a bigger station. Shawbury was chosen and as Calveley was now vacant No 11 (P) AFU was able to move its 130 Oxfords here from Shawbury. This was accomplished in a single afternoon on January 31 1944, quite an achievement, and training continued from the new base the next day, Wrexham and Cranage being used as RLGs. All these aircraft needed parking areas as there was insufficient hangarage to house them all so bar and rod tracking was laid as hardstandings. There is plenty of this tracking still to be seen today and one house on the boundary even has a garden fence made from it.

In December 1944 the unit's function changed when it was proposed to cease twin-engined training, all pupils being sent to other Oxford AFUs to finish their courses. The new establishment was to be 58 Harvards, 39 Hurricanes and four Ansons, but Masters were assigned initially pending a full allotment of Harvards. The pupil population was to be 200 in training plus 50 in a Reserve Flight. Of this capacity, two-thirds were to be fed to special Typhoon/Tempest OTUs and the remainder would go to normal fighter OTUs.

The course length would be eight weeks

Wreckage of Hurricane LE391 of No 11 (P) AFU Calveley after hitting a house on May 29 1945 (via A. Saunders).

Top *Tower and fire tender shed at Calveley.* **Above** *Firing butts at Calveley.*

in winter and six in summer with each pilot being given 40 hours flying. After 25 hours the Harvard pilots would be selected for transfer to Hurricanes and be destined for the Typhoon/Tempest OTUs. The residue would complete their training on Harvards. Flying in this new scheme began on January 2 1945 and by the middle of February the Masters had been entirely replaced by Harvards. The organisation was now 'A' and 'B' Flights with Harvards at Calveley, 'E', 'F', 'G' and 'H' Flights also with Harvards at Wrexham and 'C' and 'D' Flights with Hurricanes at Calveley.

Germany was now almost beaten and this fact was reflected in the winding-down of training units. No 11 (P) AFU was no different and all flying ceased at 16.00 hours on May 31. Flying had gone on 22 hours a day and the people of the Cheshire Plain suddenly found that their sleep was no longer disturbed by the drone and rasp of circling Harvards, for a few months at least.

The AFU disbanded on June 21 1945 and Calveley became 5 ACHU. This looked like the end of flying here but there was a brief respite when 22 SFTS formed with 30 Harvards on October 22. This school went to Ouston in May 1946 but not before considerable work had been carried out on the airfield, including the resurfacing of the east-west runway and the touch-down areas of the other two. Temporary repairs had been made already in 1944 owing to the loose surface but it was all to no avail as the airfield was abandoned in October 1946.

Proposals in June 1947 regarding its use by the Ministry of Civil Aviation came to nought and the runways soon began to deteriorate. The last known visitor was a Spitfire of Woodvale's THUM Flight which force-landed on the disused aerodrome in the early 1950s after engine failure. Coincidentally, the first wartime visitor had been Anson K6265 which also made an emergency landing due to engine trouble on February 28 1941 when construction had barely started.

Although the runways have been broken up, many of the buildings are intact and used for various light industries.

The three 'T1' hangars are now timber stores and a large agricultural depot has been built on the eastern perimeter close to where the three Blenheim Type blast pens used to be. The eight Blister hangars have all gone but the gun testing butts remain, still containing much of the original sand. With permission, it is possible to drive round most of the old perimeter track but beware of the numerous gates while you are swinging the nose of your imaginary Harvard from side-to-side!

The control tower, a common 12779/41 type, is in quite a good state of repair with a rack for Very cartridges still in place beside the door to the balcony. The control room door with the inscription 'OUT OF BOUNDS TO ALL RANKS EXCEPT ON DUTY' has now been removed, unfortunately, and a zig-zag trench in front of the building has been filled in recently. To the south by about 200 yards the original tower, a small square type, has been demolished and only the concrete base is left. The briefing room, alas, is now used by cattle and the floor is inches deep in manure. The airfield is a convenient turning point for low-flying military aircraft and in 1974 two Harriers collided just north of it with fatal results.

Cardiff (Pengam Moors), South Glamorgan

See Pengam Moors

Carew Cheriton, Dyfed

SN055030. On A477, 4 miles NE of Pembroke

At dawn on October 1 1940 the peace of a new day was shattered when enemy bombers roared in from the sea, dropped their loads on the airfield and made off unmolested. One airman was killed, four others were seriously injured, a Bellman hangar was completely wrecked, two Ansons were burned out and a Hawker Henley damaged. Another raid on October 10 caused little damage after two Ansons were followed back to base by a single bomber.

The object of the Luftwaffe's wrath owed its position to a First World War airship station known as Milton which was built in the later 1930s as a landplane base to complement nearby Pembroke Dock's long-range flying boats. It was intended to use Ansons for coastal patrol and shipping defence, leaving the boats free to roam farther afield. Part of 217 Squadron moved in during August 1939, the remainder staying at Warmwell in Dorset. Months of uneventful convoy escort duty followed but, even though they only carried a pitifully small bomb load, the Ansons' deterrent value was incalculable. No U-boat commander was confident enough to disregard them.

A detachment of Wellingtons of 75 Squadron was also here in November 1939 but soon returned to East Anglia. In May 1940 personnel of the Royal Netherlands Navy Air Service who had escaped when Holland was over-run were attached to 217 Squadron to gain experience on the Anson. Their previous aircraft, the Fokker T 8W, was being forced into retirement because spare parts were unobtainable and the Dutch crews were to form 320 and 321 Squadrons and be equipped with Ansons. No 321 Squadron came into being at Carew Cheriton on June 1 1940 and was immediately detailed for patrol work over the Irish Sea. On July 8 the 217 Squadron detachment went to St Eval and was replaced by 'B' Flight of 48 Squadron which brought six Ansons from Thorney Island.

On July 19 1940 an He 111 dropped 11 bombs on the aerodrome, causing little damage although three civilians employed by the contractors building the new runways were injured. The enemy was trying to mine Milford Haven from the air at this time and Pembroke Dock used to send up an ancient Stranraer to try and scare them away. Carew also was invited to carry out night patrols against the mine-laying aircraft but had no success. Its Ansons did, however, chase off two Ju 88s which had attempted to dive-bomb a convoy on July 31.

A serious raid was made on the aerodrome by six aircraft on April 15 1941 in which many high explosive bombs and incendiaries were dropped. There were 12 fatal casualties and seven Blenheims and one Hurricane were damaged. The station was fully operational within 12 hours after the runway had been repaired. Carew hit back a few days later when three of its Blenheims intercepted four Ju 88s off southern Eire and claimed one as damaged. A decoy site near the airfield attracted a stick of bombs in October and this was probably the last time that Carew came under fire.

Coastal Command Development Unit spent a year at Carew, forming here on

Unusual 'one-off' tower at Carew Cheriton (A.J. Ayers).

November 22 1940 and moving to Ballykelly early in December 1941. Its purpose was to carry out service trials of new airborne signals equipment and to examine and develop their tactical employment. It was modelled on the Fighter Interception Unit which had a similar function in Fighter Command and the initial establishment was a Hudson, Beaufort and Whitley. In addition the unit was to have a flying boat section at Pembroke Dock as soon as aircraft were available. In the meantime boats from other units would be borrowed for trials whilst they were attached to Pembroke Dock for maintenance.

The tests were many and varied, the most important being ASV radar development, bomb and depth charge attacks on submarines and surface vessels by night with the aid of parachute flares and, later, Leigh Lights. A trial installation of Beam Approach was made in the flying boat fairway in Milford Haven, the inner and outer marker beacons being fitted to two power boats. An unlikely test was the feasibility of using the Hudson as a dive-bomber. A tail parachute was fitted to slow it down but despite this precaution it was found that the bomb doors would not take the extra speed and were almost invariably torn away.

On October 22 1941 three Beaufighters were detached from Bircham Newton along with seven Blenheims from 248 Squadron at Aldergrove. Several combats were made with Fw 200s and Ju 88s during patrols over the Irish Sea but none were conclusive. Two Beauforts of 22 Squadron reinforced the aircraft available to thwart any attempt by German battleships

to leave the port of Brest. One of 236 Squadron's Beaufighters used St Eval as a forward base for a reconnaissance of Brest on December 19 1941 which led to the award of the Distinguished Flying Medal to its crew, Sergeant Mooney and Sergeant Philips. The detachment of 236 Squadron's Beaufighter 1s also provided anti-aircraft escort for the BOAC DC-3 service from Lisbon into Chivenor or Whitchurch and another of its duties was to act as escort for the Irish Mail steamer.

Important visitors passed through Carew on January 6 1942 when Prince Peter of Greece and General Sikorski flew into Pembroke Dock and were taken on to Hendon in Flamingo X9317 of 24 Squadron. Runway repairs caused yet another detachment, this time Blenheims from 254 Squadron, over to Angle during the early summer of 1942. Another lodger unit at Carew was Coastal Command's 19 Group Communications Flight which spent most of the war here, operating a number of different types, including Lysander T1440.

The last operational aircraft to be based here were a few Hurricanes of 32 and 238 Squadrons which were detached from Pembrey in the spring of 1942, the airfield then being transferred to the control of Training Command on July 24 1942. Two lodger units were now accommodated, namely 'B' Flight of No 1 AACU which towed targets for the School of Anti-Aircraft Defence at Manorbier and No 4 Armament Practice Camp which gave weapons instruction to the crews of Whitleys, Sunderlands and Beaufighters of Coastal Command. In October 1942, for example, two Beaufighters and a

Oxford of No 10 Radio School, Carew Cheriton (via Dr A.A. Duncan).

Wellington from Talbenny and one Whitley from St Eval were based here for a week's training.

A further transfer to Technical Training Command followed on October 5 1942 and on December 11 No 4 Radio Direction Finding School arrived and simultaneously absorbed the ten Oxfords of 1447 Flight which was formerly at Hooton Park. These aircraft became 'A' Flight of the school which was soon renamed 10 Radio School. At the end of January 1943 5 OTU at Turnberry gave up 16 of its Ansons to form the school's second flight for the training of wireless operators who were then to be posted to 5 OTU. Air Ministry planners then changed their minds and decided to abandon the system of intakes linking up to OTUs and switched to a regular weekly intake of 46 pupils for a five-week course. Routine work continued apart from little diversions such as when five of the Ansons were loaned to HQ TTC Communications Flight at White Waltham for transport duties to and from airfields in France and Belgium. The aircraft came back proudly painted with Invasion Stripes.

No 4 APC had left for Talbenny and from December 1 1943 the Martinets of 'C' Flight, 595 Squadron, Aberporth, were detached to Carew to continue the co-operation for Manorbier. In April 1944 they were doing the same thing for ships of the US Navy off Milford Haven. The spring of 1944 also saw an attachment of one Oxford and three Hurricanes of 587 Squadron. No 10 RS disbanded on November 13 1945 and the RAF station closed officially on November 24 1945. In recent years it has been completely cleared

and only a few stretches of concrete remain, conveniently used for a Sunday market. The only surviving building is a very unusual control tower.

Cark, Cumbria

SD375745. ½ mile S of Flookburgh, off B5227

Best described as the fighter station that never was, Cark was used solely by training aircraft. It was built in 1941 on the edge of Morecambe Bay with accommodation for at least one 9 Group fighter squadron. Six dispersal pens were sited off the eastern perimeter track and were capable of protecting 12 aircraft. Almost all of the hangarage, which consisted of one Bellman for major servicing and 14 Blisters, was in a dispersal area on the north-west side of the airfield rather close to the living quarters.

The station was taken over on March 17 1942 by Flying Training Command before Fighter Command ever used it. The same day a new unit, the Staff Pilot Training Unit, formed here under 25 Group. Its object was to train pilots in day and night flying before posting them as instructors to Air Observer Schools. Ansons were operated and a Tiger Moth was provided for communications between Cark and Millom because the latter was to act as parent station until Cark became self-supporting. The first course of pupils commenced training on April 30 and several more passed through before the SPTU disbanded on paper on November 14 1942 and was re-designated 1 SPTU.

The Henleys and Lysanders of 'F' Flight, 1 AACU, had been lodgers since

January 1 1942 and on October 1 1942 became 1614 Flight. 'R' Flight was also here in 1942 with Henleys and Defiants. Their target tugs were a common sight over Morecambe Bay dragging drogues to and fro for the aspiring gunners. No 1614 Flight became 650 Squadron on December 1 1943 and stayed at Cark until November 18 1944 by which time it was flying Martinets and Hurricane IVs.

Owing to the proximity of the Cumbrian Mountains Cark's medical staff often found themselves attending crashes on the fells, particularly when the official Mountain Rescue Unit at nearby Millom was already committed elsewhere. On January 11 1945 the MRU moved over from Millom, their first call-out being to a 51 OTU Mosquito which crashed on Hellvellyn on February 10. Trials were held to examine the feasibility of using dogs in mountain rescue but they were not as successful as hoped.

An 'At Home' day was held on September 15 1945, several training aircraft being on view alongside operational types like the Tempest, Spitfire, Lancaster, Halifax and Mosquito. Less than 3,000 people attended which shows the lack of private transport in those days and a widespread indifference to aeroplanes either because of their familiarity or because people were sick of the war.

No 1 SPTU disbanded on December 31 1945 and the airfield was then disused for many years. It has now, however, been revived for private flying and parachuting and is often quite busy. Only the east-west runway is in use, the other two being fenced off, and the old tower is now a dwelling.

Chepstow, Gwent

ST520965. On A466, 2 miles N of Chepstow

On June 6 1942 a Spitfire pilot from 53 OTU had cause to make an immediate emergency landing when the engine caught fire. After a crash-landing from which he escaped unhurt he was annoyed to learn that he was within two miles of a usable landing ground. Its operators were well pleased, however, to have confirmation that its camouflage was so effective that he had failed to notice any indication of its presence. The site was 7 SLG on the racecourse at Chepstow, which had come into use on May 13 1941 under the control of 19 MU at St Athan.

A winged thoroughbred replaced the horses—the Spitfire—and many were stored here when 38 MU at Llandow took over on February 21 1942. Like many other SLGs it was protected by a local Home Guard platoon reinforced from time to time by any available Army unit which happened to be billeted in the vicinity. A team of Airedale dogs and their handlers also made anti-sabotage patrols.

The aircraft were shielded by 11 hides made from wire wool and netting but these were replaced by bays cut into the surrounding woodland in the middle of 1942. As was customary at SLGs, holdings of aircraft were kept to a level which ensured ease of concealment. For example there were 34 here in May 1943, consisting of Spitfires, Mustangs and a few Bostons and Albemarles. The SLG was returned to its owners on March 31 1945 and racing was soon resumed.

Chetwynd, Salop

SJ725245. Off A41, 2½ miles NW of Newport

As soon as it was completed in 1941 Chetwynd was taken over by 5 SFTS whose base at Tern Hill was about to be disrupted by runway construction. The new airfield was grass, however, and was waterlogged many times that winter. When the unit became 5 (P) AFU in April 1942 its 'E' and 'F' Flights were detached to Chetwynd with their Miles Masters. Synthetic night flying was often done here using sodium flares and blue screens or goggles in the aircraft which gave the pupil the impression of a night approach and landing.

Unlike most other RLGs Chetwynd survived the post-war contraction of the RAF and continued to be used for circuits and bumps by 6 FTS which had replaced the AFU at Tern Hill in April 1946. Tiger Moths and Harvards were used at first but the former were replaced by Prentices and then both were superseded by Provosts for all-through training. When 6 FTS moved to Acklington in August 1961 the RLG was inherited by the helicopters of CFS. A building used as a crew room survived and air traffic control is done from a runway caravan which is mounted permanently on a concrete plinth.

Childs Ercall (Peplow), Salop

See Peplow

Church Broughton, Derbyshire

SK215320. On A50, 2 miles E of Sudbury

Several times in 1943 and 1944 a school-boy aircraft spotter recorded a Wellington with yellow undersurfaces trailing smoke from its tail. He dismissed it as a smoke-laying experiment but in fact it was a jet engine being tested by Rolls-Royce. The early trials were done from the company's airfield at Hucknall but in April 1944 most of the work, which included an Experimental Flight of Meteor jet fighters, was moved to Church Broughton on a lodger basis.

Construction of this airfield was begun in 1941 but it was to be August 1942 before it was taken over by 27 OTU as a satellite to Lichfield to replace Tatenhill. The latter was retained until October 1942 by which time the first hangar had been completed at Church Broughton and the Wellingtons of 'B' Flight with their maintenance personnel were able to move over from Tatenhill. At the same time No 1429 Czech Operational Training Flight was attached, also equipped with Welling-tons. Another lesser-known unit here was 93 Group Instructors' Pool which formed in April 1943.

Training went on until June 22 1945 when the OTU disbanded, the only flying done here since having been civilian gliding. Aircraft occasionally took off from Church Broughton on leaflet raids over enemy-held territory and a board in a dispersal hut was visible until quite recently detailing the code letters of the aircraft for the night's operations.

The main buildings are to the north-east of the main road whereas the airfield itself is virtually adjacent to it, most of the dispersal points being on the eastern perimeter. Land was requisitioned from two farms and a small copse, known locally as Pennywaste Wood, was not deemed to be a hazard and was left as camouflage for parked aircraft. Today, a 'B1' hangar remains in good condition but the tower was demolished years ago. Recently an enthusiast recovered one of the runway lights and was surprised to find that it worked when tested.

Condover, Salop

SJ505045, Leave A49, 3 miles S of Shrewsbury, for Condover. Airfield is 1 mile S of village on Frodesley road

Situated in picturesque countryside between the Shropshire Plain and the border hills of the Church Stretton area is a three-runway airfield which was never used to its full potential. Planned as a satellite to Atcham, its first visitor was a Miles Magister on October 17 1941 when the Commanding Officer of Atcham landed on one of the still-unfinished runways to inspect progress. However, as work went on, the airfield was re-allocated to Shawbury as a RLG, perhaps because the Americans now had charge of Atcham and no-one expected how much the flying there would be expanded over the next couple of years.

Condover opened officially on August 21 1942 when the Oxfords of 4 Group of 11 (P) AFU from Bridleway Gate took up residence and it soon became Shawbury's most important RLG. This made it all the more embarrassing when a Pathfinder Lancaster returning from operations made an emergency landing and had to be dragged clear of the runway so that night flying could continue.

No 4 Group received pupils from 3 Group at Shawbury as soon as they had had some experience of flying Oxfords solo and were able to benefit from

'B1' hangar at Church Broughton (B.H. Abraham).

Tower at Condover (B.H. Abraham).

navigation and cross-country training at Condover. They were then posted back to Shawbury for more advanced cross-country training and night flying. When 11 (P) AFU changed its HQ to Calveley in January 1944 the satellite's aircraft, ground instructors and senior personnel went to Cranage leaving the airfield in the hands of 5 (P) AFU at Tern Hill for two detached Flights of Masters. Flying ceased for most of July 1944 whilst the runways were repaired, the aircraft going to Bratton and Atcham during this period.

The AFU began to re-equip with Harvards in January 1945 and more and more of them were seen flying from Condover. When the USAAF left Atcham in March Flying Training Command decreed that Condover would be reduced to a care and maintenance basis and its aircraft transferred to the former station. This instruction was postponed, however, and the satellite remained in use until June 1945. Around this time the Admiralty was looking for a Beam Approach satellite for Hinstock and also a place to store 300 reserve aircraft. Condover was tentatively offered by the RAF to fill the training requirement but there was insufficient hangarage for aircraft storage. The plan was dropped when Peplow was acquired for training and the 300 aircraft were sent elsewhere, probably to Stretton.

Today the former technical and domestic sites to the west of a narrow road between the villages of Condover and Frodesley are used as a small industrial estate, the airfield having been sold off by the Air Ministry in 1961. The flying field is on the opposite side of the road, all its runways having been taken up for hardcore leaving only the perimeter track. It started life in 1942 with four Blister hangars and as activity stepped up acquired five more plus a 'T2'. Of these, only the skeletal structure of one Blister remains near a wooded area known as Lightgreen Coppice. On the north-west side the watch office stands in reasonably good condition, the words 'Flying Control' being clearly visible in white paint on the wall above the observation balcony. No dispersals were built during the war, parking being done on two large rectangular hard-stands whose concrete has now disappeared.

Cosford, Staffordshire

SJ790045. Between A41 and A464, 1 mile NW of Albrighton

The RAF's Aerospace Museum at Cosford rivals the main museum at Hendon in size and variety of aircraft on display. The collection includes some unique examples of research and development aeroplanes, the sole survivors of some aircraft types and the world's largest collection of German wartime rockets. Another unusual feature is that civil aircraft are on show, most of which have been acquired by the good graces of British Airways who have supplied a VC-10, Viscount and Comet. The museum built up gradually, some of the exhibits being originally intended for the training school. The larger types such as the Vulcan and Victor were landed on the short runway with no trouble.

The airfield itself is interesting too because of its varied examples of hangars, which range from the impressive 'C' Types of the pre-war period to the low-profile Lamellas for dispersed storage and the utility 'B1s' and Bellmans of the war years. The control tower is the only 'fort' type still in existence in the North-West. The station dates back to August 1938 when No 2 School of Technical Training opened to teach technicians how to service all the aircraft on order for the expanding RAF. During the war over 70,000 engine and airframe mechanics and armourers attended courses here.

On March 15 1939 No 9 MU came into being and occupied the first 'C' Type hangar to be completed, the first aircraft to be received being Anson N5055 a few days later. The unit took some time to get into its stride, however, owing to delays in posting-in personnel and completing the hangarage, but was fully operational by the time the war started. Spitfires were the most important aircraft handled, N3028 and N3029 being the first, both being sent to 66 Squadron at Duxford. Fairey Battles were stored and, in October, 14 Blenheims were dispatched to the Rumanian Government, flying initially via Bordeaux. Another unusual job was the supply of two Gloster Gauntlets to the Finnish Air Force.

The opening months of 1940 were notorious for the havoc which the wet and snowy weather wrought on the country's grass airfields. Cosford was no different and many aircraft became bogged and almost immovable, including a Spitfire which had its flaps damaged. Matters improved with the spring and a flow of Lysanders and Blenheim IVs went to France to reinforce squadrons of the British Expeditionary Force. With the fall of France the reverse occurred when four French aircraft, three Dewoitines and a Potez, were flown in by French airmen. They did not stay for long, however, leaving for St Athan a week later.

Throughout 1940 a sub-unit of the MU was at Castle Bromwich storing Battle airframes and later in the year a few Audax, Hector and Tutor aircraft were sent to Desford in Leicestershire to release vital hangar space for Spitfire preparation. A dozen Robin hangars were erected around the dispersal areas to house the fighters and were heavily camouflaged.

Cosford's turf was marginally less muddy than Tern Hill's in February 1941 so a detachment of the latter's Miles Masters used it for circuits and bumps. The MU had now added Wellingtons to its inventory and three Northrop Nomads were stored pending a decision as to what to do with these obsolete dive-bombers.

The blitz on the Midlands drew a handful of stray incendiary bombs but on March 11 1941 two high explosive bombs narrowly missed a Lamella hangar and slightly damaged two Lysanders inside. Construction of a single 3,600-ft runway was started in the autumn of 1941, work being hindered slightly by a Spitfire which crash-landed on it, fortunately without injury to pilot or labourers.

The work was slow and the new runway was not brought into use until July 23 1942 when the officer-in-charge of flying took off and landed on it in a Wellington. A week later the first Horsa glider prepared by 9 MU was towed away by a Halifax. At this time the unit had an Indian test pilot, which was sufficiently unusual to merit the Ministry of Information sending a photographer. Late in September 1943 two Hotspur gliders were towed off by Lysanders, the first to be collected from the MU in this way.

Cosford was still committed to Spitfire preparation, the most important being a batch of 470 which were tropicalised for use in the Middle East. During the same period a dozen more were converted for Royal Navy service. Glider production was increasing too, resulting in the formation of a special Tug and Glider Flight at Cosford in April 1942 for ferrying and testing. Indicative of the strenuous efforts being made was the total of 91 Spitfires and 60 Horsas delivered in the space of a single month in the spring of 1943.

No 12 Ferry Pilots' Pool had formed at Cosford in July 1941 to handle all the Spitfire deliveries from the MU and the assembly plant on the airfield which was a branch of the main factory at Castle Bromwich. Originally a sub-pool of 6 FPP at Ratcliffe, it soon became a separate organisation and, in 1943, the first all-woman ferry pool in ATA.

When hostilities ceased 9 MU had its share of aircraft storage and scrapping. Spitfires were the most numerous type, followed by Horsa and Hadrian gliders. In July 1945 there were 382 aircraft on charge, including a solitary Whitley. A Meteor visited on two occasions in December 1945, despite the shortness of the runway and the poor performance of these early jets.

No 9 MU remained in residence until 1959 when it disbanded and was replaced by 236 MU which was responsible for the receipt and issue of service motor transport before it, too, disbanded in 1966. The RAF Hospital, established during the

TSR 2 XR220 in the Aerospace Museum at Cosford.

war, and No 2 School of Technical Training continued to function. Flying is now restricted to 633 Gliding School. There was a flight of three Varsity aircraft based here up to about 1970 and at that time Shackletons were often seen doing touch and go landings!

This is one of the RAF's least publicised stations but without its graduates the RAF would soon grind to a halt. Some 50 specialist courses are run here, covering such diverse subjects as photography, physical training, electronics and weapons.

Cranage, Cheshire
SJ730695. On B5081, just N of Byley

Just before midnight on May 3 1941 Flying Officer Verity of 96 Squadron was airborne from Cranage in a Defiant for a patrol over Liverpool. He arrived there to find the city centre and dock area burning furiously. Circling at 10,000 ft he could pick out the bombers silhouetted against the fires. Other Defiants could be seen, too, and ack-ack was bursting amongst this confusion of aeroplanes. Verity

chased a Heinkel but lost it as soon as it left the fire zone. Telling his air gunner that the next target would have to be attacked from above against the background of the fires, he dived at a Ju 88, banking steeply at the same time so that the gunner could get it in his sights. Tracer bullets were seen to enter the top of the fuselage before it disappeared into the darkness. A few minutes later somebody shouted over the r/t that an aircraft had crashed. It was later confirmed as the same Ju 88 when the wreckage was found in Cheshire.

The large grass airfield, which was Merseyside's main line of aerial defence at that time, had never been intended to serve as a fighter station. It was built to house 2 School of Air Navigation which formed on October 21 1940 with Ansons. After the Battle of Britain the Luftwaffe turned its attention on ports and industrial targets.

Cranage lay close to the route from the south to Manchester and Liverpool convenient for patrol lines to be flown against enemy raiders. As a result 96

Cranage is now a collection of empty fields beside the M6.

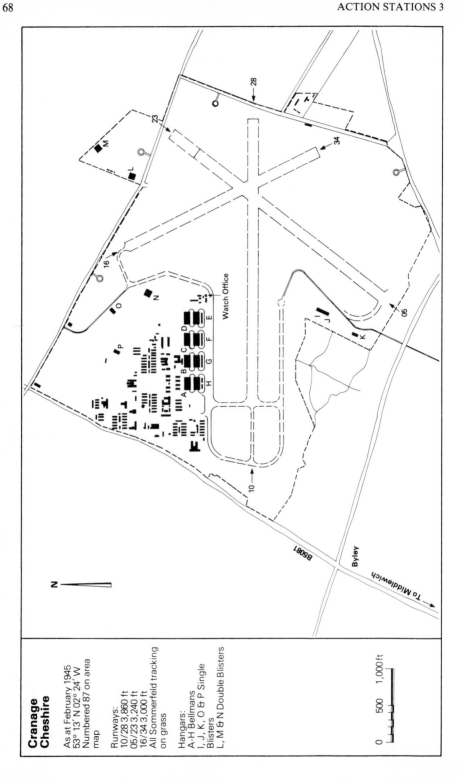

Cranage
Cheshire

As at February 1945
53° 13' N 02° 24' W
Numbered 87 on area
map

Runways:
10/28 3,860 ft
05/23 3,240 ft
16/34 3,000 ft
All Sommerfeld tracking
on grass

Hangars:
A-H Bellmans
I, J, K, O & P Single
Blisters
L, M & N Double Blisters

Watch Office

To Middlewich
Byley
B5081

28
23
34
16
05
10
M
L
N
O
P
A B C D
E
F
G
H
J
K

N

0   500   1,000 ft

Squadron was formed here on December 18 1940 from 422 Flight previously based at Shoreham. The aircraft were Hurricanes, hardly suitable for night fighting, but they were soon to be reinforced by Defiants. 'A' Flight was detached to Squires Gate, 'B' Flight remaining at base.

The squadron was not impressed with Cranage and the CO observed that a thick coppice of silver birch trees on the boundary would make excellent natural camouflage for a dispersal point if the AMWD could be prevented from uprooting the trees. They were persuaded not to and the coppice became 96 Squadron's dispersal. Plans to build fighter pens came to nought, as did a plea to build two concrete runways so that the winter weather would not hinder operational sorties. There was no attempt at dispersal of accommodation, all of the buildings being built pre-war style in a compact area with a block of eight Bellman hangars.

In March 1941 the squadron began to convert to Defiants and a preference for the Hurricane was slowly overcome. Most operational patrols were still flown with the Hurricane and during one of these on March 12 Sergeant McNair shot down an He 111 at Widnes, narrowly avoiding entanglement in balloon cables as he did so.

Two other combats the same night were inconclusive and one almost resulted in the loss of a Defiant. An He 111 was intercepted and chased over North Wales, the Defiant pilot suggesting that it might have crashed in the mountains but nothing was reported. Flying alongside another Heinkel the gunner aimed at it but the guns failed to fire. His pilot kept station with the bomber hoping that his colleague would cure the fault. The German gunner at last sighted the fighter and got in two bursts, one of which stunned its pilot. Luckily he came to in time to get the aircraft out of a spin and returned to base.

In May 1941 96 Squadron was living up to its Latin motto which translates as 'We stalk by night'. On the night of the 6th 11 Defiant and two Hurricane sorties were flown. Flying Officer Verity made two of them, shooting down an He 111 and claiming a Ju 88 as probably destroyed. The next night he was again successful when a Ju 88 was sent down in flames and another was claimed as a 'probable'. Sergeant Taylor made contact with another He 111 and shot it down near Malpas in Cheshire. Sergeant A.E. Scott, meanwhile, in Hurricane V6887 was ranging farther afield and despatched a Ju 88 off the North Wales coast.

During the summer German activity almost ceased and most of the patrols were uneventful. Aircraft were operated from advanced bases at Tern Hill and High Ercall when patrols over Birmingham were required. The squadron was posted to the new aerodrome at Wrexham on October 21 1941 and 2 SAN found itself once again in sole charge of Cranage. Day flying had been carried on normally during the winter months but night flying was severely restricted by enemy action and the possibility of falling victim to a prowling night fighter by mistake. The requested runways were never built but as a compromise three strips of Army track wire mesh were laid.

At nearby Byley a new shadow factory had just been completed for Vickers-Armstrong as a secondary assembly plant for the Wellington factory at Hawarden. Many hundreds of aircraft were produced here and towed to the airfield along a connecting taxi-way. Another lodger formed in July 1942 in the shape of 1531 BAT Flight with Oxfords.

No 2 SAN was re-named the Central Navigation School on August 14 1942, still using Ansons. The aerodrome surface was now badly deteriorated and in April 1943 the bumpy Army track was replaced with PSP. Some Wellington aircraft were allocated to the CNS and it was proposed that it would also receive some heavier types such as Halifaxes and Lancasters. Cranage was too small and the permanent station at Shawbury was selected instead.

First 11 (P) AFU had to leave Shawbury for Calveley and take over Cranage as a satellite, mainly for the repair and maintenance of the unit's aircraft. This complicated re-arrangement was completed early in February 1944, the BAT Flight being left behind at Cranage to become a detachment for the AFU. On paper at least the airfield passed to the control of 90 ITW, a ground school, between May and October 1944. The servicing echelon and BAT Flight stayed on, however, and the USAAF's 14th Liaison Squadron with Stinson L-5s was also here for a few months before moving to Ibsley on June 29 1944.

When 90 ITW disbanded on October 28 the airfield returned to 11 (P) AFU. When the AFU changed to single-engine training in January 1945 a big reduction in aircraft

Flight shed for the Wellington factory amidst the Cheshire lanes.

establishment meant that all major servicing could be done at Calveley, releasing Cranage for use by another unit. No 12 (P) AFU had recently taken over Hixon and Cranage was allocated as a satellite for its Beauforts and Blenheims. No 1531 BAT Flight soldiered on as a lodger unit, finally disbanding on June 1 1945.

Cranage then closed for flying but the former Vickers works at Byley was later used as a depot by the Ministry of Supply and the second Cierva Air Horse helicopter and a Tudor fuselage were stored here until about 1958. The airfield buildings were occupied by a USAF support unit for storage until 1957.

It is hard to realise that this peaceful spot on the Cheshire Plain once fielded almost the entire night fighter defence of the North-West. The kills were few but the effect on Luftwaffe morale must have been considerable. The AA gunfire was impressive enough but the thought of fighters lurking in the blackness was even more daunting.

Wandering amongst the ruined buildings, one looks in vain for some memorial to those events of 1941 but there is only broken concrete choked with bushes. The M6 carves its heedless way through the north-east corner and close by, the old dispersal bays can still be seen in the woodland. Cranage is yet another airfield which had its moment of glory and faded into oblivion.

Crosby-on-Eden, Cumbria

NY480610. On B6264, 3 miles W of Brampton

With the line of Hadrian's Wall along its northern boundary and the site of a Roman camp actually on the airfield, Crosby is steeped in history. It made some history of its own when it became one of the main bases for long-range fighter crew training when 9 OTU moved from Aldergrove with Beauforts and Beaufighters.

Crosby was occupied first by 59 OTU on February 20 1941 with the satellite at nearby Longtown, although the aircraft did not arrive until the middle of March. The airfield was far from complete and the living quarters at first had no light, no permanent water supply, no roads, drainage or telephones. Despite this, the first course of 37 pupils, which included 13 Canadians, was posted in. Most of the instructors were ex-Battle of Britain pilots and many of the 71 Hurricanes on strength in May were also veterans of the Battle. Conditions quickly improved and in October General de Gaulle inspected Free French pupils at the unit and watched a flypast.

Day fighter training went on until August 8 1942 when the OTU left for Milfield so that 9 OTU could be posted in. At the same time the station was transferred to 17 Group Coastal Command. In preparation for the arrival of the OTU runway extensions had been started and three 'T2' hangars erected to add to the three Bellmans already in use. Later in the war 18 spectacle-type hard-

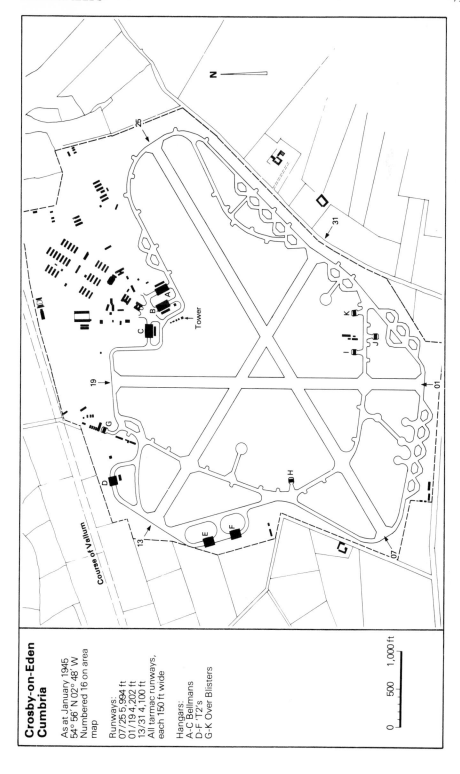

**Crosby-on-Eden
Cumbria**

As at January 1945
54° 56' N 02° 48' W
Numbered 16 on area
map

Runways:
07/25 5,994 ft
01/19 4,202 ft
13/31 4,100 ft
All tarmac runways,
each 150 ft wide

Hangars:
A-C Bellmans
D-F T2's
G-K Over Blisters

Course of Vallum

Tower

N

0   500   1,000 ft

standings were built, the perimeter track becoming a 'dual carriageway' at several points. The first trainees were hindered by all the building work in progress so a detachment was sent to Thornaby in November 1942 to finish their course.

Flying training was organised as a Beaufort Conversion Squadron, a Beaufighter Conversion Squadron, an Air Firing Squadron and an Instrument and Night Flying Squadron. Ranges at Carlaverock and Burgh-by-Sands were used for firing. It was not all work, though, as Gracie Fields and an all-star cast gave an ENSA concert at Crosby on August 18 1943.

No 9 OTU disbanded on August 11 1944 by which time its aircraft were carrying unusual identification codes in the form of Greek letters, and 109 OTU formed the same day with Dakotas. The station now came under Transport Command but not before a request by the Royal Navy to use it for working up new squadrons was refused. During the final week of September 1944 seven Dakotas and crews were sent to Down Ampney and Blakehill Farm to reinforce squadrons from 46 Group who were heavily committed at Arnhem. The OTU crews were given the routine task of carrying freight to B56 at Brussels and returning with casualties.

In January 1945 a regular service was started connecting Crosby with Pershore and Aldergrove. It was very dependent on weather but pupil crews were given useful experience in Transport Command work as there was no shortage of freight and passengers to be hauled. Crosby also saw some operational aircraft around this time as six Lancasters of 186 Squadron diverted in after a raid on Geilenkirchen followed

Above *Tower at Crosby-on-Eden with modern control room.* **Right** *Harvard on the apron at Crosby in July 1973.*

by ten more from 195 Squadron on the same day.

No 109 OTU was re-organised as 1383 TCU on August 1 1945, still with Dakotas. Stirlings appeared on August 14 1945 when 301 Czech refugee children were flown into Crosby from Prague. The TCU disbanded in May 1946 and the aerodrome was abandoned on August 6 1946. It saw limited use in 1946/47 by BEA who operated Rapides to the Isle of Man and Belfast.

The airfield now slowly deteriorated until purchased by Carlisle Corporation in December 1960 for renovation as Carlisle Airport. It was managed by Cumberland Air Services who ran charter services and a flying club. Later the firm founded Northern Air Schools to give professional pilot training but was absorbed by CSE Aviation in 1969. The latter took over airport management until March 1980.

It is not hard to imagine Beaufighters sitting on the hardstands, particularly the one on the edge of the small wood near the western perimeter. The dispersal areas are so extensive that it is very easy to get lost, as I did in thick fog, by taking a wrong turning whilst doing an air traffic runway inspection.

Dale, Dyfed

SM795065. On B4327, 5 miles W of Milford Haven

Strange to relate, this satellite station's aircraft saw as much action as those based at its parent, Talbenny. Manned and opened up on June 1 1942, its first aircraft

were the Wellingtons of 304 Squadron which arrived from Tiree on June 15, supporting the Wellingtons of 311 Squadron based at Talbenny. No 304 Squadron's first operational trip was an ASR patrol carried out by seven aircraft on July 10. Wellington 'T' was lucky enough to find a U-boat and attacked it with depth charges. The results were uncertain and strike aircraft called out to the position did not sight anything. On July 27 the same Wellington attacked an Arado Ar 196 floatplane but again without confirmation.

Dale was built on a peninsula with several of the runway approaches over sea cliffs. A particularly tragic accident as a result of this occurred on August 11 1942 when Wellington HX384 'T' of 304 Squadron was taking off on an anti-submarine sweep. The runway into wind was unserviceable and the aircraft failed to get airborne in the strong cross-wind and went over the cliff into the sea. Superhuman efforts at rescue were made but there were no survivors in the rough sea.

Despite such hazardous operations as a high-level attack on a tanker in La Pallice harbour on August 25 and shipping raids in the Gironde Estuary, all 304 Squadron's losses were due to bad weather or mechanical failure. At the end of March 1943 the squadron was transferred to Docking in Norfolk.

The next resident was Coastal Command Development Unit from Tain during April 1943 with a variety of aircraft. They were joined for a short period that summer by 303 FTU whilst the Drem lighting system was installed at Talbenny.

A complete change of role came on September 5 1943 when the Royal Navy exchanged its base at Angle for RAF Dale. It became the base for 794 Squadron, a target-towing unit, with a mixed fleet of Defiants, Fulmars, Masters and Martinets. There was a lull in activity after the squadron went to Henstridge on November 22 1943 but an increasing need by the Fleet Air Arm for larger aircraft led to the formation of 762 Squadron at Dale on April 1 1944. This was a twin-engine conversion unit equipped with Blenheims and Beaufighters and later Wellingtons and Mosquitoes. As few RN air stations had runways long enough to take these types Dale was an ideal choice. The unit moved to Ford on December 8 1945.

It had been joined by 790 Squadron on August 30 1945, a Fighter Direction School which co-operated with the ground training station at nearby Kete. A night fighter school, 784 Squadron, arrived on February 1 1946 equipped with Fireflies and Ansons. The school disbanded on October 1 1946 and became 'B' Flight of 790 Squadron. When the latter left for Culdrose on December 13 1947 Dale closed down.

Despite its position in the wilds of this area of outstanding natural beauty the airfield has survived quite well. The tower and hangars are used by a farmer and the runways have so far escaped the fate of those at Angle across the estuary.

Darley Moor, Derbyshire

SK175420. On A515, 3 miles S of Ashbourne

The sound of high-revving motor cycles now assaults the ear instead of the aircraft engines which once reigned supreme. A motor cycle club uses two of the old runways for racing and a screen of trees has been planted round the western perimeter track to muffle the noise.

Very close to its parent station at RAF Ashbourne, this satellite was first occupied by part of 81 OTU before the unit moved to Whitchurch Heath on September 1 1942. It re-opened on June 12 1943 when 'A' Squadron (later Flight) of 42 OTU arrived. Its equipment was ten Ansons, nine Oxfords, two Martinets and two Lysanders and training was started immediately although it was often interrupted by the bad weather which plagued both stations. On August 11 1943 a demonstration was held here to show members of the OTU how a daylight parachute dropping operation would be carried out. This had a dual purpose because it would also prove to the local farmers that container dropping would not harm their land! Two Blenheims supported by a Master 'fighter' laid a smoke screen on the Dropping Zone and three Whitleys then flew over in line astern and dropped four containers each. The airfield was again the scene of a demonstration on October 18 1943 when a Whitley/Horsa and Master/Hotspur combination used it for a satisfactory glider towing trial.

After students had passed out from their courses they were sent to Albemarle, Halifax and Stirling units of 38 Group and many took part in the Normandy Invasion, Arnhem and the Crossing of the Rhine. One would-be pilot was distinctly unwelcome as he happened to be an Italian prisoner-of-war who had escaped from a local camp. He was caught at Darley Moor on January 7 1944 and admitted that he was hoping to steal an aircraft and fly back to Italy.

In February 1945 42 OTU was absorbed by 81 OTU at Tilstock and Darley Moor was closed on February 10 1945 and reduced to care and maintenance. Not many buildings are left now, the tower and single hangar having been demolished soon after the war. A large plantation of trees was cut down when the airfield was constructed, the wood being used on the Officers' Mess fire. Part of this woodland still exists and aircraft dispersal bays can be seen under the trees. Down a nearby country lane stands the Nissen hut which served as the operations block and the Link Trainer hut which is now a private residence. Further away from the airfield are the remains of Nissen huts which after the war became the homes of displaced persons, many of them Lithuanians. The A515 cuts through the main HQ and administration site but its buildings are no

more, just heaps of rubble in which ash saplings have taken root.

Defford, Hereford and Worcester

SO900440. 1 mile W of A4104 at Defford village

Serrate, Boozer, Window and *Village Inn,* whimsical names which were to be the stuff of victory and all devised in the peaceful town of Great Malvern in the depths of Worcestershire. So prolific was the output of the Telecommunications Research Establishment that the nearby airfield which it was allocated was often crowded with aircraft of every conceivable Allied type so that operational tests could be carried out. In August 1945, for example, 107 aircraft were attached to the Telecommunications Flying Unit, as it was known, and throughout the war its work was considered so important that any aircraft required for trials was handed over without question, despite the protests of the unit from whom it was requisitioned.

Defford began life as a satellite to Pershore's 23 OTU but its construction was slow and it was not in use until September 1941, some six months after the parent station had become operational. Facilities were spartan, a mobile watch office being employed at first and only day circuits and bumps were possible. The situation was just beginning to improve in May 1942 when the Ministry of Aircraft Production took over the satellite for the TFU.

In February 1942 parachute troops were dropped on the French coast at Bruneval in an audacious raid to steal the essential parts of Germany's new Wurzburg radar. In this they were entirely successful and an up-to-date picture of the enemy's radar capability was obtained. The TRE was at this time based on the South Coast near Swanage with its flying unit at Christchurch and Hurn and, if the British could get away with such a coup, so might the Germans.

The answer was to move the scientists and their equipment to a less vulnerable part of the country and Malvern was chosen. No 23 OTU was deprived of its satellite and it now became the permanent wartime home of the TFU. The move was accomplished between May 22 and 25 1942 and the interrupted trials of improved types of AI radar on Blenheims and Beaufighters were resumed without delay. Concurrently, they were working on ASV installed in Swordfish P4008.

Radar research was just one branch of TRE's activity; radio aids to navigation and bombing were also under development. Not all of the experiments were successful: for example, searchlights directed by a ground controller in the same manner as he would vector a night fighter on to an enemy bomber. *Village Inn* was another device with a protracted development period but no general use, it being a radar-controlled tail turret from which the gunner could open fire on an attacking aircraft without necessarily seeing it first. A number of Lancasters were loaned to TFU for these trials after early attempts with Wellington Z1568.

One of TRE's greatest achievements was H2S, a radar which produced a 'map' of the ground below the aircraft on a cathode ray tube. Areas of land and water could be differentiated and also built-up areas and open countryside. It was to be the nemesis of many a German city, cloud no longer preventing accurate bombing. The prototype installation was made in a Halifax and a Stirling at Defford late in 1942 and in May 1943 a Fortress, 42-5793, was sent here for the USAAF's initial H2S fitment. Other Fortresses were attached at intervals from the USAAF Pathfinder base at Alconbury resulting in an embarrassing shortage of parking spaces on the airfield with all these American visitors.

TRE had a naval section too, which attracted types like the Barracuda, Firefly and a Martlet, FN212. Avenger JS464 was here for some months for trials with the *Eureka* radio beacon system. Other maritime work was carried out in association with Coastal Command Development Unit and included blind torpedoing (apparently unsuccessful), homing on to enemy ASV transmissions and a radar-controlled Leigh Light.

An unusual and popular aircraft 'owned' by TFU for most of its career was a Boeing 247D, DZ203. It was used for blind approach experiments and in June 1944 was shipped back to the USA for the fitting of an all-electric auto-pilot and American automatic approach equipment, returning later in the year.

The code names mentioned at the beginning of this section were clever devices intended, in the case of *Boozer,* to warn a bomber crew when they were 'painting' on a night fighter's radar. *Serrate,* another product of TRE, enabled RAF Mosquitoes to home on to the radar transmissions of enemy fighters. *Window* was delightfully simple, consisting of metal strips of the same length as the wavelength of the radar to be jammed. Dropped to a pre-determined pattern it simulated an invasion force approaching the Pas-de-Calais and drew the Germans' attention away from the real fleet on its way to Normandy. Although invented quite early in the war, the use of *Window* (or *Chaff* as the Americans called it later) was banned at first in case the enemy imitated it.

Tests were conducted as early as May

Defford under construction on June 24 1941. Photo taken from a Wellington at 9,000 ft (Public Record Office).

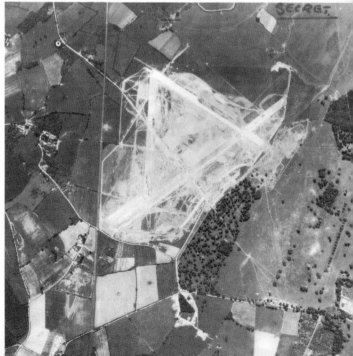

1943 on a means of projecting AI indications, artificial horizon and other information on to the windscreen of Mosquito DZ301. This was far ahead of its time and only in the last decade has the so-called 'head-up display' been perfected.

The volume of experimental work undertaken at Malvern and Defford was so large that it is impossible to cover more than a few of their most important inventions. Suffice it to say that without this unending research RAF aircrew losses would have been crippling. As fast as the German scientists produced something new in the electronics field their British opposite numbers devised a counter-measure.

In recognition, the TRE became the Royal Radar Establishment after the war and flying continued from Defford until September 1957 when it moved to Pershore. Today, the RRE still controls part of the aerodrome, the rest being farmed and one runway is used occasionally by light aircraft. Another runway has rails running along it on which a huge radio telescope can be moved for tracking purposes.

Fairwood Common, West Glamorgan

SS570915. On A4118, 4 miles W of Swansea

Opened as a fighter station in 10 Group on June 15 1941, Fairwood was occupied two days later by 79 Squadron's Hurricanes which were transferred from Pembrey. No 600 Squadron's Beaufighter IIs followed but were soon replaced by the Spitfires of 317 Squadron from Colerne.

The increased flying in the South Wales area with the building of new aerodromes revealed a gap in ASR coverage and three Lysanders were detached to Fairwood for inshore searches. No 317 Squadron provided fighter cover for bombers making a daylight attack on the harbour at Le Havre and all its aircraft returned safely, claiming two enemy aircraft destroyed and one damaged.

A week before 317 left they shot down a Ju 88 into the sea ten miles south of base. Their replacements on July 21 1941 were 504 Squadron's Hurricanes which took part in the great daylight attack on Brest on July 24. No 79 Squadron, which participated as well, stayed until December 1941, the airfield having become a full Sector Station on October 25. No 312 and 615 Squadrons' Spitfires and Hurricanes were the next to arrive, to be joined by 615 Squadron's Spitfires and 263 Squadron's Whirlwinds in February 1942.

On the night of April 26/27 1942 the Luftwaffe made its second *Baedecker* raid on Bath. No 125 Squadron, flying a mixture of Beaufighters, Defiants and Hurricanes from Fairwood and Charmy Down, flew layer patrols over the city, saw seven enemy aircraft, had two combats and claimed one probably destroyed and one damaged. One of 125's Beaufighters shot down a Ju 88 off the Pembrokeshire coast on June 27 1942 and during the same month the pilot of the Fw 190 which had landed at Pembrey, was entertained in the Officers' Mess

Modified wartime tower at Fairwood Common (W. Gibbs).

before being taken to London for interrogation.

Fighter squadrons continued to rotate through the station, staying for short periods and engaged in protecting convoys and sweeps over the Irish Sea. Most were Spitfire-equipped but 536 Squadron arrived on October 28 1942 with Turbinlite Havocs. On February 16 1943, 11 enemy raiders dropped bombs in the area, some of which hit the camp and killed three WAAFs. The Beaufighters of 125 Squadron were scrambled and shot down two of the Do 217s.

The first Mosquito unit to be based here, 307 (Polish) Squadron, arrived in April 1943 and during its stay was engaged in convoy escort and operational night patrols. Its replacement, 264 Squadron, helped defend Plymouth on the night of August 11 1943 with its Mosquitoes. A third Mosquito squadron, No 456, came in November 1943 for re-training on Mk XVIII aircraft and moved to Ford at the end of February 1944. On March 27 1944 two Beaufighters of 307 Squadron diverted in after a patrol from their Exeter base. One had just shot down a Ju 88 near Wells.

With the departure of 68 Squadron in June 1944 Fairwood ceased to be a base for operational squadrons and became solely a training station for these units. This had been its partial role since October 1 1943 when 11 APC formed here. The APC had a unique facility in the form of a stretch of disused railway track on which pilots could learn the art of train-busting. A driverless railway engine was sent down the track to act as a target for practice rockets and cannon fire. A total of 29 squadrons passed through before the APC closed on July 1 1945, the average stay being about ten days depending on the type of training or conversion required.

No 18 APC also opened at Fairwood on August 8 1944 and a total of 11 more squadrons were attached until it, too, disbanded on July 1 1945, the last squadron present being No 609 with Typhoons. An At Home day in September drew 10,000 visitors who saw for the first time at close quarters most of the fighter types which had operated over South Wales for so long.

A detachment of 595 Squadron had been here since early in 1945 for target towing but in April 1946 the whole squadron moved in from Aberporth so that it could be closer to its main customers, the School of AA at Manorbier. However, the dilapidated domestic buildings at Fairwood displaced the squadron to Pembrey at the end of October 1946 and Fairwood was then inactivated.

In the 1950s Swansea was looking for a site for a civic airport and since Fairwood was the obvious choice representations were made to the Air Ministry and the land was acquired. Since 1965 it has been equipped to handle aircraft up to Viscount size and scheduled airline services resumed in 1972 after a lapse of three years. ATC gliding takes place mainly at weekends and a number of private aircraft are kept here.

Great Orton, Cumbria

NY310540. 2 miles S of Thurstonfield on unclassified road

Opened in June 1943 but not fully completed until six months later, this airfield was built as a satellite to Silloth for eventual transfer to Crosby when Mawbray opened. The latter airfield on the Cumberland coast was never built and Great Orton stayed under Silloth's control principally for the use of 6 OTU's Wellingtons.

On October 20 1943 a detachment of eight Hurricanes and one Master of 55 OTU moved here from Longtown and stayed until May 1944. The parent unit at Annan, Dumfries, became 4 Tactical Exercise Unit on January 26 1944, then 3 TEU on March 20, by which time it also had Typhoons. The TEU's Typhoon Conversion Squadron was formed at Great Orton on April 7 1944. Another lodger was 1 Coastal Engine Control Demonstration Unit, a section of 1674 HCU, equipped with Wellingtons and based here from November 17 1943 before moving to Aldergrove on December 19.

Great Orton was also host to detachments of 281 and 282 ASR Squadrons which flew search missions over the Irish Sea with Warwicks. The 281 Squadron detachment came from Davidstow Moor on April 18 1944 and moved to Wick in September 1944. Its place was taken by five aircraft of 282 Squadron from St Eval until the end of November when it was relieved by 281 again. The airfield's ASR role ended on January 2 1945 when the Warwicks left for Mullaghmore, but it had a similar job on land in the post-war years when a Mountain Rescue Team was based here for a while.

Above *Hurricane P3039 of No 55 OTU* (via J. Huggon).

Left *Great Orton tower in January 1967* (J. Huggon).

Great Orton had a fleeting contact with the bomber offensive when a Halifax and two Lancasters diverted in on August 26 1944. Next day 12 Lancasters from 630 Squadron at East Kirkby landed on diversion. They were part of a large force of aircraft which had carried out the first RAF raid on Königsberg, capital of East Prussia. This attack entailed a round trip of almost 2,000 miles. After 6 OTU disbanded the airfield was put on care and maintenance from April 16 1945 and was occupied the following month by 249 MU who used it for bomb storage until 1952 when it closed.

The airfield nowadays presents a dismal picture as all three runways have been taken up and most buildings levelled. The control tower, however, still stands and gives rise to some conjecture. As it faces along the perimeter track rather than towards the runways, did someone perhaps get the plans the wrong way round when it was built?

Halfpenny Green (Bobbington), Staffordshire

SO825910. 3½ miles SW of Wombourne

The Blackburn Botha was an underpowered, unloved aircraft which still draws a shudder from people who remember flying in it. One of them was Mr F.W. Shaw who joined the first course at 3 Air Observers' Navigation School in this obscure corner of Staffordshire. (Literally a corner as the Shropshire, Worcestershire and Stafford borders all meet at the airfield.) Mr Shaw was not impressed with the Botha, as the following account shows.

'Every inch of the fairly long runways (for that time) was used; on occasion, the aircraft were swivelled around at the far end so that the tailwheels were literally lying in the edge of Farmer Jones' field. Then, with a thunderous ear-splitting roar, the engines were opened up to full revs and maximum boost, and the brakes released. The noise must have beaten Concorde into a cocked hat! Nothing happened for some seconds which felt like eternity and then gradually the beast would amble gently forward, for all the world like an old lady out for a Sunday afternoon spin on her bicycle. Only no old lady ever made the noise and created as much smoke and flame as did these over-weight and underpowered monstrosities. Half-way down the runway we would still be ambling and one could catch the first sight of the crash wagon and ambulance which had been conveniently sited at the point of no return where the runway ended, and just to one side. The white asbestos suits of the members of the crash party stuck out like sign-posts and on my first take-off I remember hoping that none of them had a hangover or was having domestic problems which might affect his efficiency.

'If memory serves me well, the Botha had a take-off speed of 120 mph. The magic figure nearly always came up just as the last few yards of the runway were disappearing into limbo and this was the signal for the pilot to pull back the control column with all his strength and which-ever of us was acting as first navigator gave him a hand too. If one was lucky—and I always was—the beast then reluc-tantly and ever so slowly took to the air, shuddered, then rose slowly with what seemed to be a bellow of triumph as the wheels left the restraint of the tarmac. With wheels and flaps up, it started to behave more like an aeroplane, although, at its best, it put me in mind of what it must be like nowadays to be driving a very old, badly-worn motor car in heavy

traffic, in low gear—hot, noisy, smelly and unstable. Having got this far we were supposed to carry on with the training exercise we had been given, knowing that the whole process had to be gone through again on our return.

'Landing was no better and in some respects much worse. The Botha had a very high stalling speed so touch-down had to be made at equally high speed. The actual point of landing was arranged with mathematical precision so that the tailwheel just kissed the edge of the tar-mac. Contact at those speeds was usually hard and abrupt and the sudden silence from the throttled-back engines made it a lot easier to concentrate on the nagging thought that we would never make it and the runway was not long enough after all. The rescue vehicles would still be there and, all being well, the aircraft would pull up level with them in a cloud of smoke from the tyres which screamed their protest to the tarmac. The firemen would take off their heavy headgear and wave cheerfully to us, as though to say "Well done, but just remember, you'll be doing it all over again tomorrow!" '

No 3 AONS formed at Bobbington, the airfield's original name, on February 17 1941 but, because it was unserviceable owing to flooding, the handful of Bothas which were allocated were kept at nearby Cosford and no pupils were posted in until May 2. They had all passed through Bombing and Gunnery Schools and were now to be given basic navigation training. A total of 19 Bothas and 15 pilots were available by June and flying started in

Halfpenny Green tower.

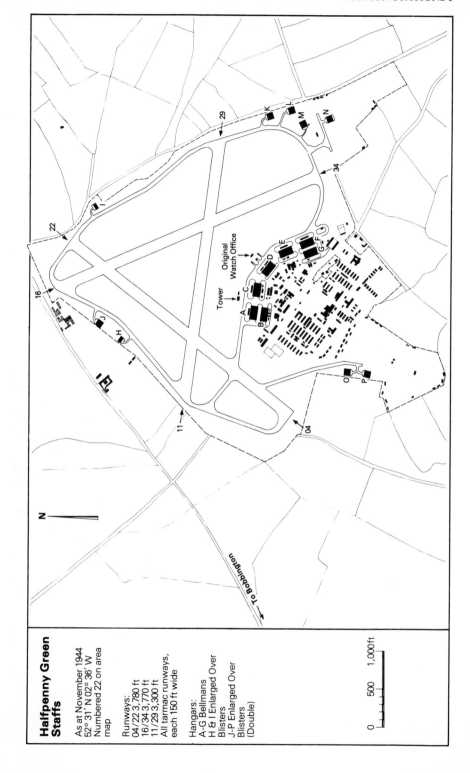

Halfpenny Green
Staffs

As at November 1944
52° 31' N 02° 36' W
Numbered 22 on area
map

Runways:
04/22 3,780 ft
16/34 3,770 ft
11/29 3,300 ft
All tarmac runways,
each 150 ft wide

Hangars:
A-G Bellmans
H & I Enlarged Over
Blisters
J-P Enlarged Over
Blisters
(Double)

0   500   1,000ft

Bellman hangars and tower at Halfpenny Green.

earnest, but two fatal accidents on consecutive days severely shook morale and the unit's Bothas were grounded, pending re-equipment with Ansons. 49 dispersed Bothas and a rapid influx of Ansons caused problems with overcrowding until the replaced aircraft began to be ferried away. Marshall of Cambridge took over most of the Anson maintenance under contract and on November 1 1941 the AONS was renamed 3 Air Observers' School. It was hoped to move the AOS to an airfield nearer the coast but none was vacant so it remained where it was.

The winter of 1941/1942 played havoc with the training programme and thwarted an attempt to start a scheme of round-the-clock flying in January. The run of bad weather continued into March and on the 25th two Wellingtons returning from operations diverted in successfully, even though one scraped a tree on approach. Courses now included many Allied nationals such as Canadians, Australians, New Zealanders and Free French and in April ten observers were seconded to BOAC. A need was now felt in the United Kingdom for an acclimatisation and familiarisation course for graduates of overseas schools in the Empire Air Training Scheme. The ten AOSs in existence were re-designated (Observer) Advanced Flying Units with a standard course which lasted four weeks and was carried out on Ansons. The Bobbington school became 3 (O) AFU on April 11 1942.

Although there was so much intensive training going on basic facilities were still poor. For example, there was no proper control tower, only a watch office bungalow of the type usually built at SLGs. Aircrew personnel under training were still accommodated under canvas as late as September 1942 but Nissen huts were available in time for winter. Ansons of the School of Flying Control moved in during November 1942. The school was actually based at RAF Bridgnorth but Bobbington was the nearest aerodrome from which live training could be carried out. It did not stay long, however, soon returning to its original home at Watchfield.

Inevitably at a training unit there were many accidents, some of them fatal. One of the most spectacular involved an Anson whose pupil pilot swung on landing and badly damaged five parked aircraft, fortunately without harm to himself. One of the staff pilots had to ditch an Anson in the Irish Sea on two separate occasions, from both of which he and his crew were picked up unhurt. Some tragic crashes were caused by the necessity of flying in less than ideal conditions in order to keep up the supply of aircrew to operational squadrons. June 1943 saw a record number of flying hours—3,917, divided into 2,712 by day and 1,205 by night.

On September 1 1943 the station was renamed Halfpenny Green after a hamlet on the northern boundary. This was

allegedly to avoid confusion with Bovingdon in Hertfordshire which had by now been allocated to the USAAF. Certainly some American aircraft landed by mistake at Bobbington but this was a common occurrence everywhere because of confusion caused by the density of airfields in such a small country. The station was sometimes host to strays like a USAAF Liberator which was lost and managed to put down safely on a runway of marginal length. A Stirling from Shepherds Grove was not so lucky when it made an emergency landing with two engines out of action, over-ran the runway and came to rest on rising ground beyond the boundary.

On April 25 1944 No 1545 BAT Flight came over from Wheaton Aston and started flying their Oxfords from here. They ignored all but the foulest weather in order to keep up the training programme and this was to lead to another expensive accident on December 13 1944. Oxford HN593 swung on take-off in a visibility of ten yards and hit five of the AFU's Ansons which were parked 50 yards from the runway. A local ruling was then brought out that beam approach training was not to be done if the visibility was below 50 ft vertically and 300 ft horizontally. Four days later the three crew members of LB515 were injured when the aircraft hit trees on high ground on a night approach. The beam approach system was installed on runway 04/22 which was the main strip during the war and there were hills off both ends. Its position in a bowl in the hills made it very susceptible to fog and an easterly wind brought industrial haze from the Black Country. It was intended to move the Flight as soon as alternative accommodation became available but it

was nearly a year—November 30 1945—before it was disbanded here.

No 3 (O) AFU disbanded on December 11 1945, all flying having ceased a month before, the station then being transferred to Maintenance Command on January 1 1946 as a satellite to 25 MU at Hartlebury. Some Dakotas are known to have been broken up here and a Horsa glider fuselage survived until the early 1960s. No 25 MU soon left, however, and the airfield came under care and maintenance, a situation which was to continue until the time of the Korean War. The peacetime training programme was now insufficient to supply the number of aircrew which it was estimated would be required for this new and unexpected conflict. Several reserve airfields were revived, including Halfpenny Green. Its runways were resurfaced by McAlpine and an Air Navigation School operated Ansons from here for about six months.

It closed again on September 14 1953 and was then looked after by RAF Bridgnorth. Occasional use was made of it by Austers of the Army Air Corps on summer exercises with the Territorial Army. It might eventually have gone the way of most surplus wartime airfields—neglect and dereliction—if it had not caught the eye of H.E. Gibson, an ex-Flight Lieutenant and former Chief Flying Instructor of 25 RFS at Wolverhampton. In 1960 he had the idea of starting a flying club at 'The Green' and approached the Air Ministry Lands Office. Persevering in the face of official inertia, he managed to obtain an initial three-month lease and moved on to the airfield in March 1961 with one Auster, G-APTR. The next step was to obtain an aerodrome licence so that it could be used for flying instruction.

Volunteers worked day and night on jobs such as painting the statutory runway markings. One day somebody tripped with a bucket of white paint and left a giant white blob which was not allowed for in Air Regulations and which had to be camouflaged with tar which is there to this day. The aerodrome was bought by a group of local businessmen and has been a hive of activity ever since, particularly at weekends, despite the usual local objections.

The South Staffordshire Skydivers Club has also used the airfield for many years, not without the occasional drama. In one incident a novice parachutist got caught under a Rapide by his static line and the instructor had to climb down it and cut him free. The pilot had his hands full, too, he had to wind on full nose-down trim and keep the stick fully forward to prevent the biplane from stalling! The trainee opened his reserve 'chute and landed safely, as did the instructor who was later awarded the George Medal for his bravery. The other near-disaster I witnessed myself from the control tower. A Rapide and Islander had climbed to 10,000 ft overhead the airfield for a mass jump of 16 parachutists who were hoping to beat the British record for a link-up, ie, joining hands in a big circle whilst free-falling. Unfortunately something went wrong; two of the jumpers from the Islander hit the Rapide, one was injured but opened his parachute, the other went through the plywood roof of the Rapide and lodged inside. Apart from broken wrists he was otherwise unhurt. Changing aeroplanes in mid-air is a rare event!

Post-war Halfpenny Green has always existed in an atmosphere of official intolerance and local hostility and there is little incentive to inject much capital. Rumours of closure continue as always but this pleasant little airfield will probably survive for a long time to come. Two legends cling to it, one, the ghost, difficult to prove. I spent many a night on the airfield alone, either in the tower or in a caravan but never saw anything. The other, that this was the 'Halfpenny Field' immortalised in the film *Way to the Stars,* is false as it was definitely not shot here. The locals, however, are certain that a film was made here but nobody knows the title. Probably it was merely a training film which will never come to light again.

Hardwick Park, Derbyshire

SK465645. 5 miles NW of Mansfield

Birthplace in 1518 of the formidable Bess of Hardwick, Hardwick Hall is just one of the surprisingly large number of historic family homes in Derbyshire. It is said to be one of the most beautiful houses in England but this did not save its grounds from requisition for aircraft dispersal.

As 37 SLG the site was prepared by Rendel, Palmer and Tritton, contractors for most if not all of the SLGs throughout the UK. It consisted of a 16-acre parking

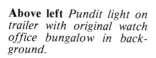

Above left *Pundit light on trailer with original watch office bungalow in background.*

Right *Halfpenny Green on March 10 1948* (Crown Copyright).

Haverfordwest tower with 'T2' behind (A.J. Ayers).

area to accommodate up to 65 aircraft and a single 1,000-yard grass runway aligned roughly north-south. It was scheduled to open in May 1941 but the first aeroplanes—two Defiants—could not be flown in until September 29 from the parent 27 MU at Shawbury. Many more were brought in subsequently but joint Army use of the park caused problems.

As the Airborne Forces began to employ it more intensively for their realistic training, the RAF expressed concern that the live ammunition being used made the SLG unsafe both for their ground-crew and for stored aircraft. This, coupled with the fact that the approaches to the landing strip had always been hazardous because of belts of trees, resulted in Hardwick Park being transferred to the sole control of the Airborne Forces on September 14 1943 and all aircraft removed. Today there is no trace of its use as an aerodrome.

Haverfordwest, Dyfed

SM955190. On A40, 1½ miles N of the town

The survey for SLG sites throughout the British Isles in the autumn of 1940 resulted in the discovery of many suitable locations for full airfields. One of these was Haverfordwest, known locally as Withybush. Its development forced the closure of the SLG at Rudbaxton, half a mile to the north, a location which had never been considered entirely satisfactory.

In October 1942 Haverfordwest's satellite airfield at Templeton 13 miles distant was nearer completion so it was decided to

set up the Station HQ there and move it to the parent as soon as the latter was completed. The official opening date was November 10 but the airfield was still far from complete as labour and plant had been withdrawn continually to other airfields under construction at St David's and Brawdy. Somewhat prematurely on November 30 four Whitley aircraft along with a ground party arrived from 3 OTU at Cranwell. They soon went back, however, when it was found that there was no hangarage and the whole place was a sea of mud. Another unexpected difficulty was the overloading of the local power station in the town of Haverfordwest which played havoc with signals and other apparatus needing a balanced power supply. At other RAF stations in the neighbourhood teleprinters could not be used at certain times because of this and the local communities eventually benefited from the improvement in power supplies.

The move of the OTU from Cranwell was now held up which in turn prevented the formation of a Ferry Training Unit at that airfield. It was June 1943 before the Whitleys, Wellingtons and Ansons of 3 OTU were seen at Haverfordwest, engaged in general-reconnaissance crew training. The Whitleys were soon replaced by more Wellingtons and the Ansons of what was known as 'O' Flight were detached to the Templeton satellite. A typical course was made up of 90 personnel comprising 30 pilots, 15 navigators and 45 wireless-operator airgunners. In December 1943 the Ansons were passed on to 12 Radio School at St Athan and the OTU disbanded on January 4 1944, to be absorbed by 6 OTU at Silloth. On the same day 7 OTU brought in its Wellingtons from Limavady in Northern Ireland. Its role was a similar one of general-reconnaissance and ASV training but the unit was redesignated 4 Refresher Flying Unit on May 16 1944. Between then and September 1944, when it was disbanded, No 4 RFU pilots delivered aircraft around the country between various Coastal Command stations and repair organisations like Brooklands Aviation at Sywell and took part in a number of exercises.

The training of photographic reconnaissance pilots was also the responsibility of Coastal Command, being carried out by 8 OTU at Dyce, near Aberdeen. At the beginning of January 1945 this unit was transferred to Haverfordwest. It was equipped with Mosquitoes and Spitfires and practised high and low level photography all over the British Isles. It was also engaged in an aerial survey of Great Britain as a secondary task. This was done on an *ad hoc* basis during training flights but in April 1945 the commitment was removed elsewhere. At the same time some rationalisation of the training scheme was carried out with photo-reconnaissance, fighter-reconnaissance and coastal courses being combined at 8 OTU. 'B', 'C', 'D' and 'E' Flights were at Haverfordwest and 'A' Flight at Templeton.

By the end of February the stragglers off courses at Dyce and East Fortune were posted to squadrons and the first three courses at the new base were at full strength and in residence. On February 27, 30 aircraft were transferred to the new satellite at Brawdy leaving a small ground party at Templeton to repair aircraft. A humorous incident took place in March illustrating how much the multiplicity of airfields in the area confused Dominion-trained aircrew. An Oxford took off for St Athan, landed at St Eval by mistake, left for St Athan but missed it a second time and landed at Carew Cheriton. The pilot gave up at this point and returned to Haverfordwest in disgust!

No 8 OTU went to Mount Farm on June 21 1945 so as to be near Benson, the main base for the RAF's photo-reconnaissance squadrons, a move it was hoped would be advantageous to both organisations. An ACHU was the last RAF unit to use the airfield and when it moved to Thorney Island Haverfordwest closed on November 22 1945.

It was re-opened in 1952 by Pembrokeshire County Council so that Cambrian Air Services could operate a short-lived Haverfordwest-Cardiff service with Rapides. The West Wales Gliding Club has used the airfield as a launching site for many years and it is one of the few available aerodromes in this part of the country for business and light aircraft. One of the runways has been withdrawn from use and the other two have been reduced in usable length because of a public road across their northern extremities.

Hawarden, Clwyd
SJ350650. On A55, 3 miles SW of Chester

At regular intervals, wing sets for the A300 and A310 Airbus leave British Aerospace's Broughton factory for transportation to the Continent where the finished aircraft are assembled. The irony is that this works and airfield, which were built to meet a threat from Europe, are now a senior partner in a European consortium to promote the cause of peace and commerce through cheaper travel.

During 1935 a system of government-sponsored shadow factories was proposed for the quantity production of aircraft and aero-engines in the event of war. Their function was to produce in quantity any type of airframe or engine that had been officially frozen in design. This in turn allowed the parent firm to develop new or improved types and, in time, to establish production at shadow factories so, it was hoped, there would be a continuing technical advance to keep the production of military aircraft abreast of operational requirements. The criteria for these factories was that they must be near, but not too near, to centres of population from which a labour force could be drawn, and possess good road and rail access.

Work was started near Chester in November 1937 on a plant for the production of Wellingtons and the adjoining land was requisitioned for a flying field. Part of this had been used formerly for RAF Sealand as a RLG. The first Chester contract was placed in May 1939 for 750 Wellingtons, the initial locally-assembled aircraft (mainly from Weybridge parts) being L7770. This was put together in a Bellman hangar as the main factory block (then the largest in Europe) was still in the final stages of construction. It made its maiden flight on August 2 1939 but flooding on the newly-completed aerodrome was so bad that the Wellington had to be flown to Weybridge for testing. Wellington assembly continued throughout the war, a total of 5,540 having been completed when production ceased at Hawarden in October 1945. A large number of these were produced by the secondary assembly-line at Byley on the edge of Cranage aerodrome but unfortunately there seems to be no recorded subdivision of numbers built at each plant.

It was a Chester-built aircraft, L7818, on which Sergeant James Ward won the Victoria Cross on the night of July 7 1941 after it was set on fire by a night fighter. He crawled out on the wing, kicking footholes in the fabric, and smothered the fire with an engine cover. Another Wellington, R1333, was subscribed by the factory employees to the sum of £15,000 and named 'Broughton Wellington'. It never went into action, however, being destroyed in an air raid on the airfield on November 14 1940.

The attack was made on the main site of 48 MU which had formed at Hawarden on March 6 1940 to deal mainly with Wellington preparation for operational use, plus other types like the Lysander, Hereford and Botha. Two of the bombs penetrated the roofs of both K and J hangars and exploded inside, destroying three Miles Magisters and Wellington R1333 and causing varying degrees of damage to 24 other aircraft of such diverse types as Botha, Henley, Hurricane and Roc. The only casualty, it is recorded, was one unfortunate rat!

Hawarden's most active users throughout the war were a succession of OTUs for fighter and fighter-reconnaissance pilots. The first was 7 OTU which took over the station on June 15 1940, No 48 MU then becoming a lodger unit. Some 25 Spitfires, 14 Hurricanes and 13 Masters were on strength initially but 10 Group decided that it should standardise on Spitfires and 58 were made available by August, together with 17 Masters and six Battles which formed a target-towing flight.

Fighter training was still a haphazard business compared with the streamlined programme which evolved by the middle of 1941. Some pilots left OTUs with as little as ten hours' Spitfire or Hurricane experience. This was at the height of the Battle of Britain when the supply of pilots presented an acute problem and it was considered that this brief training period was sufficient for the type of defensive warfare being waged in 1940. No 7 was one of three fighter OTUs and was the only one specialising in the Spitfire. The course was a mere two weeks at this time and was concerned mainly with converting

the trainee pilot on to the Spitfire with a little basic instruction in operational flying. Some had trained on Masters and Hurricanes but others had flown nothing more advanced than a Lysander or Hart biplane. Things were not quite as bad as in the First World War when pilots sometimes went into action with as little as 12 hours' solo flying behind them, but many young men were shot down over the Home Counties on their first operational flight, easy meat for veterans of Hitler's Condor Legion from the Spanish Civil War.

There was an opportunity to hit back on home ground, so to speak, as an unofficial Battle Flight of three Spitfires was kept at Hawarden permanently armed and available for use by any of the instructors. The North-West had virtually no defences at this time owing to the operational squadrons being heavily committed in the South. The CO of the OTU, Wing Commander J.R. Hallings-Pott, DSO, had a personal, unofficial link with 7 Group of the Observer Corps at Manchester who would notify him of any enemy aircraft in the area. The Flight's first combat took place on August 14 1940 when an He 111 which had bombed Sealand was engaged and brought down at Saltney.

Three weeks later, on September 7, a Ju 88 took off from Buc near Paris to photograph the results of four consecutive nights of bombing on Liverpool. The bomber was spotted at 20,000 ft over the Wirral by an alert ROC post and the information was passed via Hawarden to Sergeant L.S. Pilkington, DFM, who was carrying out exercises with a pupil. Sergeant Pilkington was, like all the 'B' Flight instructors, a veteran of 73 Squadron which had seen much action in France. He sent his unarmed companion back to base and, after a running fight across North Wales, the Ju 88 crashlanded on a mountainside in Merionethshire, the crew being taken prisoner. A Do 215 sent down into the sea off Anglesey on September 18 1940 was the Battle Flight's last victim.

The OTU, which was renumbered 57 OTU on December 28 1940, suffered severe disruption during the autumn and winter of 1940 owing to the flooding of the aerodrome and most of the flying was done from Speke, Sealand and Cranage. Only a single short runway had been laid for Wellington testing and this is still in use today as a taxiway, known as the

The Broughton Wellington
7th. Nov. 1940.

Above *The 'Broughton Wellington' at Hawarden on November 7 1940* (Clwyd Record Office). **Below** *Ground collision involving Spitfire and Master at Hawarden in 1940* (Vickers-Armstrong). **Bottom** *Vickers' flight shed at Hawarden in 1944 with a Lancaster and Wellington XIV* (Vickers-Armstrong).

Vickers Track. Contractors were hard-pressed to build all the runways which were so badly needed that wet winter, but Hawarden had priority because of its Spit-fire OTU. As soon as the weather improved in the spring of 1941, work was started by Gerrard of Manchester. While this was going on, the airfield and its surrounding dispersal fields were crammed with staked-out Bothas, Wellingtons and many other types. The situation was eased somewhat by SLGs being taken into use at Aberffraw, Anglesey and Tatton Park in Cheshire, 48 MU giving up storage facilities at Elmdon and Ansty in Warwickshire as these were considered too far away.

Aircraft ferrying within Great Britain was done mainly by the Air Transport Auxiliary, a civilian organisation which came initially under the MAP and was eventually absorbed by RAF Transport Command. Its pilots were recruited amongst professional and amateur flyers ineligible, for health or age reasons, for the RAF, thus enabling service pilots to be released for operational flying. No 3 Ferry Pilots' Pool at Hawarden was the first branch establishment of the main Ferry Pool at White Waltham and functioned smoothly until ATA was disbanded in November 1945. 'B' Flight of 4 FPP (later to be renumbered 9 FPP) was also attached from October 11 1940 until being disbanded on January 31 1941. Another short-lived lodger unit was 3 Delivery Flight which formed on April 7 1941 and moved to High Ercall on January 10 1942. It was responsible for the delivery of fighter aircraft to units in 9 and 12 Groups.

Future aces like Johnnie Johnson and 'Screwball' Beurling flew their first Spitfires at Hawarden and in the summer of 1942 the OTU did so much flying that it achieved the all-time OTU record for the highest monthly total of flying hours, logging 5,282 during June. Circuit congestion was so bad with no satellite available that Vickers complained to the Air Ministry that it was interfering with Wellington testing. No 57 OTU was then banished to Eshott in the wilds of Northumberland in November 1942. This respite was brief, however, as 41 OTU equipped with Mustang 1s replaced it on November 14. Its task was Army co-operation instruction which became known as fighter-reconnaissance after Army Co-operation Command disbanded on June 1 1943 and transferred all its units

to Fighter Command. The satellite at Poulton was ready for use in March 1943 and took some of the load off the main aerodrome.

Operational aircraft were never based here but it was a welcome haven for aircraft diverting when their bases were fogged in. On June 9 1944, for example, 13 Halifaxes from 420 and 425 Squadrons came in from a raid on marshalling yards in Northern France, as did a Lancaster on July 30. USAAF aircraft on the southern ferry route from the Azores sometimes found their way in on the rare occasions that Valley was closed. Most of them were Liberators but on January 13 1944 two C-54 Skymasters of Air Transport Command flew in direct from the Azores. General George Patton visited on at least one occasion in his Dominie transport, although the HQ of his 3rd Army, near Knutsford, was served more conveniently by Cranage. On July 16 1944, 1,044 US troops were transported from Hawarden to Normandy in 59 C-47s, taking off at intervals of a few minutes. This operation was repeated on a smaller scale on August 7 when 21 C-47s emplaned 420 troops for France.

In September and October of 1944 Seafires from 808 and 885 Squadrons of the Fleet Air Arm were temporarily attached to 41 OTU for tactical reconnais-sance training. The OTU was reorganised in March 1945, the fighter-recce wing moving to Chilbolton in Hampshire and retaining the desigation 41 OTU while the day fighter wing located at Poulton was to move to Hawarden and become 58 OTU on March 12. A total of six courses had passed through before the unit became redundant and closed down on July 20 1945. Control of the airfield now passed to 41 Group Maintenance Command and all the aircraft in open storage were moved within the aerodrome boundary so that the extensive dispersal fields could be de-requisitioned.

A total of 1,091 aircraft was in stock at the end of June, including those at the Sub-Storage Site at Hooton Park. The types were mainly Halifaxes and Wellingtons but Vengeances, Masters, Martinets, Hotspurs and Ansons were also present. The figure rose to 1,127 in July and to a peak of 1,177 in September. Most of the aerodrome was jammed with parked aircraft but the runways and a narrow safety strip were left clear so that more aircraft destined for the axe and blow-torch could land. Destruction was

The King and Queen at Hawarden in 1942 with General Manager B.A. Duncan. The Wellington (BJ708) was issued to No 75 Squadron and was lost on operations on August 27 1942 (Vickers-Armstrong).

but one function of the MU; it continued to prepare new aircraft for the RAF and refurbish surplus ones for the newly-revived European air forces.

No 4 Ferry Pool, later 4 (Home) Ferry Unit, took over where the ATA left off and many interesting aircraft passed through their hands, such as a Lancastrian and several ex-Luftwaffe Ju 52s en route to Belfast. On the closure of Atcham in April 1946, the detachment of 577 Squadron moved to Hawarden with its Oxfords, Spitfire XVIs and a Vengeance for target-towing. Most of the flying was Army co-operation work for Western Command whose HQ was at Chester. Two months later, on June 15, the detachment disbanded after 2½ years of operation from three different bases. It had provided training for 27 different Army and Navy units, amounting to 17,500 flying hours.

Vickers had switched to building Lancasters in June 1944 and had delivered 235 when production ceased in September 1945. At this point, the aircraft on the production line were replaced by prefabricated aluminium houses, better known as 'pre-fabs', intended as a short-term solution to a housing shortage caused by war damage and a rising population. Aircraft construction returned in 1948 when de Havilland took over the factory to help cope with large numbers of orders for Doves, Vampires, Hornets and Mosquitoes which the main factory at Hatfield could not accommodate. The last Mosquito built first flew in November

1950 and the vacant space in the factory was re-allocated to production of the Dove, a type which was destined to be built in greater numbers than any other British civil aircraft since World War 2. There was a lot of activity in the 1950s with Vampires, Venoms, Chipmunks, Doves and Herons always to be seen, as well as the first Comet 4s for BOAC. On the other side of the field the RAF graveyard contained a succession of Horsas, Wellingtons, Ansons and even a few Halifaxes which had survived the hundreds present not long before.

The RAF station closed on March 31 1959 and with it went 47 MU which had come from Sealand eight years before as an aircraft packing unit. The other based units, 48 MU and 173 Squadron, (the latter formed out of 4 (H) FU on June 7 1952) had disbanded on July 1 and September 1 1957, respectively. No 631 Gliding School soldiered on with its Sedberghs and Cadets until it left for Sealand in May 1963.

In the early 1960s, de Havilland tried to produce some revenue by the encouragement of passenger services through what was now known officially as Hawarden Airport. The Liverpool-based firm, Starways Ltd, started a London route mainly with Viscounts and DC-3s in April 1962 and this continued when the company was taken over by British Eagle who brought the schedule to an end in December 1966. Since then, there have been other short-lived attempts to operate

Hurricane 5500M (ex-PG499) at Hawarden Battle of Britain Display on September 15 1956 (C.P. Whalley).

services, the most recent being Air Wales' Cardiff run which was suspended in June 1979.

Under the reorganisation of the British aircraft industry de Havilland became part of Hawker-Siddeley and then British Aerospace. Almost all the Doves and Herons were built at Chester and another success story, the HS 125, is now approaching the Dove's production total. The '125 and wings for the Airbus look like keeping the factory busy for many years to come.

Hell's Mouth, Gwynedd

SH270285. On unclassified road, 2 miles W of Abersoch

In heavy rain on May 22 1942 two West-land Whirlwind fighters of 263 Squadron were vectored on to an enemy bomber far out over the Irish Sea. Radio contact with base at Fairwood Common was lost and the leader decided to break off the chase and turn east while there was still enough fuel left to reach the coast. By a miracle they found the small airfield at Hell's Mouth and came down safely, literally on the last few drops of petrol. The squadron diary recorded that this was the greatest duration operational flight ever made by Whirlwinds.

The airfield where they landed was prepared in 1937 as a range for 5 Armament Training Camp at nearby Penrhos. The high prevalence of sea mists soon forced its closure but it was later re-opened under Flying Training Command

as a RLG for the Ansons of 9 (O) AFU, also at Penrhos. Its use was spasmodic but it often served as a haven for lost aircraft making an unexpected landfall on this narrow peninsula. On September 25 1944, for example, a P-38 Lightning from Atcham appeared in the circuit and landed without incident.

A good imagination is required today to visualise what the airfield looked like as only a few air raid shelters are left. The three Bellman hangars on the eastern side have gone and a section of perimeter track is now part of a minor road. Perhaps its name was the most dramatic feature of this forgotten site.

High Ercall, Salop

SJ605185. On B5062, 1 mile W of Crudgington

This was one of the post-Expansion period airfields and was constructed by G. Walker & Slater Ltd. Unlike most of its contemporaries it had three runways from the start and thus escaped the effects of rain and mud. Some 300 acres of Shropshire farmland was utilised, some hangars being built first so that cement could be stored in them. Workers were brought to the site daily in a fleet of hired buses from all over Shropshire and the Potteries.

No 29 MU was the most important resident and was to remain here until disbandment in February 1964. Originally a civilian-manned unit, it formed on October 1 1940 to deal with anticipated deliveries of American aircraft. The first to be handled were a few Curtiss Mohawks but apart from these and a handful of other types most of the aircraft

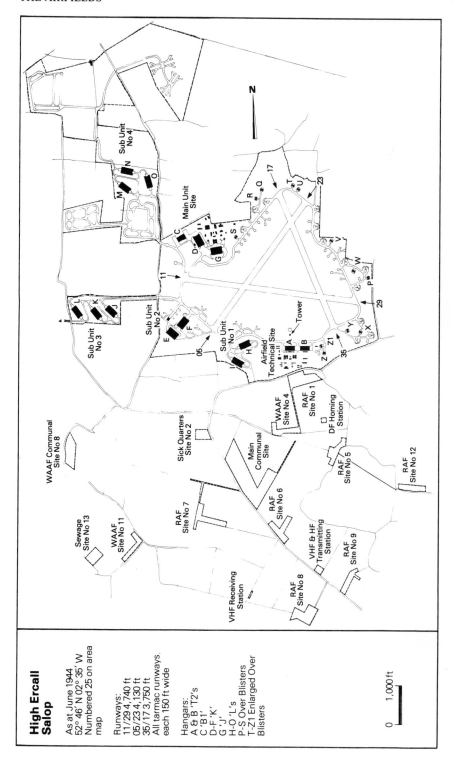

High Ercall Salop

As at June 1944
52° 46′ N 02° 35′ W
Numbered 25 on area map

Runways:
11/29 4,740 ft
05/23 4,130 ft
35/17 3,750 ft
All tarmac runways, each 150 ft wide

Hangars:
A & B 'T2's
C 'B1'
D-F 'K'
G 'J'
H-O 'L's
P-S Over Blisters
T-Z1 Enlarged Over Blisters

0   1,000 ft

for storage and preparation were British. As at most ASUs dispersals overflowed from the main airfield into the surrounding fields and many 'L' type hangars were built to supplement the 'J' and 'K' hangars on the main site.

Even as late as June 1941 the station's domestic facilities were still far from complete. An airman there at the time recalls that there were no roads and no toilets on the living sites. Cooking was done on a field kitchen and plates had to be washed under a cold tap outside the dining hall! To get a wash and shave they had to take a new dustbin across a couple of fields to a farm, beg some water and then wash in the upturned lid. Once piped water was available the freezing winters, typical of this part of the country, ensured that the supplies froze up regularly. When this happened snow and icicles had to be melted for washing purposes.

Envious eyes had lighted upon those runways and it was arranged that 306 Squadron's Hurricanes would use the airfield in the event of their base at Tern Hill becoming flooded, a likely prospect in the wet winter of 1940/41. The Lysanders of 13 Squadron from Hooton Park also took up temporary residence in February 1941. A less welcome visitor on March 7 1941 was a Luftwaffe bomber which caused minor damage but fortunately no casualties.

On April 10 1941 the station became a night fighter airfield in the Tern Hill Sector, the first squadron to arrive being No 68 from Catterick. Its Blenheim Ifs were swiftly changed for Beaufighters and the first victory came on June 17 when an He 111 was shot down near Bristol. When 68 Squadron went to Coltishall on March 8 1942 it was replaced by 255 Squadron with Beaufighter IIfs. On June 6 1942 No 255 Squadron was transferred to Honiley, High Ercall receiving in exchange 257 Squadron's Hurricanes which were superseded by Typhoons just before the squadron left for Exeter on September 21 1942.

Another new based unit from June 1942 was 1456 Flight with Havocs fitted with a Turbinlite in the nose. The idea was that a fairly large searchlight-equipped aircraft would be accompanied by a single-seat fighter in close formation. The latter would act as executioner once the searchlight aircraft had found and illuminated an enemy bomber. The Shropshire Flight was only operational for one month (August 1942) during which it made two unsuccessful contacts over Manchester. It became 535 Squadron in September 1942 but advances in radar resulted in the disbandment of all ten Turbinlite squadrons in January 1943.

One of the first USAAF units to arrive in the UK was the 31st Fighter Group with its HQ at nearby Atcham. The Group's 309th Fighter Squadron was based at High Ercall with Spitfire Vs which left for an advanced base at Westhampnett in Sussex on August 4. The following day they took part in the 8th Fighter Command's first mission, a practice run over France with experienced RAF pilots. After the 309th left the 27th Fighter Squadron, 1st Fighter Group, ferried in its 25 P-38F Lightnings from Iceland, the Group's other two squadrons going to Atcham.

At the beginning of October 1942, 13 P-39 Airacobras were flown in from Burtonwood for the USAAF's 92nd Fighter Squadron whose pilots arrived a few days later. After some practice flying the squadron moved to the West Country but soon exchanged these unsuitable fighters for Spitfires. This was the last USAAF unit to be based here but American aircraft visited from time to time. The airfield proved a haven for B-17 42-89238 of the 384th Bomb Group on September 15 1943. Shot up over France, lost and carrying three wounded crewmen, she got down safely.

High Ercall was also used as a rear airfield for fighter squadrons either resting from operations in the South of England or re-equipping. Typical examples in 1943 were 247 Squadron converting from

Hurricanes to Typhoons for mobile tactical work and 41 Squadron changing to an improved mark of Spitfire. On May 1 1943 High Ercall assumed full Sector Station responsibility from the Atcham Sector when the latter aerodrome was handed over to the USAAF.

Until December 1942 crew training for intruder squadrons had been provided by night fighter OTUs but there was now a need for specialisation. No 60 OTU was a direct result of this and traced its birth to No 2 Squadron of 51 OTU at Twinwood Farm in Bedfordshire. The latter unit was sufficient early in 1942 but the RAF now realised that in the Mosquito it had an ideal night intruder aircraft and that many more crews would be required for it in the future. The new OTU formed at High Ercall on May 17 1942 with an initial course of 12 crews. The aircraft strength was 24 Mosquitoes, two Ansons and an Oxford.

The Mosquito was a magnificent aircraft but in certain configurations, for example with one engine failed, it was sometimes more than an inexperienced pilot could manage. The following extracts from a diary kept by a navigator who attended a course at High Ercall conveys something of the flavour of those days:

'The first time that I flew with my pilot in a Mosquito we had not been airborne very long when one of the engines overheated and had to be shut down. There was bags of flap from the control tower but the pilot was very calm and we landed on one engine. The next day he was sent for by the CO who congratulated him and told him that we had had only a 50-50 chance of making a successful night landing. It was one of those cases where ignorance is bliss as it did not strike us that there was any danger!

'March 25 1944—I saw an Oxford prang, a one-wheel landing. The pilot tried to take off again, hit a hangar with a wing and went into the deck. There were four in the kite and they all walked away. Soon afterwards a Mosquito came in for a single-engined landing, so fast and reckless that I'm sure the pilot was in a flap. I thought he was going to pull it up off the ground again but found out later that both throttles had jammed. It looked as though the crew would be killed for sure but both walked away from the wreck.

'April 5 1944—There was a crash again at twilight tonight. I heard a noise like a motor bike back-firing, looked out and saw a Mossie overhead with black smoke pouring from the port engine. It circled the 'drome losing height. When up-wind he put the wheels down, tried to make an emergency landing and disappeared over a hangar. We listened, heard a faint crash and later a column of smoke showed he was on fire, poor fellow.'

No 60 OTU merged with 13 OTU in March 1945, losing its number and moving to Finmere. Control of the station then reverted to 41 Group Maintenance Command and the airfield and its dispersals were taken over for the storage and eventual scrapping of hundreds of Halifaxes. By the end of July 1945 there were 920 in store and this figure rose to 1,527 by the end of the year. Aircraft from almost every squadron, including veterans of scores of operational flights, were jammed together like a miniature version of the vast B-17 dumps in the Arizona Desert.

The Halifaxes were finally disposed of by 1950, Spitfires following them to the smelter, although not in such large quantities. The MU remained the sole user apart from intermittent visits by aircraft from CNCS at Shawbury. One of the MU's last big tasks was the storage of Percival Prentices, most of which were bought by Aviation Traders at Southend. The MU closed in February 1962 and the airfield reverted to care and maintenance but was soon sold off for agriculture and the runways broken up. The main site remains much the same with the addition of some modern buildings and is now run by the Road Transport Industry Training Board. All the original 'L' hangars around the perimeter are still in good condition.

Hinstock (Ollerton), Salop

SJ660260. 1 mile NNW of Childs Ercall on unclassified road which follows eastern perimeter track

If you follow the minor road from Childs Ercall village for about a quarter of a mile you will pass a ruined guard-house and immediately afterwards reach the brow of a hill. Stretched out in front of you is one of Shropshire's most interesting disused airfields. On the right is a small Admiralty 'S' hangar, on the left a Blister hangar used as a tractor garage. The road follows the course of the old perimeter track downhill to a group of two Pentad hangars and another 'S' type. The gradient is severe even for a hastily-built

wartime airfield and taxiing a tailwheel aeroplane with a following wind must have been very tricky. On the west side of the field are the one-time living quarters dominated by an imposing three-storey control tower of the classic Navy design, topped by a small observation post. The single runway aligned north-east/south-west was never permanent, being made of wire mesh, although its outline can still be seen from the air. At the north-east end the concrete building which housed the inner marker beacon of the beam approach equipment can still be seen.

Known mainly as a Royal Navy airfield, its origins were rooted in the Ministry of Aircraft Production's programme of SLGs. Starting life as 21 SLG, it was called Ollerton after the village just to the south of it. On October 17 1941 a detachment of one officer and 25 NCOs and airmen were sent to the SLG by the parent unit, 37 MU at Burtonwood. The two grass runways were still unfit for use and so much further work was needed that the opening-up party was withdrawn. It was expected that it would be ready to receive aircraft in the middle of April 1942 and 16 hides would be built by then to protect them. However, it was destined not to be used by 37 MU, being transferred to 27 MU Shawbury when it opened on April 20. They used the field for storing types like the Battle, Master and Magister.

In 1942 the Royal Navy was looking for a suitable airfield to set up an instrument-flying school and the MAP were persuaded to release Ollerton for this purpose. It was transferred to the Admiralty on July 23 1942 and renamed Hinstock, probably because of possible confusion with Tollerton near Nottingham. Construction of buildings and taxi-track

Below left *Enlarged Over Blister shelters farm equipment at Hinstock.*

Right *Naval three-storey tower at Hinstock.*

took nearly a year and it was commissioned as HMS *Godwit* on June 14 1943. In the meantime it had been a satellite to Stretton housing the Oxfords and Ansons of 758 Squadron, the Naval Advanced Instrument Flying School which had reformed on August 15 1942.

Like all beam approach training machines Hinstock's aircraft were marked with yellow triangles to warn other aeroplanes to give them a wide berth. It was found that young FAA pilots with less than 300 hours could pass out on the beam in eight days after some Link Trainer experience first. This little airfield in the green oceans of Shropshire certainly gave them a thorough initiation into the techniques of instrument flying.

In June 1944 the squadron operated 40 aircraft plus 20 in reserve but some of these were detached elsewhere. Another squadron, 739, the Blind Approach Development Unit, joined it from Lee-on-Solent in February 1943 with Oxfords and Swordfish aircraft but went south again to Worthy Down on September 14 1943. No 758Z Flight was formed late in 1944 at Hinstock as a Calibration and Development Flight working in close co-operation with the RAF's Signals Development Unit at Honiley. Eight Ansons were used, some fitted with ASV radar for demonstration purposes. Some training of naval Flying Control personnel was also undertaken and the VHF and HF Direction Finders at various naval establishments calibrated.

Other short-lived squadrons based here were 702 which reformed on June 1 1945 with Harvards and Oxfords for instrument training but soon shipped out to Australia in August; 734, an Engine Handling Squadron in residence from

September 1945 to the following February with a few Whitley GR VIIs; and 798 equipped with Harvards, Barracudas and Fireflies for advanced conversion courses. The latter came from Halesworth in January 1946 and was disbanded in April.

No 758 Squadron also disbanded in April 1946 but its replacement, 780 Squadron, had already reformed at Hinstock in February with Oxfords and Harvards for a similar role. This squadron was scheduled to receive some four-engined aircraft including some Lancasters and now that nearby Peplow with its three concrete runways was vacant, Hinstock was abandoned in February 1947 in favour of the former RAF station. The proximity of the two airfields had always caused problems and it is a tribute to the close liaison between the Flying Control sections that no circuit collisions occurred. This proximity was once useful as on December 13 1944 one of Peplow's Albemarles just managed to get down safely at Hinstock before the fog, which had already covered its own base, closed in.

Hixon, Staffordshire

SJ995265. Between A51 and A518, 3 miles N of Stafford

The peace of a Sunday morning on March 4 1945 was disturbed by the sudden arrival at Hixon of 23 Douglas C-47s bearing the black and yellow fin stripes of the 27th Air Transport Group. A variety of personal markings was to be seen and some had traces of the codes carried when they belonged to operational Troop Carrier Groups of the US IXth Air Force. One aircraft, 42-100667, had the name 'Nancy

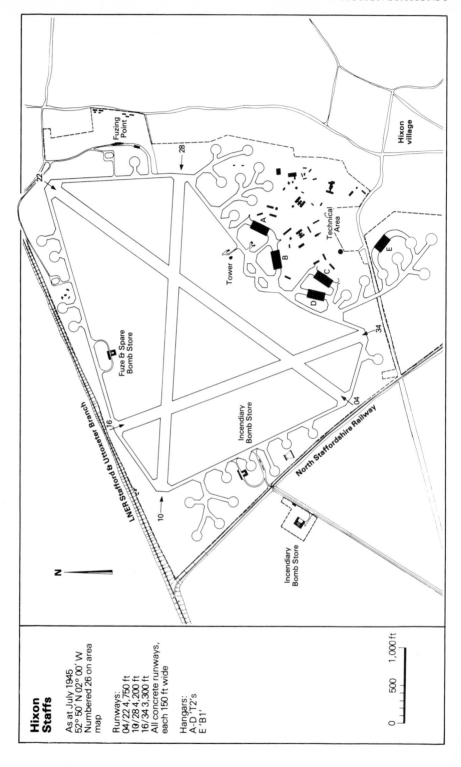

Hixon
Staffs

As at July 1945
52° 50' N 02° 00' W
Numbered 26 on area
map

Runways:
04/22 4,750 ft
10/28 4,200 ft
16/34 3,300 ft
All concrete runways,
each 150 ft wide

Hangars:
A-D 'T2's
E 'B1'

0   500   1,000 ft

N

Fuzing
Point

Hixon
village

Technical
Area

A
B
C
D
E

Tower

Fuze & Spare
Bomb Store

Incendiary
Bomb Store

Incendiary
Bomb Store

LNER Stafford & Uttoxeter Branch

North Staffordshire Railway

22

28

34

04

16

10

Pants' in bold white letters on her nose and two dark blue bands around each cowling. This was just one of the periodic American invasions of a typical RAF bomber OTU.

The visitors were usually B-17s and B-26s, however, as Hixon was one of the nearest airfields to the Combat Crew Replacement Centre at Stone. There were other US Army camps in the district and this was probably why the bunch of C-47s flew in. On June 30 1944 the airfield had a distinguished visitor when General George S. Patton Junior flew in to inspect a prisoner-of-war camp at Rugeley. USAAF liaison types were common and included a Piper L-4 44-3660 named 'The Cactus Queen', Oxford V3730 with its serial in yellow on the fin American-style and Fairchild Forwarder 43-14442 coded WD-AA which was painted bright crimson all over and belonged to the 4th Fighter Group at Debden. Cessna UC-78s too were frequent arrivals, some with invasion stripes, others like 43-31807 with jazzy markings of red engine cowlings and stripe from nose to tail over silver paint. The Beech UC-45A was not so familiar but one or two examples, including 44-86898 'Froggie Bottom Express', called in during 1944. Marauder 5W-P of the 394th Bomb Group on August 10 1944 was one of the more war-like types which landed from time to time.

The American colour relieved the drab night camouflage of the RAF Wellingtons which occupied Hixon for most of its active life. Its first movement came on May 15 1942 when a Wellington touched down on No 2 runway which was still only partially complete and had to be specially cleared for the occasion. Another Wellington landed close on its heels, both being assisted by an improvised smoke generator (there being no windsock in place yet) and green Very lights. These first aircraft came from 12 OTU at Chipping Warden and were intended for ground instruction. It was the end of July before three Wellingtons, towards the preliminary establishment of 30 aircraft, arrived.

The leisurely opening-up period had begun on May 13 1942 when the first party of airmen was posted in, RAF Lichfield being the parent station until the infant struggled to its feet. Hixon in turn was parent to Whitchurch Heath when it opened in July 1942. No 30 OTU formed on June 28 1942 for night bomber training and within a few months found itself

sending aircraft over enemy territory. The first operation in which the unit took part was to Essen on September 16 1942. Four aircraft took off but two were forced to turn back with unserviceabilities, always a problem with worn-out training aircraft. The other two bombed the target and returned safely, one landing at Tatenhill. This was to be the OTU's last operation for some time although many *Nickel* raids were carried out over Northern France.

No 25 OTU at Finningley disbanded in January 1943 with many of its aircraft and ground-crew being transferred to Hixon. In turn they were sent on to the new satellite at Seighford to help with the servicing of the 26 Wellingtons which had been detached there. Group now decreed that 30 OTU should be made up to full OTU status and be re-equipped with newer Wellington IIIs and Xs.

In April 1943 the training scheme at Hixon was modified to a straight-through flight system. This meant that pupils spent the whole of their OTU flying time in one Flight which changed its function as required by the stage of training. Intakes were so allotted that at any one time one Flight was doing day and one Flight night conversion at one aerodrome and the other two Flights were doing day and night operational flying respectively. The new scheme enabled the various departments to know exactly what was going on at any one time and to plan ahead. In the past each Flight contained pupils in four different stages of training and the planning of flying programmes was a very complicated matter.

The *Nickels* continued in 1943 building up to the night of June 22/23 when 16 air-craft went to Paris, Orleans, Le Mans and Reims. One crew was posted missing, one of the few lost from Hixon in the course of these trips. A bombing raid within operation 'Starkey' was flown by four Wellingtons on August 30 1943 when an ammunition dump at Foret d'Eperlecques was attacked.

Some Curtiss Tomahawks were attached to the OTU for fighter affiliation in 1943 and all were painted with the sharks' teeth markings traditionally associated with these aircraft. They were joined later by Masters, Martinets and Hurricanes which were often seen over the Midlands making dummy attacks on the Wellingtons. In June 1944 the engineering staff were pleased to be informed that an emergency air bottle for the lowering of Wellington undercarriages, designed at Hixon, had

Wellingtons on the grass at Hixon with camouflaged 'T2's in the background. The Wellington in the foreground (BK347) crashed on Whernside, Yorkshire, on April 21 1944 and pieces can still be seen at the site (Imperial War Museum).

been officially adopted by Bomber Command.

The airfield being required for other purposes, 30 OTU moved to Gamston on February 2 1945 having fallen in arrears on its night flying commitment owing to consistently poor weather. One day the airfield was packed with Wellingtons, the next they had all gone and their dispersals were now occupied by 37 Beaufort IIs. These were trainer aircraft with the turret position faired in but they were still finished in Coastal Command camouflage of grey and white. Some had single letter codes, others double ones such as AE, AG and so on in black behind the roundel and repeated on the nose. The unit they belonged to was 12 (P) AFU which had been transferred from Spitalgate on February 8 1945. A satellite at Cranage was also available until the AFU disbanded on June 21 1945.

This was virtually the end of flying at Hixon as it now became a sub-site for storage by 16 MU at Stafford and remained so until November 5 1957. The land was sold off in August 1962, the use being divided between farming and light industry on the main hangar site. The tower has been left standing and shows an unusual modification in the form of a large picture window which replaces the three separate openings in the upper storey. Parts of the old runways are used by a Tiara, one of the several light aircraft flown from here for many years by the same private owner.

When twilight descends upon this old airfield it is not hard to imagine the scene nearly 40 years ago with Wellingtons waddling round the perimeter track, waiting for a 'green' from the runway caravan and roaring off down the dim flarepath, some never to return.

Hoar Cross, Staffordshire

SK128223. 1½ miles SW of Tatenhill airfield

Search as ye may, you will find no evidence that there was ever an airfield here, or that Hellcats, Whitleys and Typhoons once lurked by the hedgerows. You will just have to take my word for it that this was the site of an SLG. I only know because of the evidence of a gentleman who, as a schoolboy, got inside an unguarded Whitley parked by the lane and thus knows exactly where it was.

The area is well off the beaten track which perhaps explains why there were no guards nor indeed personnel whatsoever present when my informant made a visit during the late war period. As 32 SLG it was opened by 51 MU on July 27 1941, being operated solely by this unit until it was closed in June 1945. A total of 58,900 square yards of Square Mesh Track was removed after this but none seems to have found its way into use for the local fences.

Hodnet, Salop

SJ615273. On A442, ½ mile S of Hodnet village

Beside the road just south of the village of Hodnet is a small building of military

Mess-room and ablutions at Hodnet SLG.

appearance which gives away the location of an obscure SLG. This hut was a combination messroom and kitchen for the personnel guarding the aircraft stored in the surrounding fields and woodland. A gap in the hedge replaced by a wooden fence shows where aircraft were towed across the road from the landing strip to the dispersal parks. The only other surviving building is now used as a changing-room for the local playing field. Villagers there during the war remember the little airfield with some affection and there are childhood memories of evenings sharing tea and toast with the airmen.

It opened on June 12 1941 as 29 SLG under the control of 24 MU at Tern Hill but was transferred to 37 MU at Burtonwood on April 20 1942. When Burtonwood was handed over to the USAAF, the SLG passed to 27 MU, Shawbury with effect from July 7 1942 but was then rescheduled for use by 51 MU, Lichfield. The latter did not use it, however, and it reverted to Shawbury in November 1942. The grass runways were not reinforced with wire mesh as the commitment was mainly for the storage of trainers like the Master and Martinet. In May 1943, a total of 35 aircraft was in store, some in hides covered with steel wool on the edge of the woods. Square Mesh Track was laid for hardstandings but this was torn up after the site closed in February 1945.

Hooton Park, Cheshire

SJ380785. On B5132, 1 mile SE of Eastham

As a war-plane the Tiger Moth would come last in everyone's choice of a suitable aircraft but, early in 1940, it found itself in the front-line of the U-boat war. Coastal Command was unable to cover all of Britain's vulnerable coastline so Coastal Patrol Flights were formed to watch for submarines and invasion from the sea.

No 3 CPF formed at Hooton Park on December 1 1939 and flew its first two sorties the same day. It was joined by 4 CPF which flew over from Aldergrove a few days later and both units shared the four daily patrols during the hours of daylight. The only sighting of any note was by Flying Officer Chambers on January 16 1940 north-west of the Point of Air. He spotted a large oil patch with turbulent air bubbles but what was causing it was never discovered. Late in January most of the Tiger Moths were replaced by Hornet Moths, no more potent than the former but offering the comfort of an enclosed cabin.

In February two daily patrols were flown alternately, covering the north coast of Wales and the Isle of Anglesey and the west coast of England from Liverpool to St Bees Head in Cumberland. No enemy submarines were ever sighted by the aircraft but we shall never know what deterrent effect they had. The last sortie was flown from Hooton on May 30 1940 by Tiger N6781 but it had to return early because of low cloud.

Before the First World War Hooton Park was a race-course but, on August 4 1914, the Government requisitioned the estate for army training purposes. In 1917 three Belfast hangars were built within what was formerly the paddock area,

Hooton Park circa 1957 (via A.P. Ferguson).

intended for the erection of American-built aircraft shipped to Liverpool. This scheme did not materialise, however, and the airfield was taken over by 4 Training Depot Station which moved from Tern Hill on September 19 1917 with a collection of Sopwith Scouts and Dolphins. On January 20 1918 there were 37 aircraft on charge and many others were passing through the aircraft repair section which had been set up here. Flying accident casualties during this period are commemorated on a plaque in Eastham Church, most of the dead being Canadians.

After the TDS disbanded in 1919 the site was unused until 1927 when a local businessman acquired most of the estate with the aim of turning it into a major airport for the north of England. The Liverpool and District Aero Club was formed with a grant from the Air Ministry, at first operating Avro Avians. A further development was the founding of a factory by Flight Lieutenant Nicholas Comper to manufacture his Swift light aeroplane.

Conveniently in February 1931 Pobjoy Airmotors Ltd set up shop next door and their engines became the standard fitting in the production Comper Swifts. Some 41 Swifts were built, the last few being completed at Heston after the company moved there at the beginning of 1933. During 1930 Comper also assembled some Ford Trimotors at Hooton. Comper's only other design to be flown at Hooton was the Comper-Cierva C 28 Autogiro, G-ABTO, which was not very successful and was soon abandoned. More publicity accrued from the airfield's use as a staging point in the King's Cup Air Race, then a long-range event taking in most of the country.

In 1930 it was designated the official airport for Liverpool and commercial services were run until July 1933 when Speke on the opposite bank of the River Mersey achieved airport status. Hooton suffered from its poor position relative to Liverpool and a short-lived passenger service was operated between it and Speke in 1936 by Utility Airways. Custom was so sparse that the cynical staff nick-named it 'Futility Airways'!

On February 10 1936 No 610 (County of Chester) Squadron was formed at Hooton as a light bomber unit in the Auxiliary Air Force. During the wave of patriotism after Munich my father was one of those who volunteered as aircrew for the squadron but, owing to the long waiting list, he joined the Territorial Army instead. Had he been accepted, and bearing in mind the heavy losses the Auxiliaries suffered in 1940, I probably would not have been around to write this book! On January 1 1939 the squadron re-mustered as a fighter unit but retained its Hawker Hinds until the beginning of the war when it received some Hurricanes. These were soon given up in favour of Spitfires when the squadron moved south to its war station.

The airfield was taken over by the

regular RAF on October 9 1939 and on the following day seven Ansons of 'A' Flight 206 Squadron landed for convoy and anti-submarine duties under the operational control of 15 Group. All civil flying had now ceased, apart from the Dragons on army co-operation work, and 18 of Hooton's considerable population of light aircraft were immobilised and stored under the old grand-stand. All were destroyed in July 1940 in a disastrous fire.

The airfield was still an impossible hotch-potch of private firms—one was a meat-canning factory—but the new CO determined to turn it into an efficient operational station as soon as possible by requisitioning. In the meantime, the first Anson patrol over the Irish Sea was made on October 11 1939. The landing ground was considered too small and so surrounded by trees that blind take-offs and night-flying would be very unsafe. The detached Flight of 206 Squadron was replaced by four Ansons of 502 Squadron at the end of November.

No 13 Squadron had been lucky to get out of France before being overrun and was now re-formed at Hooton on May 25 1940 with 11 Lysanders and one Gladiator. They moved to Speke on June 17. No 15 Group disbanded the CPFs with effect from May 30 1940 and 12 Hornet Moths left for Colerne. More refugees from the South in June were the Ansons of the School of General Reconnaissance whose Guernsey base was soon to be under new management. The School was transferred to Squires Gate the following month. The detachment of 502 Squadron was now sent to Aldergrove, being replaced by 48

Squadron's Ansons from Thorney Island on July 16 1940.

A few days later one of the Ansons chased an enemy aircraft which had just dropped two bombs on a convoy, but could not catch it. From dawn to dusk continuous patrols were flown by two aircraft to cover the inbound convoy track in Liverpool Bay, and from time to time they were fired on by mistake. No 13 Squadron was now back in residence and carried out a daily dawn patrol down the Welsh Coast to Pembrey in the hope of catching an unwary U-boat.

In March 1941 the station agreed to accommodate 701 Squadron whilst the latter was non-operational and five Walruses duly arrived. Merseyside was under heavy night attack at this time and the airfield was at the receiving end of many stray bombs which is probably why 701 Squadron only stayed a few days before moving on to Arbroath. In June 1941 Sealand began to use the aerodrome as an RLG and in July No 13 Squadron moved to Odiham. Its example was followed by 48 Squadron whose aircraft had all left for Stornaway by July 27.

The pre-war firm of Martin Hearn Ltd was now known as 7 Aircraft Assembly Unit which, as its name suggests, assembled Bostons, Harvards and Canadian-built Hampdens, and later maintained Halifaxes and Mosquitoes in a hangar complex on the south-east corner of the airfield. The landing-ground had

Personnel of No 11 Radio School, Hooton Park, in 1943. A Botha lurks in the background (via A.P. Ferguson).

Anson K6234 of No 48 Squadron at Hooton Park in 1938 (Richard T. Riding).

been extended but the bigger aircraft expected necessitated the construction of runways, a task which was commenced by A. Monk & Co Ltd in December 1941.

Lysanders detached from 116 Squadron at Castle Bromwich were based intermittently from October 1941 for AA calibration work but a planned move of the CCDU from Carew Cheriton was cancelled. No 1447 Flight was formed with Oxfords, Lysanders and one Fairey Battle on March 19 1942 for air-to-air gunnery practice off the North Wales coast with fighter aircraft. This lasted until December 1942 when Hooton was transferred to Technical Training Command. The Flight's ten Oxfords were then sent to Carew Cheriton to form the nucleus of 10 Radio School, the vacuum being filled by the Bothas of 3 Radio School from Prestwick. The unit was re-numbered 11 Radio School and the Bothas were gradually replaced by Ansons but some were still on charge when the School disbanded on August 3 1944. The last one, W5673, was flown to Sherburn-in-Elmet for reduction to produce on September 23 1944.

Martin Hearn Ltd, as well as assembling aircraft, had also constructed gliders like the Kirby Cadet during the war and repaired Mosquitoes. Three battered Mosquito fuselages, including DZ410, languished at Hooton until at least 1954. DZ410 is not completely extinct as a friend of mine removed a piece with the serial number on it. The firm went on to build gliders for Slingsby, including Tutors, Kites and Sedberghs, and serviced Sabres and Lockheed T-33s for the Royal Canadian Air Force.

In June 1946 No 610 Squadron reformed with Spitfire XIVs, giving way to Spitfire 22s, then Meteor 4s and finally Meteor 8s. It was joined by 611 Squad-ron's Meteors from Woodvale in March 1951. Hooton's third auxiliary squadron was 663 which formed in 1949 with Tiger Moths and Auster 5s and were replaced by Chipmunks and Auster 6s and 7s. Liverpool UAS and 19 RFS were also here from 1948 until 1951 when they moved to Woodvale to make way for the two Meteor squadrons.

The disbandment of the Royal Auxiliary Air Force in March 1957 marked the end of flying at Hooton, all the Meteors being ferried to Kirkbride for scrapping or conversion to target drones. One in its original 610 Squadron markings was to be seen at Tarrant Rushton, as late as August 1960, awaiting attention.

The airfield was acquired by Vauxhall Motors in 1962 and a huge car factory was built on the south-eastern half, engulfing the old Martin Hearn base which once consisted of three Bellman hangars, two Robins and three Blisters. Only half of the main runway is left and it is used for the open storage of completed cars. The main site with its three Belfast hangars dates back to the First World War and a single 'B1' hangar remains intact. There was never a proper control tower, only a hut which served as a watch office. As a lad I went to several Battle of Britain Displays here and on one never-to-be-forgotten occasion made my first flight, a ten bob trip in Rapide G-AHPT.

Hornby Hall, Cumbria

NY575295. Just off A66, 3 miles E of Penrith

Hornby Hall opened on March 17 1941 as 9 SLG for use by 22 MU at Silloth for aircraft dispersal, two Wellingtons being flown over initially. Battles, Blenheims, Bothas and Hudsons soon followed, the adjacent woodland being used as natural camouflage for the parked aircraft. The site was so well hidden that a visiting Piper Cub pilot could not distinguish the grass runways and landed in one of the dispersal fields by mistake. This aircraft had come to pick up the ATA pilot of a Spitfire which had force-landed near Appleby. Another visitor was an Anson of 2 AOS at Millom which landed on August 22 1941 to investigate the crash of one of the School's Bothas on the nearby hills.

In January of the following year all the aircraft were removed and the SLG was handed over to 12 MU on a temporary basis for Wellington storage. The parking areas were fenced to permit sheep and cattle grazing which helped the camouflage and in July there were three Bothas and 11 Wellingtons present. The SLG reverted to 22 MU's control during the summer and when the unit received its first Mustangs some were sent to Hornby, the first arriving on September 24 1942.

April 1943 saw a Halifax of 78 Squadron make an emergency landing on the strip with an oil pressure drop on both inner engines. The pilot stated that but for the fact that he saw a smoke generator and a Hudson and Oxford land he would not have recognised the place as an aerodrome and considered the camouflage excellent.

With the introduction of a scheme whereby an MU would specialise in a limited number of operational types, 22 MU was allocated the Hurricane and Sea

Hurricane and many of these passed through Hornby before the SLG's official closure date of July 2 1945. It was then taken over by the Ministry of Works for the accommodation of German prisoners-of-war, even though the last of many Anson aircraft was not flown out until July 31. A Robin hangar converted into a barn and a few small buildings are all that remain.

Hutton-in-the-Forest, Cumbria
NY470350. 3 miles NW of Penrith

The first trial landing here was made by an Anson on June 1 1941 and a platoon of the Home Guard was formed from the civilian employees at the SLG for its protection. The parent 22 MU was mostly civilian-manned and Hutton's average strength was two RAF officers, eight other ranks and 43 civilians. In November a platoon of the Border Regiment took over the guarding of the parked Blenheims, Hurricanes, Bothas and Hudsons.

In March 1942 ten Blenheims and 12 Bothas were picketed out and on July 8 the first of many Venturas, AE669, was dispersed here. Landing with a cross-wind it pulled up with only about 80 yards to spare. The next month a Wellington made a safe landing at Hutton. Subsequently a test flight was made and the take-off proved satisfactory. Work was done on many Mustang aircraft and 8 SLG, as it was known, finally closed in August 1945. Since then the sole Robin hangar has been removed along with some of the huts, leaving only a few small buildings today.

Robin hangar at Hornby Hall (J. Huggon).

Small firing butts at Hutton SLG (J. Huggon).

Inskip, Lancashire

SD450370. On unclassified road, 2½ miles NE of Kirkham

At night the red lights on the 600-foot wireless masts at Inskip warn aircraft to keep away from what was once a busy airfield. The four runways no longer exist as they were dug up in 1974 by McAlpines and the hardcore used for the Broughton-Blackpool motorway.

The Admiralty purchased 600 acres of land in June 1942 and the construction of an airfield to be known as Elswick was started. The name was changed to Inskip in April 1943 after another nearby village and the station commissioned on May 15 1943 as HMS *Nightjar*. It was to be used for the operational training of anti-submarine and two-seat strike crews.

The first OTU Squadron, 747, arrived in May 1943 with Swordfish and Barracudas. In July 1943 it was joined by 766 Squadron also with Swordfish and on August 23 by 735 Squadron which formed here with yet more Swordfish for ASV radar training. No 747 Squadron moved to Fearn on January 26 1944 and 735 Squadron to Burscough on March 17 1944.

Three Squadrons re-formed here during the spring of 1944; 737 for ASV training with Swordfish and 760 and 763 Squadrons for anti-submarine operational training, the former with Swordfish and the latter with Avengers. No 737 Squadron left for Arbroath on August 28 1944, 760 disbanded in October 1944 but 763 soldiered on at Inskip until August 1945.

Several first-line Squadrons spent time here in 1944, including 787, 813 and 838, all with Swordfish. The following year Fireflies came on the scene, the first being with 1791 Squadron which arrived from Lee-on-Solent on April 19 1945 and moved to Drem on June 18 1945. It was followed by 1792 Squadron from Lee also for night fighter training and this Squadron stayed until August 9 1945. Two days later 816 Squadron brought more Fireflies for training before leaving for Macrihanish on October 11 1945.

No 766 Squadron which had been here almost since the airfield opened, went to Rattray in February 1946 and Inskip then closed for flying. The Navy retained it as a Transport Pool, the 32 'S' Sheds being useful, and also as a storage depot. When the Navy's world-wide communications network was modernised the site was chosen as a radio station. It is now one of the Navy's most important transmitter sites and the old control tower has been converted into accommodation for junior ratings.

Jurby, Isle of Man

SC360985. On A14, N of Sulby Glen

Built on the flat northern extremity of the island, this pleasant airfield escaped the attention of the Luftwaffe throughout the war, only to suffer heavy damage from a friendly aircraft just a few weeks after it ended. On May 20 1945 a Sunderland of 423 Squadron, Castle Archdale, had an engine catch fire whilst on convoy escort. An emergency landing on the nearest shore base seemed the best course of action (it had been successful at Angle three years before) but the fire had spread to the wing by the time the boat touched down at Jurby. The crew jumped out and ran as there was a full load of depth charges on board and there had been no time to jettison them. An attempt was

Mosquito RR299 at Jurby, circa 1968 (via Dr A.A. Duncan).

made by the station fire crew to control the blaze but they were ordered to retreat. Luckily there were no casualties when it blew up but almost every window on the airfield was shattered and the hangars were very badly damaged by the blast.

When the war started there was a wholesale movement of training units away from the east coast. Many were redesignated Air Observer Schools and replaced the existing Armament Training Schools, each of which had an associated bombing range and whose role had been to provide weapon training facilities for operational units. No 5 AOS (ex-5 ATS) was a typical example; it opened at Jurby on September 18 1939 with a mixed collection of aircraft including Wallaces, Blenheims and Battles. The unit was renamed 5 Bombing and Gunnery School on November 1 1939 and went on operating the same obsolete types for the armament training of graduates of Air Observer Navigation Schools on the mainland. The title reverted to 5 AOS on July 19 1941 in accordance with a new scheme of all-through training to replace the two stage AONS-B&GS sequence. There was now to be one course covering navigation and weaponry.

The School soon had many Herefords on strength but they were unpopular and prone to engine fires. A total of 28 was visible on the airfield on July 27 1941, accompanied by 12 Blenheims, 10 Henleys, three Ansons, four Hampdens and 20 Hurricanes. In August 1941 a USAAC Major was attached to study the training of air gunners. He was one of many American personnel in Britain at this time seeking help on how to improve their own country's unprepared state.

Three Hurricane squadrons were based here for varying periods between January 1941 and March 1942. They were 258, 302 and 312 and all were employed on convoy escort over the Irish Sea. A Spitfire squadron, 457, was here from August 1941 to March 1942 also on day patrols and, earlier, 307 Squadron's Defiants had carried out the same duties in the autumn of 1940. Bomber squadrons, too, were represented by brief detachments of Whitleys and Wellingtons of 166 and 215 Squadrons respectively in 1939 and early 1940.

There being no local MU, Jurby was responsible for salvaging all crashed aircraft on the island and a compound on the Ballawoirrey road often contained some interesting scrap. On August 27 1944, for instance, there was the wreck of a USAAF Liberator which had crashed on Snaefell on July 6 and several Hercules engines from a Halifax.

There was much barrel-scraping in the spring of 1942 when 'Bomber' Harris was trying to assemble enough aircraft for a Thousand Bomber Raid. Jurby lent three Hampdens which were flown to Syerston, although one crashed on the way. For technical reasons they were not flown on the raid but one of the observers took part as a supernumerary crew member.

A visit to Jurby on February 3 1943 revealed 60 Ansons, 15 Blenheim IVs, six Blenheim 1s and ten Lysanders on the airfield. A year later the same local spotter noted that all the Blenheims had gone but three Martinets and a Manchester fuselage were in evidence. No 5 AOS was disbanded on February 1 1944 and the Air Navigation and Bombing School was formed in its place. Now that all basic navigation training had moved overseas with the Empire Air Training Scheme it was the only unit of its type in the UK. Its task was to develop training methods and to provide a yardstick by which to measure the competency of graduates of the EATS schools. Ansons were operated at first, being joined by Wellingtons in October 1944.

The station often found itself organising rescue parties for aircraft which had flown into the nearby mountains. The unofficial mountain rescue team stayed on after the war and became a recognised body. Jurby also handled many Lodestar aircraft early in 1945 bringing Norwegian collaborators via Leuchars in Scotland to the many internment camps dotted around the island.

On May 31 1945 the title of the Bombing School was changed yet again, this time to 5 Air Navigation School but still equipped with Ansons and Wellington Xs. Now that the EATS had been wound up there was a need for the re-establishment of basic observer training in the UK and this was one of the schools set up to do it. It moved to Topcliffe in Yorkshire on September 17 1946, being replaced by 11 Air Gunnery School which flew its Wellingtons over from Andreas. The AGS disbanded on October 15 1947 leaving Jurby to care and maintenance.

No 1 Initial Training School re-opened it on April 12 1950, being responsible for the ground training of pilots and navigators. It, too, disbanded on July 24 1953, but in September the Officer Cadet Training Unit moved over from Millom, having a peak intake of cadets of 240. Almost ten years to the day, in September 1963, the OCTU closed and in February 1964 the Isle of Man Government bought the airfield from the Air Ministry for £133,000. It was used as a diversion in the event of Ronaldsway, on the south end of the island, being closed by sea fog, a

common occurrence. The air traffic staff and other ground services were re-deployed to Jurby when necessary. This practice was discontinued in the early 1970s and part of the airfield is now a light industrial site. The runways and control tower are kept in good condition, however, and it would be a simple matter to put it back into service.

Kingstown, Cumbria

NY390595. On A7, 2 miles N of Carlisle

In November 1942 two German pilots escaped from a prison camp in Westmorland and stole a Magister from this airfield on the outskirts of Carlisle. Posing as Dutchmen they pursuaded ground-staff to start the trainer for them, took off and headed south. Their absence from the camp had been concealed and their intention was to land at an airfield in East Anglia, re-fuel and fly to the Continent. The plan went awry, however, because after re-fuelling successfully they got lost and eventually landed in a field near Great Yarmouth. Still claiming to be Dutch officers they were taken to RAF Horsham St Faith but their incredible luck ran out at this point because all RAF stations had finally been alerted that the aircraft was missing. They were arrested and put back behind barbed wire. All agreed it was a 'jolly good show' but the unit from which the Magister had been taken was very embarrassed.

Kingstown could claim to be the second municipal airport to be founded in Britain after Manchester's Barton. In its first few years, however, only the occasional light aircraft used it. On March 23 1933 the first commercial aircraft landed after a flight from Croydon via Blackpool,

Rapide G-AEBX of Railway Air Services at Kingstown in 1937 (via J. Huggon).

Magisters R1853 and T9735 of No 15 EFTS near Kingstown, summer 1940 (via J. Huggon).

although another year elapsed before scheduled services were started. The Isle of Man was the most popular destination and several companies operated on this route.

The Border Flying Club was formed in June 1935 and flew from here until September 1939 when its aircraft were impressed into the RAF. An RAFVR school, 38 E & RFTS, was established in June 1939 and additional hangars and buildings were erected and a concrete apron laid down. Tiger Moths and Harts were used but the school closed down soon afterwards. Two Flights of Henleys from 1 AACU were sent here for exercises in July and August 1939 and, on November 24 1939, the Ansons of 3 AONS arrived from Desford. They left for Weston-super-Mare on June 3 1940 to be absorbed by 5 AONS.

No 15 EFTS had been at Redhill in Surrey but was moved north to a safer area for training on June 3 1940, its 40 Magisters flying via Shawbury. Training restarted almost immediately at Kingstown, so great was the demand for new pilots. Until early 1941 the instructors were on duty from before dawn until after sunset and civilian ground crew worked even harder to keep the Maggies in the air. Most of the trainee pilots were British but a special Flight was set aside for Poles.

The airfield suffered poor drainage because of its clay sub-soil so RLGs at Burnfoot and Kirkpatrick were opened in the autumn of 1940 to reduce wear and tear. Early in 1942 Tiger Moths replaced the Magisters on the unit. The type of work altered also, full *ab initio* training

being abolished in favour of the grading of pupils. Each individual was given about eight hours' instruction on which his future as a Service pilot was judged and, if he went solo in this time or showed that he would be able to do so without much more instruction, he would be sent to an overseas training school to complete the course.

In 1945 there were 108 aircraft on strength together with 73 flying instructors and it was the proud boast of the engineering staff that they could usually maintain 95% serviceability. The work decreased in scale until 15 EFTS closed at the end of 1947, by which time it had flown some 270,000 hours and given instruction to over 12,000 pupils, some, of course, during its early days at Redhill.

It re-formed on April 1 1948 as 15 RFS with Tiger Moths and, from 1949, six Ansons. In 1952 the RFS re-equipped with Chipmunks and from then onwards these aircraft were used to give refresher courses to already qualified pilots and the Ansons gave navigation and signals refresher training. After the unit closed in March 1953 Kingstown quietened down considerably, being used only by a few civil firms. One of these was Manx Airlines which operated an Isle of Man service with Rapides up to the airfield's closure in 1957. The small grass field, which on one occasion managed to accommodate a Lancaster, was incapable of extension because of the railway on the west side, 14 MU's storage site to the north and the village to the east. Therefore Carlisle Corporation looked elsewhere and eventually acquired Crosby.

Kirkbride, Cumbria

NY225550. 1 mile S of Kirkbride village

On a summer's day in 1945 an RAF Mitchell crew were detailed to take their aircraft to an MU in Cumberland. It was a much-loved aeroplane which had carried them unscathed through an operational tour over North-West Europe and they assumed that it would be overhauled and returned to service. After landing they were marshalled to join scores of other Mitchells and then learned to their dismay that their pride and joy was destined for the scrap heap. It was almost a betrayal of a trusted friend and there was time only to remove the clock from the instrument panel as a souvenir.

Peace meant that hundreds of aircraft could be packed close together but it had not always been like that at Kirkbride. Back in 1938 it was planned as one of the Aircraft Storage Units to deal with the projected wartime needs of the RAF. The location was remote but well dispersed in case enemy bombers could reach this far. It was hoped to open the station in May 1939 but building work fell behind schedule and the official date was June 5 1939 with 12 MU forming here on the same date.

Even then, no buildings were fully completed on the main site and its four sub-sites and the Equipment Officer found himself in a make-shift hut. An 'E'-type hangar became fit for use on July 31 but no aircraft were seen until September 5. They were four Avro Tutors which

came by rail as the landing ground was still not ready for use until later in the month when a Magister was flown in for the Station Flight. Things picked up in October when Fairey Battles and Ansons began to be delivered from the manufacturers.

The possibility of airborne attack was faced by the issue of two Lewis guns and 12 magazines of ammunition to cover the airfield, a token gesture if ever there was one! The IRA, too, was considered a potential threat and precautions were taken against its activities.

December 1939 brought bad weather which closed the airfield for days at a time, there being no concrete runways yet, although the construction of three was started in January 1940 by Sir Robert McAlpine Ltd. Delivery of aircraft was spasmodic but improved with the drier weather and, by April, Spitfires, Ansons, Hampdens and Bothas were passing through. The same month 1 OTU from nearby Silloth used Kirkbride for night flying training with their Hudsons. This was to be repeated many times over during the next few years. In August many of the surrounding fields were requisitioned for aircraft parking and the Commanding Officer sought permission to disperse aircraft at RAF Kingstown on the northern outskirts of Carlisle. The opening of SLGs at Wath Head and Hornby Hall made this unnecessary and an attempt to set up a satellite to 55 OTU at Kirkbride was successfully evaded.

A Colonel of the USAAC visited in

Left *Unusual style tower at Kirkbride in January 1967* (J. Huggon).

Top right *The former ATA HQ at Kirkbride* (J. Huggon).

Above right *Meteor F 8 WA776 of No 610 Squadron at Kirkbride on April 23 1957* (J. Huggon).

April 1941 to learn the general principles of running an ASU. The numbers of Spitfires being dealt with were increasing rapidly and were now joined by Wellingtons and Hudsons. All these aeroplanes needed ferry pilots so an ATA pool, 16 FPP, formed here at the end of July 1941 and stayed until disbandment in August 1945. Halifaxes and Airacobras began to be seen late in 1941 and, on November 11, a test landing was made by a Liberator. As suspected, the runways were too short for safe operation of this heavy bomber and extensions were approved but not carried out until 1943, owing to more pressing commitments elsewhere.

The MU's routine was interrupted on April 13 1942 by the sudden appearance of a Hurricane of 59 OTU minus its airscrew. After a hurried downwind landing it was found that the fighter had collided with another Hurricane, which crashed fatally. Shortly afterwards a Hudson from Silloth overshot the runway and hit a lorry on the Kirkbride-Wigton road. Fortunately the injuries were slight but the road was blocked for hours.

Mid-1942 saw the arrival of Mitchells,

Venturas and Fortresses for preparation. The former's tricycle undercarriage was sufficiently unusual to merit a special conversion course for the MU's test-pilots. A few rarities like the Sikorsky Kingfisher and Vultee Vigilant were also being worked on or stored.

Mitchells, Wellingtons, Halifaxes and Bostons were the most numerous types handled in 1943 but unusual aircraft such as Brewster Bermudas landed from time to time. The following year the first Vultee Vengeances arrived and Albemarles were being fitted out for squadron service. The end of the war caused a sudden change of accent from preparation to disposal. For example, in July 1945, 930 aircraft were held at Kirkbride and its SLGs, this figure reaching 1,206 at the end of November. Some of these aircraft were selected for long-term storage and, in October, 396 engines were being maintained by periodic running.

No 12 MU remained active until June 1960 and, towards the end of its life, was notable for the hundreds of Meteors lined up here waiting to be scrapped. The airfield is still used by light aircraft and most of the buildings are intact.

Knowsley Park, Merseyside

SJ465945. Off A58, 1 mile N of Prescot

Few visitors to Knowsley Safari Park are aware that it was an SLG and Wellingtons once lurked amongst the trees instead of lions and monkeys. Sited on Lord Derby's land, it was known as 49 SLG and was intended for use by 37 MU at Burtonwood from the autumn of 1941. It was so water-logged, however, that no aircraft could be dispersed here at first, a decision under-lined by the fact that a Magister force-landed here in November 1941, its wheels sinking about three inches into the soft surface! The ground dried out somewhat in the spring of 1942 and the SLG opened on May 13, 19 Wellingtons being flown in by the end of that month. Even then some got bogged down in the process.

Despite the usual attempts to camou-flage such a site a Gauntlet and Gladiator en route to Speke made precautionary landings owing to bad weather on June 14 1942. Asked how they located the disguised aerodrome, the pilots stated that it was very noticeable from the air and could not be mistaken for anything else!

When Burtonwood was handed over to the USAAF for a Base Air Depot, 37 MU disbanded and all its holding of aircraft and personnel were transferred to 48 MU at Hawarden. Knowsley Park went too, the official change-over date being July 8 1942. The following month the MU was instructed to assess the SLG's suit-ability for four-engined aircraft. It was found acceptable and some Halifaxes were flown in to join the Wellingtons already being prepared or stored. By the end of 1944 there was no longer a serious need for dispersal of aircraft and No 48 MU's SLGs were closed down so that the aircraft could be consolidated conveniently at the parent airfield and its nearby sub-site at Hooton Park. Knowsley was relinquished in December 1944, the few Robin hangars being dismantled, and there appear to be no other surviving buildings.

Lawrenny Ferry, Dyfed

SN010062. 4 miles NE of Pembroke

Overshadowed by its near neighbour at Pembroke Dock, this marine base was commissioned on February 1 1942 but it had been used by 764 Squadron from as early as May 1941 when this unit, the Seaplane Training Squadron, was displaced from Pembroke Dock. It was

equipped with Walruses but a few of the rare Sikorsky Kingfishers joined them later. The squadron disbanded on October 24 1943, the station then reverting to care and maintenance under Lee-on-Solent. There is no record of any further use by aircraft and, apart from the slip-way, little remains to show its existence.

Lichfield, Staffordshire

SK145130. On A38, 3 miles NE of Lichfield

This station had several notable achieve-ments to its credit. It was the only airfield in North-West England from which air-craft took-off for the thousand bomber raid on Cologne on May 30/31 1942, it pioneered many flying control procedures which became standard throughout the RAF, and it was claimed to be one of the busiest in the country, some 113,800 take-offs and landings having been made between December 1942 and June 1945. In addition, it was control airfield for the Birmingham Balloon Barrage and all aircraft for Castle Bromwich and other airfields in the Birmingham area had to land at Lichfield before proceeding. Another factor contributing to its heavy traffic was that it was on the track of all aircraft flying through the corridor formed by the south of the Pennines and Birmingham and there were many diver-sions owing to weather or emergency. A minor point, but one which seemed to be known throughout the RAF was its proximity to the LMS main line railway, resulting in many aircraft arriving with personnel going on leave.

Planned as an Aircraft Storage Unit, Lichfield opened on August 1 1940 when 51 MU formed here under 41 Group. The first aircraft to be received were Hurricanes, Oxfords and Ansons, and SLGs at Blidworth in Nottinghamshire and nearby Hoar Cross were later taken into use. Tradition has it that Amy Johnson, then an ATA ferry pilot, was flying the first aeroplane to land here. There was still plenty of space, however, and the MU became a lodger unit when 27 OTU formed on April 23 1941. The first intake of pupils for night bomber training arrived on May 25 and, within a few days, Ansons and Wellingtons were flown in and instruction got under way. Most of the crews were from Australia and New Zealand and, on July 24 1941, the Prime Minister of the latter inspected a parade of his countrymen.

In July the first *Nickels* were carried out

when three Wellingtons dropped leaflets over Northern France. This was to become the culmination of each course so that the airmen could gain some experience of operations before being posted to a squadron. Although enemy occupied territory was not penetrated deeply it could still be dangerous and several Wellingtons were lost on these sorties. Bombing practice was carried out on the range at Cannock Chase and night flares were dropped to enable photographs to be taken. A satellite was opened at Tatenhill on November 2 1941 so as to take some of the load off the parent station, but the runways were not long enough for Wellingtons to operate with any safety margin and it was given up and replaced by Church Broughton in August 1942.

A strict security clamp descended towards the end of May 1942 and all personnel were confined to camp. The rumoured thousand bomber raid was on and the OTUs were throwing their weight into Bomber Harris's calculated risk which could either destroy a German city or decimate his force, and, worse still, cripple his training organisation if things went wrong. The ground crews worked 24 hours a day to get as many Wellingtons serviceable as possible, spurred on by the knowledge that this was a tangible opportunity to hit the enemy. On the evening of May 30, 21 aircraft took off from Lichfield at carefully planned intervals—target Cologne—each with one 500-pound bomb and 360 four-pound incendiaries. Three were forced to return early with crew illness or mechanical problems but 18

The 'haunted' tower at Lichfield.

Wellingtons bombed the primary target and all came back safely. The results were difficult to observe as the city was partly hidden by a pall of smoke but the defences were still able to put up a heavy barrage which caused some damage. Wellington X9608 brought back its 500 pounder after the release mechanism failed over Cologne but N2760 had the opposite experience, in that its bomb fell through the doors somewhere on the way to the target and the crew had to be satisfied with dropping the incendiaries only. The feared heavy losses to Bomber Command and its OTUs did not happen and reconnaissance showed that Cologne was devastated.

It had been planned that if this first raid was a success, a further strike would be mounted the following night before the thousand force was dispersed and its OTU participants resumed their normal routine. The target this time was Essen but, because of haze over the highly industrialised Ruhr Valley, the attack was not concentrated and the effects did not match those of the night before. No 27 OTU sent 19 Wellingtons this time but, again, three aircraft aborted through sickness and malfunction. There were no casualties but Flight Sergeant H. Richardson and his crew in Z- DV559 had a narrow escape. Their aircraft was held in a searchlight over The Hague at 8,000 feet and dived to 200 feet over the sea. While the gunners fired at the light an enemy fighter came on their tail. The rear gunner gave it a short burst and the aircraft was then hit by light flak from a ship which broke some of the geodetic framework, punctured the tailwheel, and passed through the navigator's seat and table.

Fortunately, he was with the pilot at the time and the unit's ORB laconically states 'An oil leak was stopped with chewing gum and the aircraft returned to base'.

No 27 OTU took part in seven more operations before the end of 1942, when it reverted to the more normal and rather less dangerous *Nickel* raids. The attack on Emden and Bremen on the night of June 25/26 1942 saw the first battle casualty when R- R1162 failed to return out of 15 aircraft dispatched by the OTU. Two more operations passed uneventfully but N- DV552 and R1526 went missing over Düsseldorf on August 31. Lichfield, for all its ostensible training role, must by now have captured something of the atmosphere of one of the main force stations in Yorkshire or East Anglia. Stark tragedy was brought right home to the ground personnel on September 13 when 14 aircraft were detailed for a raid on Bremen. An elderly Wellington, L7815 from the first production batch, had its port engine catch fire just after take off. The Australian captain nursed it round the circuit but stalled on the final turn to land. There were no survivors from the blazing wreck and four of the station fire crew were injured when the bomb load exploded.

Three days later, 12 aircraft participated in a raid on Essen with one failing to return. In addition, X9876 had its port aileron shot away and a hole blown in the leading edge over the outskirts of Essen. The target was bombed despite control difficulties but it took 4½ hours to reach the English coast at an indicated airspeed of 95 mph. The crew baled out near Andover and all landed safely. This operation was a fiasco which in no way reflected upon the courage of the airmen, most of whom were pupils. The ageing Wellingtons, many of them veterans of operational use two years before and withdrawn to OTUs, were just not up to the demands put upon them and no further operations (apart from *Nickels*) were undertaken until some newer Mk IIIs and Xs were available. Of the 12 aircraft which took off for Essen, six were forced to return early, two of them because sections of fabric blew off the wings making control difficult, one was missing and two bombed targets of opportunity because of inability to climb and turret unserviceabilities. Only three were able to bomb the primary target.

Nickel raids on French towns were resumed with more success but there were

occasional losses to *flak* and fighters. Routine cross-country flights were not without their hazards either. For example, on June 14 1943 two Wellingtons, BK672 and BK843, disappeared without trace and were presumed to have crashed in the North Sea. A few bombing operations were mounted in August and September 1943 against objectives in France, one of which was Boulogne. In all, 27 OTU dispatched 142 aircraft against various targets, plus some 274 leaflet dropping sorties. The heavy traffic played havoc with the runways and perimeter tracks at Lichfield which had been rapidly constructed in the hectic days of 1940/41 and Flying Control had to inspect them at least six times in each 24-hour period. Frequently, flying had to be suspended temporarily whilst a gang of men rushed to the runway to carry out immediate repairs. In 1943, deterioration was so bad that it was decided that complete resurfacing was the only solution. Due to the flying commitments, it was impossible to close the station but careful planning enabled the work to be completed in five and a half months, with minimal disruption to training.

Many operational aircraft returning from raids found Lichfield a useful diversion in 1944, including eight Lancasters and Halifaxes on August 5 and nine USAAF B-17s on November 16. In August and September 1944, the US Postal Service ran a C-47 service from Prestwick to Lichfield with mail brought over on the transatlantic C-54s. The mail was sorted here and flown on to the south of England. The reverse process was then done in the opposite direction with mail being flown to Prestwick for onward transmission to the States.

The Rolls-Royce Development Flight took over a hangar in April 1944 but what they flew from here is uncertain. The closing down or change of role of OTUs in the North-West in October 1944 brought Canadian personnel from Gamston to finish their training and RAF pupils from Peplow. No 27 OTU officially ceased to be a Royal Australian Air Force OTU on January 22 1945 as most Australian aircrew were being kept in their native land in preparation for a concentration on Japan as Germany collapsed. It closed on July 8 1945, having trained over 1,000 crews for Bomber Command, and control of the airfield was returned to Maintenance Command.

No 51 MU's main task had been the

preparation of Typhoons, together with Fortresses and Liberators for the RAF. It had been joined on April 4 1941 by 82 MU which worked as a packing unit. Amongst the aircraft handled by the latter were Spitfires and Hurricanes for Russia. No 82 MU disbanded on October 31 1945. The airfield and its sprawling network of dispersals were now devoted to the storage of aircraft pending their being broken up for scrap. On July 31 1945, the holding was 781 aircraft but this rose sharply until, on the day of the Battle of Britain Display in September, there were 900 Typhoons, 500 Liberators, and 150 Fortresses to be seen overflowing into the surrounding fields. Sommerfeld Flex-Boards, devised by the inventor of the runway mesh which also bore his name, were used to support the heavy bombers on doubtful ground when the hard-standings were full. These boards had originally been used for freeing bogged-down aircraft. One Fortress, at least, survived, being taken by road to Cranfield College of Technology in April 1946.

Lichfield was retained by the RAF post-war and became the base of 6 ANS, formerly known as 104 Refresher Flying School, in February 1952. Once again, Wellingtons were seen in the Staffordshire skies but were not to last long. No 99 MU were there for three years before disband-ment on March 1 1957. The airfield was finally closed in April 1958 and was then used for light industry and storage. Since this time there have been alleged sightings of a headless figure in flying kit on the airfield and lights flickering on and off in the control tower. Guard dogs refuse to go within 50 yards of the ruined tower

which stands on the south east side of the vast and deserted flying field. The tower certainly has a creepy atmosphere, particularly on a wet day when water drips and the wind sighs through the broken window frames, but this is perhaps inevit-able if one knows the legend. Lichfield had more than its fair share of tragedy and here is one aeronautical ghost story more convincing than the average. The hangars present a contrasting picture; they are freshly painted and well-main-tained. The runways have been resurfaced for vehicle testing and the only things missing are the aircraft.

Little Sutton, Cheshire

SJ365763. On A5032, 1 mile S of Little Sutton

If you follow the minor road out of Little Sutton towards Wales, you will see on the left a large pasture with a Blister hangar and a few huts on the edge of it. Had you been there on February 20 1945, you would have seen an Anson of 1 Ferry Unit, Pershore, blocking the road after it had skidded through the hedge, perhaps the largest aircraft ever to have landed here. The northern boundary of what was once an RLG for RAF Sealand is now encroached upon by a row of houses, but it is easy to see how small an airfield if once was. Opened early in 1941, it was used initially by aircraft of 5 SFTS and, to a lesser extent, by RAF Hooton Park which lies only two miles to the north. When Sealand became the base of an EFTS, Tiger Moths moved in in force,

Enlarged Over Blister at Little Sutton.

although the proximity of Hooton must have caused some problems. While Sealand's single runway was being constructed in the late summer of 1942, most of 24 EFTS's flying was done from the RLG. After the EFTS left for Rochester on March 11 1945, it was little used and was finally de-requisitioned in May 1946.

Llanbedr, Gwynedd

SH570260. Access road from A496 at Llanbedr village

Enjoying one of the finest locations in Britain, Llanbedr occupies a narrow coastal strip with the mountains just to the east and Harlech Castle on its crag to the north. It opened on June 15 1941 initially under Valley's control and was intended to be a forward airfield for day operations against enemy raiders in the Irish Sea. Its first occupants were not fighters, however, but six Ansons with pupils and instructors detached from 6 AONS at Staverton for several months, beginning on August 24.

The expected Spitfires followed in October 1941, flown by 74 Squadron, who then embarked on a series of convoy patrols. The first combat was on November 26 when two aircraft were scrambled to intercept three Ju 88s over Cardigan Bay. Unhappily one of the Spitfires was shot down against a claim of one Ju 88 probably destroyed. The squadron was posted to Northern Ireland in January 1942 and was replaced on the 8th of the following month by 131 Squadron from Atcham.

Everyone agreed that Llanbedr was a delightful spot, even though they had requested a move to the south to get a crack at the enemy. Dusk patrols were inaugurated, flown on three approved routes across St George's Channel at about 100 feet so as to silhouette the enemy against the horizon. Little or no radio assistance was possible and the 300-mile route was carried out on dead-reckoning with a landfall on the Irish coast. Alas there was to be no success until after a move to Valley in March 1942.

The next fighter squadron was 232 which stayed from May until August 1942 with a short break at Merston to take part in the Dieppe Raid. At this point a radically different type of aircraft came on the scene when eight Lightnings of the USAAF's 48th Fighter Squadron flew into

Llanbedr for a few days of training which included air-to-air firing. During the next few weeks all the pilots of the 48th and 49th FSs arrived on short detachments from Atcham. The Lightning squadrons were soon considered operational under 9 Group and on September 26 two aircraft were scrambled from Llanbedr and climbed to 17,000 ft off Carnsore Point, Eire. No contact was made and the pilots found it bitterly cold at this altitude, a foretaste of a problem which would plague the early P-38s in European skies.

After 41 Squadron's Spitfires left for High Ercall in February 1943 there was a lull until December when 306 Squadron stayed for a week, later returning for a few weeks in March 1944. The Czech 312 Squadron, no stranger to these parts, spent some of December 1944 here. The airfield was now an Armament Practice Camp and squadrons came and went in quick succession.

The USAAF's 2025th Gunnery Flight, equipped with about a dozen Lysanders, had been in residence since at least March 1943, operating mainly in conjunction with Atcham's Thunderbolts. These aircraft used the cannon range at Dyffryn and also dropped practice bombs on a buoy anchored just off the coast. USAAF bombers on liaison flights were occasional visitors but a stray B-24 on March 11 1944 had come all the way from Marrakesh, missed Valley and landed at the first airfield it saw.

No 129 Squadron spent March 1944 here converting from Spitfires to Mustang IIIs. In April the Typhoons of 195 Squadron were based briefly, preceded by 302 Squadron's Spitfires getting some bombing practice in readiness for the Invasion. The end of hostilities found 631 Squadron's Spitfires at Llanbedr and the MRU from Llandwrog was also here for a while before disbanding. No 631 Squadron was renumbered 20 Squadron on February 7 1949 and disbanded on October 16 1951. It was followed by 5 CAACU equipped with Mosquitoes, Beaufighters, Vampires and Meteors.

The approaches at both ends of one of the runways are unique in that they are both over the sea. This fact resulted in the airfield being selected for the pilotless target aircraft necessary for guided missile development. The rockets were fired both from the air and RAE Aberporth and over the years Fireflies, Meteors and Jindiviks have been employed, the first pilotless

Llandow tower, a 518/40 pattern now used as offices (A.J. Ayers).

sortie being flown by a Firefly in February 1954.

Being distant from other airfields, but surrounded by training and low flying airspace, Llanbedr attracts a large number of aircraft on diversion. Student pilots from Valley also use it for touch-and-go landings when target work permits.

Llandow, South Glamorgan

SS960715. B4270 crosses site

The date was June 7 1942, the place Quinville on the Cherbourg Peninsula. A lone Spitfire pilot attacked a motor vessel and was then chased by four Fw 190s. Turning into them he fired a two second burst which scattered them and enabled him to escape into the clouds. A common enough happening in 1942 but the difference here was that the Spitfire belonged to a training unit, 53 OTU, and its pilot was a pupil! He got lost on a training flight (so he said) and was lucky not to suffer disciplinary action.

This was to be almost the only taste of combat the airfield from which he took off was to enjoy. The other took place on August 6 1940 when a Ju 88 dropped four heavy bombs on the station, causing slight damage to a hangar on the main site. Dating back to 1937 when 614 Squadron formed here with Hinds and Hectors before moving to Pengam Moors in September 1939, it re-opened as an Aircraft Storage Unit on April 1 1940 run by 38 MU.

One 'L'-type hangar was available at first and three Lysanders were brought in by road a few days later. Some Tiger Moths, a Fairey Battle and two Fox

Moths followed and then three Blenheims direct from the makers at Woodford. Spitfires and Whitleys were to be among the main types to be stored and the first were flown in during August. The runways were not all completed until late in the autumn and, to begin with, only one was usable.

Eleven Super Robin hangars were rapidly erected and more 'L'-types were built to a final total of seven. As the aircraft commitment steadily increased two 'K'-types, one 'J', two 'T2's, one 'A1' and 12 Blisters were added. The MU became responsible for Albemarles and Bostons in 1943 and then Mustangs and Lancasters. Stocks of aircraft had reached 499 in May 1945 and 856 by November of the same year. Fields were packed with Lancs waiting only to be dismembered and melted down.

From July 1 1941 the airfield was shared by the Spitfires and Masters of 53 OTU which had formed originally at Heston on February 18 1941 for single-seat fighter training. Hundreds of pilots from all over the world were taught how to fly the Spitfire here until the OTU moved to Kirton-in-Lindsey on May 9 1943. It was replaced by a more mundane organisation on July 1 1943 when No 3 Overseas Aircraft Preparation Unit was created at Llandow. It was responsible for the preparing for ferrying abroad of Beaufighters, Wellingtons, Warwicks and Ventura Vs, a routine task which it performed faithfully until moving to Dunkeswell in August 1945.

The only excitement after the OTU left was caused by the mass escape by German prisoners-of-war from a camp at Bridgend on March 10 1945. They were all recaptured within days after a search operation on a vast scale, three being tracked down to a pillbox on one of the MU's sites.

No 614 Squadron reformed as an auxiliary fighter unit on August 26 1947 at Llandow. It was equipped with Spitfires but converted to Vampires in the summer of 1950 and flew these until disbandment in 1957, the aircraft carrying the red and green colours of Wales as squadron insignia. 'A' Flight of 663 Squadron's Auster AOP 6s was also in residence here between July 1949 and March 1957.

Llandow was unfortunate enough to be the scene of what was up to that time the world's worst air disaster. On March 12 1950 Avro Tudor G-AKBY of Fairflight Ltd was returning with a load of rugby supporters from a match in Belfast when it dived into a field in the circuit. Of the 83 occupants only three survived.

Today the main site is surrounded by a high fence and used for storage, all the original buildings remaining intact. A go-cart racing circuit takes in most of the three runways and parts of the perimeter track.

Llandwrog, Gwynedd

SH435590. On small peninsula, 4 miles SW of Caernarvon

Built on a peninsula jutting into Caernarvon Bay and opened in January 1941, this station has a permanent place in the annals of the RAF because here was the birthplace of the Mountain Rescue Service. Before the war the infrequent crashes in the hills were dealt with by the police and local civilians, with some help from the nearest RAF station, but this was totally inadequate for the wartime toll of aircraft accidents. The MRS was exceptional in that it arose from a need recognised on a local level rather than as a directive from Air Ministry. In the early stages of the war it became apparent that the discovery of a missing aircraft in the mountains was often a matter of chance and the subsequent removal of casualties a difficult problem.

During the last five months of 1942 there were ten major accidents in the Snowdonia area of North Wales, from which a total of 40 dead and eight injured were recovered. The accidents were attended by Station Sick Quarters staff from Llandwrog, the nearest airfield, with local assistance. A typical call-out was to Boston Z2186 of 418 Squadron which had flown into the 3,000 foot summit ridge of Carnedd Dafydd on October 17 1942. The wreck was spotted on the mountain two days later when the cloud lifted and the first person to reach it was a local doctor. The pilot was rescued though suffering from exposure and a broken leg, but sadly his two crew members were dead.

However, the accident which really emphasised the necessity for a specially-trained rescue team occurred on November 20 1942. At 12.00 hours a Hawker Henley target tug from Towyn was reported to have crashed on Silyn Mountain in the southern fringes of Snowdonia. The SSQ party from Llandwrog searched in thick mist for four hours without success. At 19.00 hours it was learned that an Anson had crashed on the side of Moel Eilio four hours previously and had been found by civilians. One airman was still alive but died before he could be treated properly. The Medical Officer who might have saved him was otherwise engaged on the fruitless Henley search. The next day an air survey sighted the Henley wreck wedged in a gully on the cliffs of Cwm Silyn. An RAF party was sent but found that the pilot's body was on the top of the inaccessible rock face and it was left to local quarrymen to recover it the following day. This solved the problem but hurt the RAF's pride to have its job done by civilians.

The following January, Flight Lieutenant George Graham, the Medical Officer at Llandwrog, was awarded the MBE for his services to mountain rescue. However, he was not satisfied with the facilities available and an accident which occurred on January 14 1943 illustrates the reason for his disquiet. An Anson crashed in Snowdonia during a night flight, the pilot struggling down to a farm despite concussion and lacerations of the face. When Flight Lieutenant Graham and two nursing orderlies reached him he was irrational and could not give any idea of the direction in which the aircraft and its other three occupants lay. Reinforced by 30 more men sent from base they split into four parties and combed the mountain slopes until the early hours of the morning, without result. It should be remembered that the men were inadequately equipped; gas capes and ordinary army boots are hardly the thing for these gale-

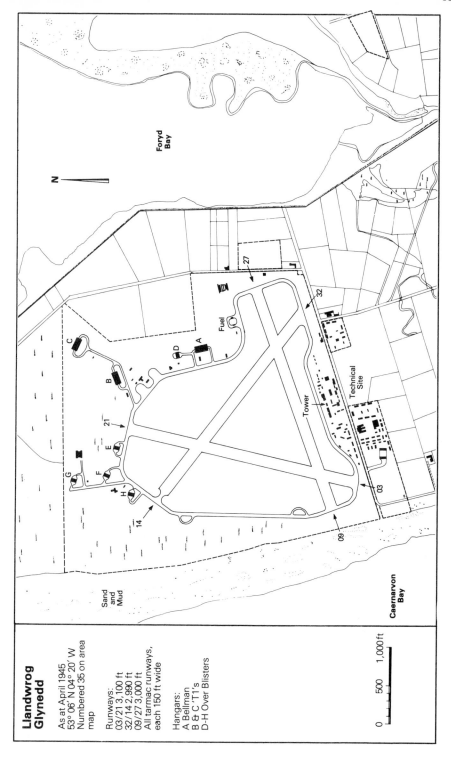

Llandwrog
Glynedd

As at April 1945
53° 06' N 04° 20' W
Numbered 35 on area
map

Runways:
03/21 3,100 ft
32/14 2,990 ft
09/27 3,000 ft
All tarmac runways,
each 150 ft wide

Hangars:
A Bellman
B & C 'T1's
D-H Over Blisters

0   500   1,000 ft

Foryd
Bay

N

Sand
and
Mud

Caernarvon
Bay

Fuel

Tower

Technical
Site

C

B

A

D

T

E

F

G

H

27

32

21

14

09

03

swept peaks in January and only the MO had any previous climbing experience.

At first light they set off again in two separate groups. The first soon found the Anson with one member of the crew still alive but, as the MO was in the second party, contact had to be made with it before the injured man could receive proper medical attention. Communications between the two groups were so bad that it was another hour and a half before he was able to reach the scene. Removal of the patient to the ambulance then required three more hours of arduous work. As well as the lack of radio their transport was unable to negotiate the steep track up from the Conway Valley and a civilian vehicle had to lend a hand.

To remedy these faults Graham proposed to set up a unit specially equipped for mountain rescue. When this had been accepted he conducted the first rescue trial in February 1943. A Jeep and a Humber four-wheel drive ambulance were selected as the most suitable transport. Trials were also carried out with radio so that search parties could communicate both with each other and also with the vehicles which would penetrate as far as possible into the mountains. Improvements to the General Service Stretcher were also suggested and this was later superseded by a lightweight version, far more suitable for rough country.

Four months later the unit was ready for action. Ropes, maps, compasses and weather-proof clothing were supplied and portable radios were now in service. The USAAF supplied a considerable amount

of equipment and an article about the unit appeared in *Yank* magazine, written by a US Sergeant who spent several days with them. The experience gained by this local unit was used in the establishment of other specialist teams to cover all mountainous areas in the British Isles, a service which operates to this day.

Llandwrog had opened as a base for No 9 Air Gunnery School equipped with Whitleys and Ansons. Two days later it was attacked by a solitary Ju 88 which came in at 50 feet from the south and machine-gunned the parked aircraft but did not drop any bombs. Whitley P5024 was slightly damaged and the raider disappeared into the mist as fast as it had come, the crew no doubt wondering which airfield it was that they had fired on!

Three of the Whitleys from 9 AGS (N1345, N1428 and T4155) were detached to Driffield for the thousand bomber raid on Cologne, one of them being reported missing. There was a short period of use by 11 SFTS who based some Oxfords here in the summer of 1941 to catch up on its night flying programme. No 9 AGS was disbanded on June 13 1942 and Llandwrog became a satellite to 9 (O) AFU at Penrhos, an unusual situation as the satellite had concrete runways and the parent was grass-surfaced. Also by this time personnel strength exceeded that at Penrhos and all night flying was done from Llandwrog. It was obviously more logical to reverse this situation and move the station HQ to Llandwrog and this was done on February 11 1942. Navigation and gunnery training went on uninterrupted until the AFU closed down on June 14 1945. Flying then ceased and the buildings were used to accommodate 2 ACHU.

Llandwrog tower with some lettering still faintly visible.

Duplicated watch office at Llandwrog beside the main building.

It would appear that Llandwrog might have had a secret secondary function in its early days as a rearward defence line airfield in the event of an enemy invasion in the south. The presence of an Iron Age fort close by at Dinas Dinlle testifies to the little peninsula's traditional ease of defence and the airfield boundary was heavily mined (there was a fatal casualty during clearing operations late in the war). Extensive accommodation was provided for a defence unit from the RAF Regiment in the technical site area on the southern perimeter. Many pillboxes can still be seen and the customary Battle HQ is just south of the approach to runway 27. Conversely, in the unlikely occurrence of an invasion via the Irish Sea, the airfield would have been a valuable prize for an enemy force and was geared to repel this threat as well. The control tower's function was duplicated by a reinforced concrete block-house adjacent to it.

There were formerly two 'T1's and a Bellman hangar plus six Blisters, but all have been taken down and based aircraft are now picketed out next to the caravan which serves as an office for the flying club. The control tower is nearby, still bearing 'FLYING CONTROL' in letters faded by the salty winds. Llandwrog was refurbished to allow its use by light aircraft and helicopters during the Prince of Wales' Investiture at Caernarvon Castle. This led indirectly to occasional use by civil aircraft until its re-opening by Keen-Air Services of Liverpool who have renamed the field Caernarvon. Pleasure flights are offered to the public in association with Fort Belan, a local tourist attraction, once the wartime base of an ASR launch.

Longtown, Cumbria

NY410683. 1½ miles E of Longtown village

A fairly large airfield with a 2,000 yard main runway, Longtown never aspired to being more than a satellite to various other airfields in the Solway area. It started life in July 1941 under RAF Crosby to take some of the Hurricanes of 59 OTU but they left on August 5 1942 and the airfield then passed to RAF Annan. The aircraft were still Hurricanes but this time from 55 OTU. In August 1942 a front-line Spitfire squadron, No 41, spent five days here before moving on to Llanbedr.

No 9 OTU at Crosby employed it for Beaufort and Beaufighter training from September 1942, sharing the airfield with 55 OTU until both units ceased flying from here in October 1943. This was to enable Longtown to accommodate 1674 HCU which moved its HQ from Aldergrove on October 19. This unit's Halifaxes were augmented by Fortresses from 1 OTU when the latter disbanded at Thornaby. The HQ of the HCU returned to Aldergrove on February 1 1944, followed by the rest of its aircraft a few weeks later.

The Wellingtons of 6 OTU at Silloth had also used Longtown as a satellite between October 20 1943 and January 5

Now demolished, Longtown tower stares out at the empty airfield (J. Huggon).

1944, No 9 OTU then taking over again. Its Beaufighters were allowed to stay even when 1332 HCU formed here on August 11 1944 with 15 Stirlings, four Yorks and four Liberators. Crews converted on to Stirlings, some going on to Yorks or Liberators, the latter including a C-87 transport version, EW628. Facilities at Longtown were found insufficient to meet the planned training output so the unit was moved to Nutts Corner, on October 7 1944.

The station was reduced to care and maintenance on October 9 1944 and was not used again until October 20 1945 when 1521 RAT Flight flew its Oxfords in from Wymeswold. The Dakotas of 1383 TSCU at Crosby did some flying from Longtown until March 25 1946, on which date a farewell dance was held in the camp concert hall. No 1521 RAT Flight disbanded on April 1 1946 and the airfield then closed.

Its runways are still intact and one or two aircraft have landed here mistaking it for Carlisle Airport. The tower was demolished in 1975, the single 'T2' and two Blister hangars having gone long before.

Madley, Hereford and Worcester

SO420375. 6 miles WSW of Hereford

During the war years Proctors and Dominies with mysterious codes painted on them like '4-61' were a daily sight over Hereford and the Severn Valley, flying from an almost forgotten field close to the Welsh Border. Virtually on the limit of suitable terrain for an airfield because of the hilly country on three sides, Madley was planned as a school for wireless operators. Its premature opening on August 27 1941 was marked by a lack of feeding and sleeping facilities and the officers and men of the opening-up party had to be billeted at RAF Hereford.

No 4 Signals School, as it was known initially, aimed to train 2,800 ground and 1,200 aircrew wireless operators. The airfield was grass-covered until it was reinforced in October 1943 with Sommerfeld Tracking, the work being done by an RAF Airfield Construction Flight. The hangarage was unusual, consisting of three of the pre-war Hinaidi type and two Callender-Hamiltons, later joined by 13 Blisters. The living sites were dispersed over a wide area in the normal manner of the period.

The aircraft establishment provided for 60 Proctor IVs and 18 Dominies and these were all to be worked hard day after day whilst trainee operators struggled over their morse keys sending and receiving cryptic messages, practice which might one day save their lives over enemy territory. A small lodger unit in the form of a detachment of 8 AACU employed a few Lysanders to train local army personnel and divided its time between here and Shobdon from July 1941 onwards.

The radio trainers were joined occasionally by visitors such as Tomahawk AH799 of 26 Squadron on May 8 1942 and two Hurricanes and two Mustangs of 239 Squadron which were attached for three days in June 1942 for an Army co-operation exercise. Two contrasting personalities passed through, namely General George S. Patton Junior on June 3 1944, for whom the RAF provided a guard of honour, and Hitler's former deputy, Rudolph Hess. Hess, who had been imprisoned in the district since 1941, was flown out from Madley in a Dominie to stand trial at Nuremburg in 1946.

The proximity of the Welsh Mountains meant that the station was continually having to send men to attend aircraft crashes and to remove casualties. As at other RAF aerodromes close to hilly areas, the teams were medical staff from Station Sick Quarters, untrained in mountain craft. However, by the end of 1943, considerable experience had been gained and a properly equipped mountain rescue party was set up on the lines pioneered by RAF Llandwrog. Most of the accidents dealt with, such as a US Navy Liberator on August 24 1944 and a Wellington from 22 OTU on November 20 1944, were fatal but a survivor was rescued from cne of the unit's own Proctor aircraft which had crashed on the Brecon Beacons on January 12 1945. An unusual accident occurred on Christmas Day 1944 when a Liberator named 'Bold Venture III' crashed near Madley and a fruitless search was made for her missing crew. It was discovered later that they had all baled out over Belgium assuming that their flak-damaged aircraft was about to plunge to destruction.

Madley survived the wave of closures when the war ended, for a time at least, and many of its Proctors found their way into civilian hands after the Radio School disbanded. The rare Hinaidi hangars and

Two of the rare Hinaidi hangars, a 1927 design, at Madley (P. Francis).

the Callender-Hamiltons still exist in good condition and naturally the one-time landing ground has returned to agriculture.

Manorbier, Dyfed
SS075975. On B4585, 1 mile E of Manorbier

One of the least known airfields in Wales, it was used solely for target towing and radio-controlled target flying from its opening in the mid-1930s. 'B' Flight of 1 AACU was here for the summer of 1937 and this routine continued until the war started when the Pilotless Aircraft Unit was permanently available for the local training of AA gunners. Never a large field, it was enlarged slightly in 1940 but autumn floods made it unserviceable and Queen Bees on floats had to be fired from a catapult mounted on the cliff which fringed the landing ground so that practice could be kept up. A salvage vessel was to hand to pick up the pilotless drone after its water landing and return it to Tenby harbour, whence it was taken by road back to base. Queen Bees were quite sophisticated devices for their time. For example, a trailing aerial wire struck the ground or water first and this contact automatically set the aircraft up for landing, in theory anyway!

Operations were almost farcical at times and practically every shoot ended in disaster. The normal procedure was a climb to 5,000 ft and the aircraft would then be guided backwards and forwards in front of the gunners who would attempt to hit it. On two occasions in 1941 they never even began because the Bee refused to climb after launching and flew into the cliffs. The drones sometimes behaved better when left to their own devices. One disappeared out to sea but was found

drifting almost undamaged some time later. Another was actually shot down by the gunners but still managed to land itself in one piece.

The enemy ignored Manorbier—its capacity for self-destruction being admirable anyway—until January 17 1941 when a low-flying raider was fired on by the local AA gunners who claimed it as damaged. No bombs were dropped but a Hamilton-Pickett retractable pillbox was soon installed on the boundary to discourage any further incidents. These obscure inventions could be raised and lowered hydraulically and it is doubtful if any survive today. Several aerodromes in southern England, including Christchurch, had one to augment their conventional fixed gun-posts.

The Pilotless Aircraft Unit was still present in 1946 and since then the airfield has been used intermittently by Army Air Corps Beavers for liaison with the army camps and ranges which ring it and make viewing impossible. One Bellman hangar was used to protect the aircraft and it is probably still there.

Meir, Staffordshire

SJ935415. On A50, 2 miles SE of Longton

At the foot of a hill and virtually surrounded by houses, Meir was one of those municipal airports whose development was doomed from the start because of its urban position. Every town wanted its

'airport', however, and Stoke-on-Trent was no exception. The actual opening date has proved elusive but is now known to have taken place on May 18 1934.

From August 12 1935 Railway Air Services called at Meir 'on request' as part of their Croydon-Belfast-Glasgow service. There was one DH 86 each way daily, except Sundays, and this continued until 1938 when the frequency was stepped up to two each way per day. There were more services in 1939 but Meir was no longer a port of call. The North Staffordshire Aero Club had kept a few aircraft here but most of the flying from August 1 1938 was done by 28 Elementary and Reserve Flying School. It was run by Reid and Sigrist Ltd under contract to the Air Ministry and operated Tiger Moths and Hawker Harts. One other notable pre-war occurrence was the use of the aerodrome as a turning point in the King's Cup of 1937 and Alex Henshaw was forced to retire from the race and land his Mew Gull G-AEXF here.

On February 12 1940 the opening up party of 1 Flying Practice Unit arrived at Meir. This unit was the first of its kind (and only one as it turned out) formed to accommodate 120 Acting Pilot Officers and 120 Sergeant Pilots who had completed advanced courses at an FTS. They were to be kept in flying practice and given some ground instruction. Problems with billeting all these men were solved by requisitioning three large houses for the

The original hangars at Meir in centre of photograph, now heavily added-to and with a helicopter pad to the left, seen in 1979 (Staffordshire Potteries Ltd).

officers and housing the NCO pilots in the Town Hall at neighbouring Longton. Reid and Sigrist were contracted to maintain the aircraft, parachutes and motor transport but it was over a month before the first machines, Hawker Hectors, were flown in, to be followed at intervals by a quantity of Hawker Hinds. The unit was informed that it was to be responsible for instructing Finnish pilots along the same lines as those given to Polish pilots at their EFTS. However, hostilities in Finland ceased and the plan was dropped, perhaps fortunately in view of the formidable political implications!

The invasion threat in the summer of 1940 had widespread effects even in such a backwater as Meir. Arrangements were made for defence against parachutists and troop-carrying aircraft and exercises were held in which all 40 Hinds and Hectors were dispersed around the perimeter within 15 minutes. The aerodrome camouflage was renewed having become indistinct after the spring grass cutting. A 'continuation' of the suburban roads on the boundary was painted on the grass so as to prevent a chance sighting from the air. This was normal practice with near built-up areas, a particularly good example being at Christchurch in Hampshire. Meir was never attacked deliberately but it did collect one or two stray bombs during the raids on the Pottery towns without any serious damage.

The FPU did very little flying, apart from occasional co-operation with troops and vehicles in the vicinity, and disbanded on June 16 1940, having been grounded since June 3. The aerodrome was now earmarked for use by 5 EFTS, whose base at Hanworth in Middlesex looked as though it might find itself in the front line of the air war at any moment. The RAF was desperately short of pilots so the interrupted training was resumed within two days of the school arriving on June 16, despite a lack of hangarage and offices. No 1 FPU's aircraft were rapidly ferried away and replaced by the Miles Magisters which were to become such a common sight in this area. Pupils were turned out at an impressive rate that summer while the weather held, 3,342 flying hours being completed in July and 134 pilots sent on to SFTS.

Unfortunately when the rains came in the autumn parts of the landing ground turned to mud and the industrial haze from the Potteries was a grave hindrance, plus the added handicap of the

surrounding hills. Visiting aircraft were few but Blenheim L1218 of 13 OTU came in from Bicester on December 5 1940 and skidded into the hedge. A Harrow inbound on December 23 did not even get this far as it had to force-land in a small field after being fired upon by the local AA defences! The EFTS flourished until it closed abruptly on December 31 1941, probably because the demand for pilots was no longer so great. No 16 EFTS then used the airfield as an RLG for its Magister fleet at Burnaston.

Throughout the war Rootes' shadow factory at Blythe Bridge produced hundreds of Blenheims and Beaufighters which were towed the half mile to the aerodrome for test-flying. Rootes also had a contract late in the war in association with Helliwells at Walsall Airport for the maintenance of RAF Mustangs and Harvards. A single rather short runway was built for the heavy twins but there were never any taxi-ways apart from the one to the factory. Production at Blythe Bridge ceased in September 1945 when the last Beaufighter X was delivered. Beaufighter VIFs had preceeded them on the production line, in turn having replaced the Blenheim V in 1942.

Post-war, the aerodrome was used mainly by Staffordshire Potteries who operated a Dove and at weekends by the Staffordshire Gliding Club. A few light aircraft were also based here until the mid-1970s but, by this time, the runway surface was almost unusable and industrial development was beginning to encroach. The remainder of the site was zoned for urban development and in 1979 the runway was taken up. Meir's use as an aerodrome is scarcely credible now and is only recalled by the road names, for example Farnborough Way and Catalina Place. The roads on the pre-war estate on the western boundary are named after contemporary airmen such as Cobham Road, Mollison Road and Kingsford Road. The Rootes factory is still there but the flight shed on the airfield side of the road was removed to make way for new houses.

Millom, Cumbria

SD140790. 1½ miles S of Millom town

This coastal airfield was built as an advanced fighter station under 9 Group but the requirement altered by the time it opened in January 1941. The first Botha for No 2 Bombing and Gunnery School

Millom from 3,000 ft on August 25 1942. Runways are camouflaged but the newly-painted 'hedges' are still very obtrusive (RAF Museum).

flew in on January 14 and more aircraft were available by the time the school opened six days later. There was so much sand blowing about the newly-finished airfield that the Bothas had to be grounded continually for engine changes due to excessive oil consumption. Despite special filters fitted to the air intakes the difficulties continued and 18 Ansons were loaned in June.

No 2 B & GS became 2 AOS on June 1 1941 and was now flying Battles, Blenheims and Ansons as well as the ailing Bothas. 'R' Flight of 1 AACU was attached as a lodger unit between September 9 1941 and January 1 1942 when it moved to Cark. Its Henleys and Defiants had originally been at Squires Gate but moved to the Furness area to be nearer to the ground units with which they were co-operating.

No 2 AOS was re-designated 2 (O) AFU on February 18 1942 and 240 Dominion-trained air observers formed its intake for each six-weekly period. The station unwillingly found itself providing rescue parties for crashed aircraft in the Lake District, a task which became more and more frequent in 1942. Skilled airmen were being diverted from their proper jobs and training was suffering as a result. This led to the formation of a specialised MRU based on the model of RAF Llandwrog, although it was not recognised officially until January 1944.

All flying ceased here on January 2 1945 and after a period of care and maintenance and use by an OCTU the airfield was transferred to the War Department on September 24 1946. It is now Haverigg Prison and close inspection is not recommended! During the war there were eight Bellman hangars in a block together with a number of Blisters dispersed around the perimeter. As an economy measure, or to allow for future extension, all three runways had narrow stubs connecting their ends with the perimeter track.

Mona, Anglesey

SH410760. On A5, 1 mile SE of Gwalchmai

Originally known as Heneglwys, the correct pronunciation of which was a mystery to the average Englishman, Mona opened in December 1942 under 25 (Armament) Group. It was not a good place to park aircraft outside over-night, exposed as it was to the winter gales, and the three 'T1' hangars were soon augmented by no less than 17 Blisters. The same site had been used in the First World War as an airship station called Llangefni after a larger village to the north-west. The mooring area appears to have been where the hangars are today. The station was completed in mid-1942 and planned as the base for 6 AGS. This unit was not formed as it turned out, and 3 AGS was transferred from Castle Kennedy on December 19 instead. The School was equipped mainly with Bothas but these much maligned aircraft were later replaced by Ansons before the unit moved back to

Castle Kennedy at the end of October 1943. In February and March 1943 a Flight of Masters was detached from 5 (P) AFU at Tern Hill to train a group of Turkish officers. The Anglesey weather delayed matters somewhat and it was March 16 before the Flight returned to base.

The last (O) AFU to be formed during the war, No 8, opened at Mona on November 15 1943 equipped with Ansons, being disbanded on June 14 1945. During its occupation it was joined temporarily in January 1944 by a detachment of Martinets when their base at Bodorgan was unserviceable. The proximity of Valley often caused confusion to American aircraft arriving from overseas, the first unintentional visitor being a B-24 from Marrakesh on March 14 1944. The following month three C-47s landed and, on April 11, the most impressive, a sleek silver C-54 Skymaster belonging to Air Transport Command.

After a period of care and maintenance it became, in 1951, an RLG for the Vampires of 202 AFS operating from Valley and later the Gnats of 4 FTS. The main runway was lengthened to 6,000 ft, the other two being withdrawn from use. A flying club operates Cessna 150s from here at weekends and evenings when Valley's training commitment allows, and there are several privately-owned aircraft based.

The tower is the original building modified with a large picture window to improve the view and a runway caravan is manned when the jets are flying, in accordance with standard RAF practice. Although it fell into disuse between the

Modernised tower at Mona (E. Doylerush).

wars, Mona has a longer span of history than most other stations in the North-West, even if nothing very momentous has ever happened here.

Montford Bridge, Salop

SJ435170. On unclassified road, 1 mile N of A5 at Montford Bridge village

This very basic satellite station opened in April 1942. It had three runways and a perimeter track with 25 rudimentary hard-standings, most of which are merely small laybys off the taxi-track. A small control tower which bears to this day the inscription 'Flying Control' stands sentinel close to the farm on the north-east boundary. Most of the huts have been demolished but the farmer, who was in the RAF in the Middle East during the war, has preserved the tower and a nearby Nissen hut which once served as the crew room.

The living sites were dispersed to the north of the aerodrome but most of the huts have now been cleared. Pierre Closterman, the French fighter ace who trained at 61 OTU, describes in his book *The Big Show* how appallingly cold it was in the Nissen huts and how the pilots used to 'borrow' coal from a dump by the railway. At the time when he was at the OTU the course lasted for eight weeks with five weeks at Rednal and the last three at the satellite. Flying went on continuously when the weather was suitable and sometimes when it was not.

Night flying in Spitfires was often done with the aid of gooseneck flares to mark the runway. On one rainy night the few local inhabitants were roused from their beds to help search for a Spitfire missing in the circuit. It was found next morning

Flight huts at Montford Bridge where trainees once waited their turn to fly a Spitfire.

in a small copse on the edge of the aerodrome, the pilot surviving although injured.

Apart from 61 OTU few other units spent any time at Montford. They included five Piper Cubs of the US Army's 83rd Artillery Division which were here for a short period in May 1944, a detachment of Oxfords from 11 (P) AFU at Shawbury which used the aerodrome as an RLG in July 1942 pending the opening of their own RLG at Condover, and a flight of Oxfords of 6 AACU (later 577 Squadron) from May 1943 to at least the middle of 1944.

When 61 OTU went to Keevil in June 1945 their satellite became a sub-site to 34 MU for the breaking up of Masters and Hotspurs, including most of the aircraft from 5 GTS at Shobdon. This work went on until about December 1945.

The airfield, which is known locally as Forton after a village which is much closer than Montford Bridge, is used for parachute dropping at weekends. The only hangars provided were four Blisters for minor repairs and to shelter the aircraft in the event of strong winds. All were dismantled soon after the war.

Ollerton (Hinstock), Salop
See Hinstock

Pembrey, West Glamorgan
SN403035. On A484, 2 miles NW of Burry Port

On the evening of June 23 1942 a Fw 190 returned to what its pilot believed was a French airfield, performed some victory rolls and, after extending the undercarriage whilst inverted, landed off a steep turn. The pilot was dismayed to discover that he had arrived at RAF Pembrey and had no time to destroy his aircraft before he was captured. The Fw 190 had been in a fight with Spitfires from the Exeter and Portreath Wings and, after shooting down a Spitfire, Oberleutnant Faber became disorientated, mistook the Bristol Channel for the English Channel and assumed he was back over occupied territory.

British Intelligence was thus presented with an intact example of Germany's latest fighter which could be used for evaluation of its capabilities against Allied types. So anxious was the RAF to obtain one that a Commando raid had been planned on an airfield near Cherbourg in order to steal one. Jeffrey Quill, the Supermarine test pilot, was to fly the aircraft back to England but the unexpected gift made this dangerous operation unnecessary.

Pembrey is remembered also as an important fighter station up to June 1941 when it was re-allocated to Flying Training Command. It opened in May 1940, at first having no runways and requiring but little rain to become unserviceable. The Spitfires of 92 Squadron were the first operational aircraft to be based, having been withdrawn to South Wales for a rest in mid-June. Routine convoy patrols were flown and no opportunity to engage the enemy was missed. On July 4 a patrol shot down an enemy bomber over Wiltshire and on the 24th a Ju 88 was sighted over Porthcawl, chased and sent down near Ilfracombe.

The squadron returned to Biggin Hill at the height of the Battle of Britain on September 9, to be replaced at Pembrey by 79 Squadron's Hurricanes which spent almost a year here mainly on convoy and sector patrols. There were scrambles when towns in South Wales or the Bristol Channel area were attacked. On one occasion nine aircraft engaged a formation of He 111s off St David's Head and claimed one destroyed and one 'probable'.

A notable victory was scored on November 20 1940 when a patrol over Pembroke Dock shot down a Ju 88 into the sea. It was later found that it had been photographing the results of the infamous Coventry air raid. Joined by the Hurricanes of 32 Squadron in April 1941, both units continued on uneventful convoy escorts until June and then moved to other airfields in the area.

A new Polish Squadron, 316, named 'City of Warsaw', formed here on February 15 1941 with Hurricanes and became operational ten days later. Bristol Channel patrols were the order of the day and on one of these, on April 1, two Poles saw a ship on fire off Linney Head. The culprits made off but not before one was probably destroyed. The first confirmed kill was to come on April 10 when an He 111 was shot down into the sea off St Ann's Head but there were no more successes before the squadron left for Colerne in June.

Night raids in the area were causing much damage and loss of life so detachments from 256 and 307 Squadrons were based at Pembrey for short periods early in 1941 as a deterrent. There were no successful combats, however. The last fighter aircraft here were four Tomahawks of 26 Squadron attached for a few days in June to participate in exercises with the School of Artillery at Sennybridge. They left before the station was handed over by Fighter Command for use by 1 Air Gunnery School on June 15 1941.

Blenheims and Lysanders formed the main equipment and personnel for No 1

Focke-Wulf 190 after landing in error at Pembrey (IWM).

Course began to arrive on June 21. The Blenheims were somewhat war-weary but late in May 1942, 34 of them were flown to Upwood to reinforce Bomber Command. The unit was told that they were to be used temporarily for low-level attacks on barges and beach targets but in fact they were really amongst the assortment of second line aircraft which 'Bomber' Harris was scraping together to make up the numbers for the thousand bomber raid on Cologne. In the event they were not needed which was perhaps fortunate and, having returned to South Wales, were soon replaced at the School by Ansons.

From time to time Pembrey was the venue for trials of various types of aircraft and equipment. In December 1941 a small detachment from Gosport investigated the performance of a new design of anti-submarine bomb, using a Fairey Albacore to drop it into 20 ft of water. A year later a Whitley carried out night firing trials with an illuminated towed target and tracer bullets but this idea does not seem to have been adopted. On April 9 1944 trials of the new Warwick aircraft were held by the Ministry of Aircraft Production and, in April 1945, it was intended that the Windsor bomber would carry out tests from Pembrey but it is doubtful if this ever happened.

The airfield found itself host to many a stray aircraft apart from the Fw 190 described above. On December 9 1942 Halifax DT551 landed with one engine out of action after a patrol over the Bay of Biscay. In January 1943 a Liberator, 41-23817, diverted in short of fuel on the way back from a heavy VIIIth Air Force attack on the U-boat base at St Nazaire. Another American visitor was Brigadier-

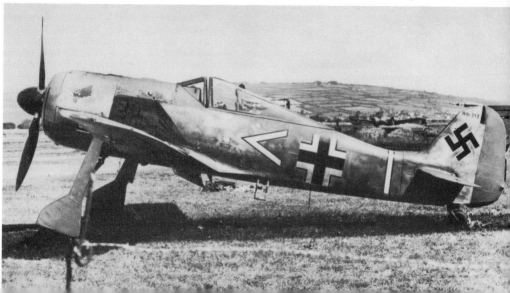

Top *Side-opening 'VR' hangar at Pembrey, never a common design* (A.J. Ayers). **Above** *Astrodome at Pembrey, another rare survivor* (A.J. Ayers).

General Hoyt S. Vandenberg, later the commanding general of IXth Air Force, who arrived in a B-17 from Marrakesh on May 19 1943 and flew on to Bovingdon after refuelling. The Marrakesh-Valley ferry route brought several Liberators into Pembrey during April 1944 and other USAAF visitors the same year included a number of C-47s evacuating wounded from Normandy.

No 1 AGS meanwhile soldiered on with occasional brief excitement like the time when an Anson had to shoot down a barrage balloon which had broken loose from a merchant ship in Swansea harbour. The Ansons began to be replaced by Wellingtons with the first six arriving in September 1944 and some Spitfires were added to augment the Martinets for more realistic fighter affiliation. The AGS disbanded on June 14 1945, having run a

total of 114 courses since its inception, each lasting about two months.

No 3 ACHU took over the accommodation but there was little flying until 595 Squadron brought its Spitfires and Martinets over from Fairwood Common at the end of October 1946 to continue co-operation for the School of AA at Manorbier. The station once more came under the control of Fighter Command and 595 later received several Vampires, some of which were detached to Valley. It was renumbered 5 Squadron on February 11 1949 and stayed at Pembrey until the airfield closed for flying in the mid-1950s. It is now on the edge of an air-to-ground firing range and the RAF retain a small part of it as an observation post. The main site, which includes two hangars, is now a chicken farm but a rare astrodome trainer survives.

Pembroke Dock, Dyfed

SM960040. Close to town centre

On June 2 1943 a Sunderland of 461 Squadron, captained by Flight Lieutenant C.B. Walker, was on an anti-submarine patrol, west of the Bay of Biscay and was attacked by eight Ju 88s. On the first pass the port outer engine was put out of action by cannon shells and further assaults mortally wounded one of the gunners and wrecked the rear turret's hydraulic system so that the guns could only be operated by hand. The Sunderland fought back through all this and three Ju 88s were sent down into the sea before their comrades gave up the struggle and returned to base. All of the flying boat's crew were wounded, and one engine and the radio were useless. The base at Pembroke Dock was 300 miles away but Walker managed to get the boat to Praa Sands in Cornwall. It was badly holed and the hull was strained so much by the violent evasive action that all the doors had jammed. As soon as it touched down the water began to pour in so the Captain desperately poured on full power and beached the Sunderland on the shore line. He was subsequently awarded the DSO, the Navigator and Flight Engineer, the DFC, and the Rear Gunner, the DFM.

This action was typical of many fought by Pembroke Dock's Sunderlands against the packs of Ju 88s which roamed the Bay of Biscay. The strategic importance of Pembroke Dock was recognised long before World War 2. On the first day of 1930 the station opened officially, beginning the development of a flying boat centre which, from 1939 until the end of the war in Europe, was to play an ever-increasing part in the war against the U-boat. Its first flying boats were the Southamptons of 210 and 230 Squadrons, the latter forming here on December 1 1934. All maintenance work on the aircraft had to be done in the open on a floating dock until September 1935 when a hangar was completed.

Two Squadrons had their home here on the day war was declared: 201 and 228 with Sunderlands. The former incorporated the national symbol of Wales in its badge. No 228 Squadron found itself amongst the first RAF units to see real action. On September 9 1939 one of its Sunderlands attacked a U-boat with uncertain results and five days later L2167 bombed the U-boat which had just sunk the SS *Vancouver City*. The Sunder-

lands stayed with the lifeboats until the survivors were picked up by another ship. On the 17th L5798 claimed hits on another submarine.

A message from the SS *Kensington Court*, that she had been torpedoed and was sinking, was received by Sunderland N9025 on September 18. The aircraft set course for the scene and found 34 survivors crammed in one boat which was dangerously overloaded. The flying boat alighted on the open sea, took off 20 of the men and brought them back to Milford Haven. The rest were later picked up by an aircraft of 204 Squadron.

After this flurry of activity, things quietened a little until December 8 when a 228 Squadron Sunderland sighted a U-boat in the act of diving. Eight bombs were dropped in a stick from low-level but the vessel was believed to have escaped. During the heavy raids in Britain in May 1941 the station caught one of at least a dozen land-mines dropped on the neighbouring town. One RAF man was killed but only slight damage was done to the beached aircraft.

When France fell and the enemy secured her west coast ports, Pembroke sprang into prominence. The task of the flying boats was to assist in the protection of convoys bringing the life blood of food and war materials to Britain. By constant patrols over the Bay of Biscay they were able to locate and attack U-boats, leaving the pens in Brest, Lorient and St Nazaire to relieve the Wolf Packs in the Battle of the Atlantic. Although the actions seldom resulted in a conclusive sinking, their patrols kept the submarines under water and reduced their cruising range while position reports helped the Admiralty to direct convoys away from their areas of operation and allow destroyers to converge for a hydrophone search.

AA opposition in the early days had been almost nil but now the submarines were equipped with multiple cannon and machine guns and their commanders often preferred to fight it out on the surface. No 210 Squadron had re-equipped with Catalinas and, on May 30 1943, one of its aircraft, FP264, was badly damaged by gunfire, one of the crew being killed. An emergency landing was made in Milford Haven but the badly holed flying boat sank almost immediately, although not before her crew escaped.

On the same day in May Sunderland 'O' of 461 Squadron sighted a dinghy off

Southampton II S1231 of No 210 Squadron taking off from Milford Haven.

the French coast containing survivors. The captain attempted to touch down but, owing to a heavy swell, the boat was submerged and subsequently sank with the loss of one crew member. The remainder were rescued by 'E' of 461 Squadron some 14 hours later, but this Sunderland was unable to take off owing to the excessive load. A Free French destroyer took on most of the men, leaving the Sunderland to fly back to Pembroke Dock with a skeleton crew.

The US Navy was anxious to play its part in the Battle of the Atlantic and, on July 20 1943, the first air echelon of VP-63 arrived at Pembroke Dock with Catalinas. A change of policy transferred the USN's anti-submarine war to land-based patrol bombers. On December 15 1943, VP-63 left for Port Lyautey in North Africa and most of its ground personnel were posted to Dunkeswell to service the Liberators of Fleet Air Wing 7.

At the end of October 1943 the station had a new establishment of three flying boat squadrons with repair and maintenance facilities and responsibility for the satellite at Angle where CCDU was based. A 'T2' hangar was erected in November for use by airmen of 78 MU doing major repairs on Sunderlands.

On D-Day the Sunderland squadrons shared in a vast operation to prevent the enemy from moving his submarines into position to harass our invasion craft. Patrolling aircraft criss-crossed every inch of the Bay, making it impossible for a U-boat to reach the Channel approaches

without being detected. Almost a year later they were to search the same area for surrendering U-boats.

The aircraft moorings were about a quarter of a mile north of the station and, during the war, they were also dispersed along both banks of the river for about a mile to the east. The actual touch-down area was two miles west of the base. The 'taxiing' instructions from here to the moorings were complicated and so unusual that they are worthy of quotation here. The Control pinnace, by the way, in 1945 had the appropriate radio call-sign 'Quack-Duck'.

'Taxi into harbour until town of Milford is passed. When past Milford keep to the buoyed channel to the northern side of the estuary as extensive mud-flats lie to the south. Past the south side chequered buoy at Wear Point turn NE so as to round the starboard buoys off Spit. Taxiing from the night-flying flare-path opposite Angle Bay is difficult at night without local knowledge and it is advisable for visiting pilots to do so only when guided by an RAF pinnace or seaplane tender. Weather permitting, aircraft may be moored at RAF buoys on each side of the estuary opposite Angle Bay. Aircraft proceeding to the RAF station are frequently towed by RAF pinnace in order to save fuel and still more to spare the aero-engines.'

In the post-war years 201 and 230 Squadrons with Sunderland MR 5s were based here but the sight of almost a hundred flying boats moored in the river, so common in 1943 and 1944, was but a memory. When the Sunderlands were retired from service in February 1957 there was no further need for a water aerodrome so Pembroke Dock was closed and placed on care and maintenance on March 31 1957.

The ownership of the RAF station reverted to the Admiralty but they readily gave permission to the Short Sunderland Trust to preserve one of the last aircraft of its type here. It was ML824 which had flown many wartime sorties from Pembroke Dock and finally served with the French Navy. She arrived on March 24 1961 and stayed until 1976 when the RAF Museum acquired her for display at Hendon.

The entrance to the station was one of the most unusual of any in the RAF, being merely a gate in a high dockyard wall. It is there still but, passing through it, one is greeted by a very different scene. Almost all the buildings have been demolished to make way for a new ferry. The two 'C'-type hangars and the 'T2' have gone but the slipway up which the boats were hauled for maintenance has survived.

Pengam Moors (Cardiff), South Glamorgan

ST215770. On coast, 2 miles E of Cardiff city centre

Adjacent to a capital city but still one of the least-known RAF stations, Pengam was originally Cardiff Municipal Airport. It started life in September 1931 named Splott after the suburb on its northern boundary, but this rather unattractive name was dropped about 1936. The area selected for the airport was flooded by spring tides so a sea wall was built to protect it. In 1932 the British Air Navigation Co Ltd operated a Bristol-Cardiff service with Fokker Spiders but this was possibly through the private aerodrome at Wenvoe, some five miles west of the city. From September 1932 Fox Moths and, later, Dragons linked Bristol and Cardiff and week-end trips to Le Touquet and Paris were arranged in 1935. The Cardiff terminal was certainly Pengam from 1935 and in the summer of 1936 Western Airways started an hourly Cardiff–Weston-Super-Mare schedule with a return fare of 9/6 (ie, approximately 50 pence). The ferry which was flown mainly by Dragons was very popular, especially on Sundays when the pubs were shut in Wales!

On April 12 1933 the Great Western Railway had set up an airline called GWR Air Services with a service between Pengam and Plymouth which was soon extended to include Birmingham. The aircraft used was Westland Wessex G-AAGW on hire from Imperial Airways but the trip made a loss and was stopped five months after it began. Railway Air Services was formed in 1934 and a Dragon service connecting Plymouth and Liverpool, with stops at Haldon and Pengam, was inaugurated on May 7 of that year. With minor variations this schedule was to operate until 1938, by which time the Dragon had been replaced by the newer Rapide.

The Air Transport Licensing Authority came into being in 1939 and Western Airways were given the monopoly of the Cardiff routes, apart from a summer service to several south coast airports flown by Great Western and Southern Airlines, a break-away section of Railway Air Services. The first night service in the UK was started in October 1938 between Cardiff and Weston and in August 1939 Western Airways claimed that this route was the most intensive in the world. It operated half-hourly from 08.30 to 21.00 hours, covering the 13 miles in ten minutes and a greater-capacity DH 86 was available at busy periods.

A month later the war brought everything to a halt and many aircraft were flown to Pengam to provide a pool for the newly-formed National Air Communications. This organisation ceased to exist in May 1940 and most were soon ferried away again. Like most municipal airports it was requisitioned and handed over to the RAF, to become the first war station for 614 Squadron which moved over from Llandow. This unit was equipped with Hawker Hinds and Hectors for army co-operation but soon left for Odiham on October 2 1939.

In February 1940 No 43 MU opened to act as a packing depot for aircraft being shipped overseas and rapid changes were made. The allotments at the airport entrance were levelled to permit exit of dismantled airframes, a site was prepared for the storage of timber for packing cases and the hangars were refurbished. A major innovation was the provision of electric light! Seven Vickers Vildebeestes arrived by road for packing, to be followed a week later by three Tiger Moths flown in from 6 MU at Brize Norton. A total of 53 more aircraft were delivered in February, mostly by road because of the poor condition of the landing ground. The types included Harts, Lysanders, Hurricanes, Gladiators

The factory on the main runway at Pengam Moors.

and a Northrop Nomad which was dispatched to South Africa.

There was so much confusion in correspondence and signals with 43 Group and 43 MU that the latter was renumbered 52 MU on March 13 1941. The same month 78 Hinds were sent to South Africa and the unit was told that it would in future pack all aircraft for the Fleet Air Arm. On May 4, 21 Magisters made a mass arrival and were joined by two Walrus amphibians and a Percival Vega Gull, the latter destined for Egypt. So much ferrying was going on by now that 2 Ferry Pilots' Pool at Whitchurch had a detachment at Pengam which was by now known as RAF Cardiff. Two urgently required Fairey Sea Fox aircraft were sent on to Kalafrana in Malta and a Fairey Albacore was received for experimental packing. The airport was now such a good target that efforts were made to camouflage it by painting the concrete apron and approach roads, and cases out in the open were strung with netting. For the protection of the whole city, the Cardiff balloons were increased to 25 in number, with the immediate result that Harvard N7122 inbound to the airfield severed a cable with its wing but still managed to land safely.

The routine of work continued into 1941, 16 more Nomads shipped to South Africa being among the less common types handled. The Luftwaffe visited the city on February 27 1941 and a stray heavy bomb damaged one of the MU's hangars which were soon to be augmented by a new Bellman. The same month a local civilian was awarded the British Empire

Medal for rescuing the crew of Dominie AW115 after it had crashed on the edge of the airport. The remainder of the year was spent chiefly in preparing Hurricanes for the Middle East and in October three Mk IIAs were transported to Liverpool Docks for onward transit to Archangel in Russia. A damaged Tiger Moth was presented to Cardiff University Aeroplane Club for ground instruction.

With winter approaching a runway of Sommerfeld Track was laid down and this allowed the airfield to remain serviceable until a concrete strip was constructed in the summer of 1942. Hurricanes passed through in greater quantities, 173 in July 1942, and the activity was recorded by the RAF Film Unit for a feature on Maintenance Command. Harvards and Spitfires were packed also, the monthly total of aircraft received rarely falling below 150 in 1943.

No 8 AACU had set up its base at Cardiff in November 1940, having moved from Weston Zoyland with an assortment of impressed civil aircraft reinforced by some Blenheims and Lysanders. It had detachments as far apart as St Eval, Old Sarum, Gosport and Gatwick but its main duty was to provide co-operation for the 9th Anti-Aircraft Division in the South Wales area. In May 1941 the unit received a Dominie fitted with a device which illuminated the undersurfaces of the wings. Viewed from the ground it produced an effect similar to that of an aircraft caught in a searchlight beam and enabled the gunners to gain experience in laying and height finding. The rest of the unit's Dominies and Dragonflies were soon fitted with the lighting but the idea faded from use when these aircraft were replaced by Oxfords. The latter plus Miles

Masters formed the major equipment of 8 AACU when it disbanded in December 1943 and was reformed as six separate squadrons.

The preparation for D-Day involved the storage of vast quantities of aviation fuel in jerry-cans on the airfield but trucks of the USAAF removed these in April 1944. The small airfield saw many unusual visitors in 1944, ranging from Avengers to Hampdens, and Thunderbolts to Marauders, the highest monthly total of aircraft being 898 in August. A detachment of 587 Squadron was accommodated for a while before transferring its Miles Martinets to Weston Zoyland in September 1944. October was notable for the gliding instruction given to Air Training Corps personnel on the airfield.

There was another flurry of activity in November when C-47s of the USAAF collected stores for the Continent and a squadron of Piper Cubs was asssembled and tested prior to ferrying to the battle-front. The number of aircraft being packed (now mainly Seafires) slowly dwindled in 1945. The RAF took over deliveries from the ATA in July and the MU finally closed on October 31 1945. Its last few Spitfires were dispatched the same day, bringing to an end an unspectacular but invaluable contribution to the war effort. Also at an end was the long, close association with the city; local Home Guard units had defended the airport, for instance.

After the war it was used by the Ansons and Tiger Moths of 3 Reserve Flying School and British European Airways, Cambrian Air Services and Western Airways. Unfortunately the short runway, cramped position and lack of night flying facilities proved its downfall when larger types of aircraft, like the DC-3, were considered by the operators. On April 1 1954 all civil flying was transferred to Rhoose and the airport became an industrial site after a period housing the Ministry of Transport and Civil Aviation's fire-fighting school before it moved to Stansted in 1960. There was a brief protest in 1956 when one of the few surviving Lancasters was burned at Pengam in an exercise.

Penkridge, Staffordshire

SJ935125. At end of private road leading off B5012, 1 mile SE of Penkridge

Unnoticed by most of the thousands of people who pass it every day on the M6

motorway, this was a place where many an RAF pilot learned the basics of flying. From the motorway a cluster of small hangars and huts can be seen fleetingly, but a closer look is much more difficult. A typical wartime concrete road leads from the B5012 past a farm, where permission must be sought before going any further, and the airfield site is half-a-mile beyond it. It is undoubtedly the best preserved of all the smaller sites in the area covered by this book, as almost every original building is intact, although some are rather decayed. There are five hangars in all and there is an interesting comparison between two Super Robins and the three smaller standard-sized Robins. Traces of brown and green camouflage paint are still discernible on those which have not been re-roofed with modern materials.

One of the huts contains an original example of a pot-bellied stove, well-known to those who had to endure winters in the hutted camps where one of these was the only source of warmth. There must have been extensive areas of bar and rod track, laid to combat the ever-present mud, as many of the fences across the former flying field are made of this, ideal for the purpose. A rusting section of the less common Channel Grid metal runway can also be seen leaning against one of the farm buildings.

The airfield, usually called Pillerton by the locals after an old building close by, opened on June 17 1942 as an RLG for 28 EFTS at Wolverhampton. All the unit's night flying was to be done from here for the time being, perhaps because the balloon barrage around the parent station was proving too dangerous. During the day circuits and bumps were carried out and, in the words of a gentleman who was familiar with the RLG at that time, it resembled a hive swarming with bees in the shape of Tiger Moths.

One day a Hurricane landed which must have given some inspiration to the struggling pupils. Another day, in August 1944, saw Anson DJ634 of 9 (O) AFU force-land after an engine failed on a cross-country flight. Apart from the usual run of broken propellers and crumpled undercarriages, Penkridge seems to have been free of serious accidents, a happy achievement for a wartime training field.

The date of closure is uncertain but it was probably during the summer of 1945 when most of the RLGs were given up because of the reduction in demand for training aircrew and it then went under the plough once more. The farmer who suffered the requisition of his land eventually inherited a metalled road where a track existed before and a fine selection of buildings in which to store his machinery, perhaps not such a bad bargain after all! A few years ago I saw a Jet Ranger helicopter operating from the edge of the airfield during an agricultural meeting, but all the fences ensure that no fixed wing aircraft could fly from here once more.

Penrhos, Gwynedd

SH335335. On A499, 3 miles W of Pwllheli.

Attacked on no less than five occasions, it is ironical that this aerodrome, like others in North Wales, might have been ignored by the enemy had it not been for the publicity which attended its construction in 1936. New airfields, schools and ranges to train the expanding RAF met with vociferous objections everywhere they were planned. When the Air Ministry purchased seven farms at Porth Neigwll (to become Hell's Mouth aerodrome and ranges) and a farm of about 250 acres, roughly three miles west of Pwllheli, opinion was split. The local people welcomed the 500 jobs which the building work would provide and were hostile to the Welsh Nationalists who thoroughly opposed the plan.

During the early hours of September 8 1936 three members of the party set fire to the contractor's offices, workshops and timber supplies. The blaze devastated some 50 square yards and 100 men were

thrown out of work. The arsonists then walked into Pwllheli Police Station and gave themselves up. There was a great deal of controversy, especially when it was deemed necessary for the trial to be held at the Old Bailey and not in the Caernarvon Crown Court. The defendants were each sentenced to nine months' imprisonment and all the publicity no doubt exaggerated the importance of the airfield to potential enemies.

The station opened on February 1 1937 as 5 Armament Training Camp with an establishment of six Westland Wallaces and five range patrol boats to operate from Pwllheli harbour. However, the troubles were not yet over as heavy seas swept away the targets on the foreshore and it was April 3 before the first training course arrived. On that day a mass formation of 34 aircraft flew in from 10 FTS at Tern Hill with Acting Pilot Officer Pattle leading a group of five Gloster Gauntlets. Pattle was to become one of the RAF's top-scoring fighter pilots before his death in action.

Aircraft from several FTSs were attached for periods of one month during 1938 and 1939 and there were several visits by aircraft of 4, 13 and 600 Squadrons which stopped for fuel and lunch on what were described as 'long distance flights around the British Isles'. The only public airing was Empire Air Day on May 28 1938 which was attended by over 11,000 spectators.

Penrhos became the home of 9 Air Observers School on September 9 1939 equipped with a collection of obsolete aircraft such as Harrows and Fairey Battles. The unit was renamed 9 Bombing

and Gunnery School two months later. Training went on routinely with one or two incidents like the occasion when the duty pilot airborne at first light spotted the conning tower of a submarine two miles south of St Tudwals. A fishing boat was suspected of giving supplies to the intruder and details were passed to Coastal Command. Three days later the suspicious activities of an Irish steamer were also reported. These incidents resulted in a Battle being kept bombed-up at readiness to meet any U-boat activity.

Real war came to the station with brutal suddenness on July 8 1940 when a single enemy aircraft destroyed three blocks of officers' quarters, killed two men, wrecked two Hawker Henleys of 1 AACU and damaged a hangar. Steps were taken to camouflage the airfield and a photograph exists showing cleverly painted hedges and lanes across it. Unfortunately, aircraft have been parked on the 'hedges' which rather detracts from the effect! The Luftwaffe was not deceived, however, and came back several times to do further damage, but inflicting no casualties. As a deterrent six Spitfires of 611 Squadron were detached from Tern Hill and were later relieved by a flight of Hurricanes from 312 Squadron at Speke. The Czechs moved to Valley in April 1941 as Penrhos had remained unmolested since the previous autumn.

Near Caernarvon, 20 miles away, a new aerodrome was opened at Llandwrog for use by 9 Air Gunnery School and the training of air-gunners was to be transferred there. On January 21 1942 this was done and in yet another change the Penrhos unit became 9 (O) AFU on the last day of February 1942. Training policy was still not finalised and on June 13 1942, No 9 AGS was disbanded and Llandwrog was made a satellite for 9 (O) AFU. The latter was by now equipped mainly with Ansons. One of these was damaged by a Halifax which force-landed and went over the edge of the aerodrome which was built on a plateau about eight feet above the surrounding fields on the south-west boundary. This undesirable feature caused the demise of many aeroplanes, including a US Navy Catalina which landed with engine trouble on November 6 1942, struck a hangar and slid over the edge backwards.

Since Llandwrog had tarmac runways it was decided to move the HQ there with Penrhos reverting to satellite. No 9 (O) AFU ceased to exist on June 16 1945, 21 ACHU occupying the vacant accommodation. The Holding Unit disbanded on March 31 1946, and RAF Station Penrhos passed into history. The main domestic site later served as a Polish Home and remains so today, a haven for those gallant soldiers and airmen who chose not to return to their ravaged homeland and who now live in retirement in their adopted country.

Access to the airfield is via a concrete road from the A499 leading to the caravan site which occupies a large area, including the bases of the long-dismantled Bellman hangars. There is a slight rise on the north-west perimeter which still has some gun posts and huts but many other buildings have been demolished. Private aircraft are quite frequent visitors in the summer months using a 400-yard tarmac strip of recent construction.

Left *Anson 1 of No 224 Squadron after a ground collision at Penrhos with a sister aircraft in 1938* (via R.C.B. Ashworth).

Right *Audax K5161 E of 5 FTS after nosing over at Penrhos in autumn 1937* (J.H.G. Wellham via R.C.B. Ashworth).

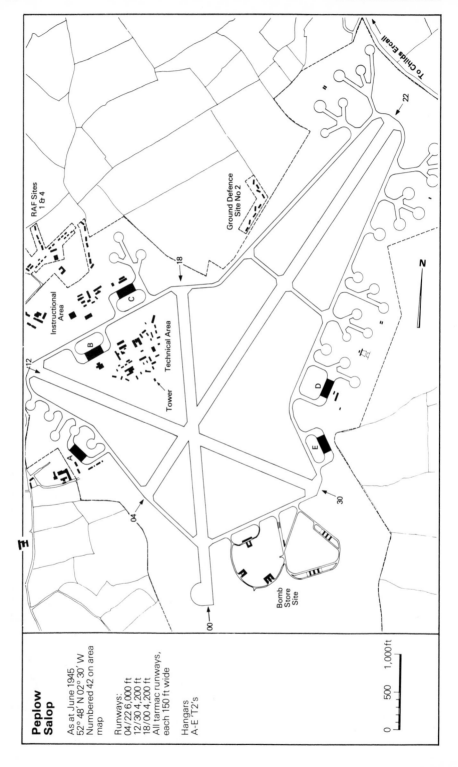

Peplow
Salop

As at June 1945
52° 48′ N 02° 30′ W
Numbered 42 on area
map

Runways:
04/22 6,000 ft
12/30 4,200 ft
18/00 4,200 ft
All tarmac runways,
each 150 ft wide

Hangars
A-E 'T2's

0   500   1,000 ft

RAF Sites
1 & 4

Instructional
Area

Ground Defence
Site No 2

Tower

Technical Area

Bomb
Store
Site

To Childs Ercall

Peplow (Childs Ercall), Salop

SJ660235. Just south of Childs Ercall on unclassified road to Sutton-upon-Tern

A very large airfield and eminently suitable for use by heavy bombers had it been in the eastern counties, is one's first impression. The road from the village utilises most of the north-west perimeter track and is flanked by four 'T2' hangars and some huts in various stages of disrepair. The feeling of size is emphasised by the fact that the buildings are set well back from the taxi-way, unlike at other airfields in this area, and the main runway is 2,000 yards long.

Childs Ercall, as it was originally called, started off much more modestly as a grass-surfaced RLG for Tern Hill's Masters in 1941. Oxfords of 11 SFTS Shawbury also used it in September and October 1941, but both instructors and pupils found it too small for this type of aircraft. A decision was made to develop the site for a bomber OTU parent station with three runways and work started late in 1942.

The SLG at Ollerton was only one mile away to the north but the restricted activity at this sort of airfield was not thought to present a problem. Unfortunately, in August 1942, the SLG was handed over to the Admiralty who had an urgent need for an instrument training base in a geographically central position. Renamed Hinstock it was rapidly enlarged and soon became very busy.

Work pulled ahead at its neighbour which opened in July 1943 but many of the buildings were not yet ready for occupation so the first crews to arrive were sent to Finningley, Hixon and Lichfield for ground training. It was some weeks before 83 OTU was up to its full strength of 40 Wellingtons, four Masters and one Oxford and, on August 20, the station's name was changed to Peplow owing to confusion with High Ercall. No satellite was available so the OTU functioned as what was known as a ¾ OTU, ie, at reduced strength. The routine of night flying, cross-countries and bombing exercises was occasionally enlivened by *Nickels* to Northern France, the first being on October 17 1943 when 11 aircraft were sent out and all returned safely. OTUs were often called upon to

Peplow on February 24 1944. About 15 Wellingtons can be discerned at dispersal (Public Record Office).

carry out ASR searches for missing aircraft, usually their own, but on January 13 1944 four Wellingtons left Peplow to look for some missing USAAF bomber crews over the North Sea, a mission which was sadly fruitless.

The following account by a Sergeant Air-Gunner who attended 5 Course after a posting from 4 Air Gunnery School at Morpeth gives a good idea of what went on at Peplow all those years ago: 'The course began in October 1943 with circuits and landings, an instructor being captain, the trainee pilot taking command after a solo check flight. This was followed by stick bombing and high level bombing practice, making a total of 38 hours day flying. In early December we started night flying with further circuits and bumps, followed by cross-country flying, air-firing, air-to-sea firing and bombing practice. During the month our crew completed a total of 42 hours night and six hours day flying. Gunnery exercises brought my total time at OTU to 94 hours by the time the course was completed early in January 1944'.

Other memories of Peplow were the numerous accidents and the sight of aircraft burning on or around the aero-

I. PEPL. 24·2·44. // PEPLOW AERODROME
52°48 N. 02°20 W.   SCALE 5700

Above *'T2' at Peplow.* **Right** *Hurricane IIC LF380 of 83 OTU at Peplow in October 1944* (via B. Martin).

drome became depressingly familiar to crews returning from night flights. One accident with an element of farce occurred when a Wellington trundled off the end of the runway after a fast night landing and stood up on its nose in the soft earth. No one was hurt but the rear gunner had to be rescued from his turret 20 feet above the ground by ladder! Social life was limited and evenings spent in Market Drayton often ended in scuffles on the returning bus between RAF servicemen and sailors from Hinstock.

In April and May 1944 Captain E. Swales, a South African, trained at Peplow, being classed as an above-average pilot. He was posted to the Pathfinder Force and, whilst flying with 582 Squadron as Master Bomber for a raid on Pforzheim, he won a posthumous Victoria Cross. His Lancaster was crippled by a night fighter but he continued to direct the operation until it was completed. Over France on the way back the aircraft became uncontrollable. Captain Swales stayed in the cockpit until all his crew had baled out but left it too late to escape himself.

As D-Day approached the *Nickel* operations to France became more and more frequent and it is pleasant to record that there were no losses to enemy action. Courses too were enlarged, No 21 consisting of 15 pilots, 17 navigators, 14 air-bombers, 14 wireless-operator/air-gunners and 27 air-gunners. All OTUs strove to maintain their output of trained crews and there was many a local scheme to improve efficiency. At Peplow aircraft were marshalled on the grass, clear of the

runways and perimeter tracks with a view to saving time on the ground taken up by taxiing from remote dispersals. This also enabled the taxi-ways, which were showing severe signs of wear, to be resurfaced and, at the same time, in the summer of 1944, the Cherrington Moor Bombing Range was constructed by unit labour under a 'self-help' scheme.

On July 20 1944 the unit's Gunnery Flight was disbanded, being replaced by a Bomber Defence Training Flight equipped with Hurricanes for fighter affiliation. All aircraft were grounded at midnight on August 8 when 25 Halifaxes from stations in 6 Group's area in Yorkshire were diverted after bombing troop and gun concentrations in the Caen district.

The loss of scores of experienced glider pilots at Arnhem forced a sudden change of policy and literally overnight, on October 28 1944, No 83 OTU closed and was re-designated 23 Heavy Glider Conversion Unit. The airmen who had not yet completed training were absorbed by other OTUs and the next day 20 glider instructors reported for duty. Albemarles and Horsa gliders were now the order of the day, but most of the glider landings were done at the new satellite at Seighford, probably because of the proximity of Hinstock and the permanent congestion of the Shropshire skies. No 23 HGCU's life was brief as it disbanded on December 31 1944. The airfield was next used by 21 (P) AFU as a satellite for Oxford training between January 26 and the end of February 1945.

No 1515 BAT Flight moved in from Poulton on January 30 1945 but there were difficulties caused by beam approach training at Peplow and Hinstock simultaneously, particularly as the beams were almost parallel. Owing to the heavier

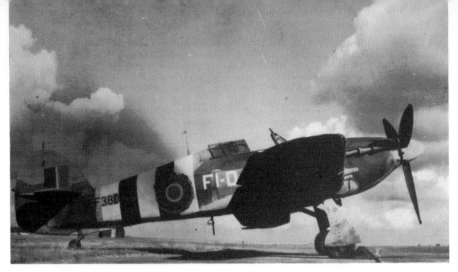

training commitment at the Navy airfield it was decided that the BAT Flight's Oxfords would only operate when the cloud base was 1,000 ft or above. Fortunately this situation only lasted for a month because the Flight then went to Coleby Grange in Lincolnshire.

Yet another change of role came after this when Peplow was loaned to the Admiralty as satellite to Hinstock. A detachment of Oxfords from 758 Squadron flew from here for a while and 780 Squadron, an advanced flying unit, reformed in February 1946 with Oxfords, Harvards and Fireflies plus a few Lancasters including PA224. The station finally closed at the end of 1949, the land being used for farming, although the runways were retained and are still in reasonable condition, being used by light aircraft and crop-sprayers. The tower was demolished a few years ago and some of the old huts near it may go next.

Pershore, Worcester and Hereford

SO975495. Off B4082, 2 miles NE of Pershore town. Road to Throckmorton crosses runway

The most westerly of all the bases used by aircraft taking part in the Thousand Raid on Cologne, Pershore supplied 34 Wellingtons which was probably the highest figure for a single OTU participating. Five aircraft each were attached to Stradishall, Oakington and Bourn but 19 operated direct from Pershore. One shot down a Ju 88 off the Dutch coast, to even out the loss of Wellington N2857 and its Canadian pupil crew on the same raid.

It was a long flight from Worcestershire and any bomber which failed to reach the target before 02.40 hours was briefed to turn back, whatever its position. Return-ing aircraft reported curious red balls, apparently stationary in mid-air, which burst into brilliant stars, and could not be certain whether they were fired from the ground nor what purpose they served. Presumably this was an early use of night fighter flares to illuminate potential targets. Training continued to be disrupted for another week because, on June 7 1942, 18 Wellingtons raided Essen, supported by five from each of the advanced bases. This time two failed to return. The third big attack in June was on Bremen and again two Pershore aircraft were missing.

Pershore had begun life quietly enough in June 1934 when the Worcestershire Flying School was started on a flat piece of land near Tilesford House. A hangar-cum-workshop was built and in 1938 the school was operating two Moths. A couple of Walrus amphibians called in one day in 1938 and it was not long before the RAF took notice of its possibilities for development as a Service airfield. When war broke out the plan became reality and Mr R.J. Bunning's little field was soon swallowed in concrete.

The station opened in February 1941 but, before any aircraft were flown in, it was attacked on the night of March 16. Only slight damage was caused, although 16 bombs were dropped. There were still only six aircraft on the airfield when a second raid occurred on April 10. It was believed that the enemy bomber saw the newly-completed and uncamouflaged runways in the moonlight and dived from 3,000 feet. One high-explosive bomb was dropped, setting alight and destroying two petrol bowsers and damaging a parked Wellington. Fortunately no one was hurt and no other damage was done. A month later, on May 10, the third and last recorded attack was made by an unconfirmed He 111. After a brief exchange of gunfire with the ground defence posts, the aircraft flew off without dropping any bombs.

On April 1 1941 No 23 OTU formed here, responsible for training Canadian crews for the new Commonwealth squadrons of the RAF. Wellingtons were the main equipment plus a few Ansons and a Tiger Moth for communications duties. The airfield was not yet finished and there was a lot of trouble with aircraft dispersal until the frying-pan hard-standings were ready. Construction of a satellite at Defford was behind schedule and, since it was unusable until September 1941, this also hampered the training programme.

The OTU's first leaflet dropping operation took place on July 20 when six aircraft from 'C' Flight visited the Paris area. Two 250 lb bombs were also carried by each Wellington and these were released over German-occupied airfields with unknown results. On the way back one Wellington flew into a balloon cable at Weybridge in Surrey. The cable cut into the starboard wing as far as the mainspar, severing the engine controls. Despite partial engine failure the pilot flew it back to base and landed safely. Bombers from operational squadrons, too, found Pershore a welcome haven. As far back as May 28 a Hampden of 144 Squadron at Hemswell had diverted in because of bad weather and, on September 27, Stirling N6087 of 15 Squadron got lost with radio failure after raiding Cologne. It was guided here by searchlight pointer.

The Americans were very anxious to learn as much as possible about British training methods and, in October 1941, the Chief Navigation Instructor of the USAAC was attached to 23 OTU. Work on the construction of a Battle HQ was started in October but it was still not completed the following May so, in the event of an invasion, it was decided to designate Cleave Orchard for this purpose. A few Nickels over northern France were made without loss during the closing months of 1941. A night operation against a secret target brought 12 Wellingtons from 103 Squadron at Elsham Wolds to Pershore on March 27 1942 because it was deemed to be the most suitable starting point. The squadron was accompanied by its own operations, navigation and intelligence staff but only two aircraft returned here, the rest landing at a number of other airfields.

Another unusual duty came after the German Baedecker Raid on the city of Bath on April 1 1942. A Wellington from 23 OTU was called upon to take a series of photographs so that a mosaic could be produced showing all the bomb damage. The OTU was deprived of its Defford satellite on May 18 1942 thus reducing the training potential. The routine was further interrupted by the participation in the Cologne and Essen attacks already mentioned but, after June 1942, the OTUs were only expected to furnish a handful of aircraft at a time to support the main force.

On July 30 seven aircraft went to Düsseldorf, X9917 being posted missing. During September trips were made again to Düsseldorf, Bremen and Essen. From the last-named, on the night of September 16/17, three Wellingtons failed to return. Wellingtons often went missing, too, on ordinary cross-country navigation flights. On October 1 1942 X3751 disappeared without trace and, almost exactly a year later, on October 2 1943, the same thing happened to X3470. No distress calls were received and an ASR search was fruitless. Like all OTUs Pershore had a depressingly high accident rate and an orange glow in the sky was a common sight to residents of Worcestershire in those days. The large Canadian War Graves section at Worcester Cemetery is a permanent reminder of the apalling sacrifice.

A replacement for the satellite was obtained on November 16 1942 when RAF Stratford was taken over from 22 OTU at Wellesbourne Mountford. 'A' Flight was detached there for initial training which was mainly circuit and landing practice. The new year began with a Nickel to Nantes and, on January 18, nine aircraft were detailed to search the North Sea for Bomber Command aircrew missing from a raid on Berlin the previous night, but no dinghies were spotted. Bombers on the way back from Western France still used Pershore on occasion, eight Wellingtons landing from St Nazaire on March 1 and 16 Lancasters from the same objective on March 23 1943. They came from farther afield too, like a Pathfinder Lancaster which had been to Dortmund.

No 23 OTU's last operation with bombs was on August 30 1943 when five Wellingtons from the parent station and one from Stratford were sent to a French target, each carrying six 500-pounders. By November 1943 the unit's strength was reduced to 40 Wellingtons, four Martinets for target-towing and a few Tomahawks for fighter affiliation. It disbanded on March 15 1944 and the airfield then found itself under the control of Ferry Command.

No 1 Ferry Unit formed here the next day for the collection and ferrying overseas of various types of aircraft which included Mosquitoes, Beaufighters, Halifaxes, Venturas, Wellingtons and Warwicks. In March 1945 16 Beaufighters were delivered to the Portuguese Navy at Lisbon. Ferrying went on without a break until the spring of 1948 when the unit disbanded. No 10 Advanced Flying Training School with Oxfords was the next resident until this unit, too, was disbanded in 1953.

In September 1957 the Royal Radar Establishment's Flying Unit moved here from nearby Defford where it had been based since 1942. Pershore's main runway had been lengthened considerably to take jets but a right of way was maintained across it, guarded by police boxes and traffic lights. The work being done was of a very secret nature and prying eyes were not encouraged. However, it was possible to see from afar the Hermes prototype with its tailwheel undercarriage which made it look like a Hastings at first glance. Many other radar test-beds, including Canberras and Meteors, were to be seen with mysterious aerials and protrusions. The airfield closed for flying in 1978 but the area radar facility still remains operational.

Perton, West Midlands

SO860995. 1 mile S of A41 at Wergs

North-west of Wolverhampton is a perfectly normal housing development like those to be found on the edge of any town or city but why, you ask yourself, are all the roads named after airfields, for example, Scampton Close and Manston Drive? The answer is that this estate itself was once an aerodrome and this is a customary way of commemorating the fact now that so many former airfields are being swallowed up by suburbia.

There was a First World War landing ground on or adjacent to the later site covering about 50 acres. It was intended for use by 38 (Home Defence) Squadron and was operational in 1916 and 1917. The Second World War airfield had a very inconspicuous career and when it opened on August 2 1941, a decision was still pending as to its future function. It seems likely that it was planned originally as a fighter station as earth-banked dispersals were provided. During the autumn of 1941 the living quarters were occupied by the Princess Wilhelmina Brigade of the Royal Netherlands Army. The first aerial visitor was probably Magister N7626 which force-landed on November 11 1941, damaging its tailwheel against a heap of rubble on an unfinished runway.

In December the Parachute Training School from Ringway, who were looking for a more suitable base, inspected the airfield with a view to taking it over. The location suffered from the same disadvantages as Ringway, namely that it was close to a densely-populated area which compromised security and was subject to industrial haze so the plan was dropped. The other reason was that 11 SFTS at Shawbury needed to clear a back-log of pilot training caused by airfield unserviceability. Perton with its three runways was offered as an RLG and 14 Oxfords flew in on January 26 1942 to stay until March. This detached Flight returned in August and soon became almost a self-contained unit with accommodation for all pupils, instructors and ground-crew. All servicing, apart from major overhauls, was carried out at Perton, a single 14-bay 'T2' hangar being erected for the purpose.

As detailed in the section on Wheaton Aston, 21 (P) AFU formed out of the Wheaton Aston and Perton detachments of 11 (P) AFU and Perton became satellite to the former. The airfield was used also by Helliwells Ltd for final adjustments and flight testing of the Boston and Havoc aircraft which they repaired and overhauled at the small Walsall Airport. Larger types like Fortresses were infrequent visitors and the pronounced dip in the middle of Perton's longest runway must have been disconcerting for their pilots.

The airfield probably closed late in 1945, certainly being active in October of that year with the radio call-sign 'Bushranger'. It was abandoned on July 10 1947 and soon returned to agriculture. Model aircraft flying went on here and an Auster was based for several years in the 1960s. It is now extensively built upon but small sections of the old runways and perimeter track are still visible. Soon it will disappear, yet another airfield gone for ever.

Poulton, Cheshire

SJ400600. On minor road, 1 mile E of A483 at Pulford

This was a mid-war airfield constructed by George Wimpey and Co and intended to be a satellite of Hawarden which lies four miles to the west, over the border in Wales. Hawarden was extremely congested in 1942 with MU work, Wellington test-flying and a fighter OTU all competing for space in the circuit. This was one of the reasons why 57 OTU moved to Eshott in Northumberland at the end of that year. It was replaced by 41 OTU which taught fighter reconnaissance with Hurricanes and Mustang Is and took over Poulton on March 1 1943 for its 3 Squadron. Sealand was also discussed as a second satellite but it was agreed that it was unsuitable and it would be better to form another OTU rather than increase the size of the existing one.

The airfield was built on the edge of the Eaton Hall Estate to the customary pattern of three runways in a triangle with a slight indentation in the perimeter track to avoid Poulton Hall Farm. As almost every building has now been demolished, it is hard to visualise that this was once a busy station. A 1941-design satellite watch tower was sited on the west side of the flying field and, although there were no hangars at first, 14 Blisters were in use in January 1945, together with a canvas Besonneau hangar of First World War vintage. This relic had been erected for 1515 BAT Flight who had been posted in as a lodger unit and were dismayed to find that there was no office, workshop or hangar accommodation available. Eight Oxfords were on charge but work got off to a very slow start because of delays in finishing the essential buildings and trouble with the installation of the Standard Beam Approach equipment. The flight eventually got itself organised and, by June 30 1945, when it moved to Peplow, it had trained many hundreds of pilots on short detachments from the parent unit, 21 (P) AFU at Wheaton Aston. Its operations rarely interfered with the fighter training going on at the same station, as SBA practice was carried out mainly in poor weather when the Mustangs were grounded.

The other lodger was not so welcome; it was the so-called Woodvale or 'W' Detachment of 12 (P) AFU. Its task was advanced training on Blenheims for pilots to be posted to Beaufighter OTUs and its nominal base was at RAF Grantham. The latter's grass surface was suffering badly from heavy usage and RLGs had to be found for most of the flying while steel mesh runways and coir matting were laid. The detachment was based at Woodvale from January 10 to February 7 1944, but a requirement for that airfield to house fighter squadrons for a short period forced a temporary move to Poulton. Here, all accommodation was in use but two Nissen huts and a Blister hangar for Blenheim servicing were grudgingly allocated. It was proposed that some of the aircraft would be further detached to Cranage but the availability of two more Blisters improved the situation and this did not become necessary. The Blenheims were only to be at Poulton for six weeks it turned out, and went back to Woodvale on March 21.

At the end of November 1943, No 41 OTU underwent a thorough re-organisation which reflected an unexpected surplus of fighter-reconnaissance pilots. Each output of trained personnel was now not to be absorbed into squadrons but instead would remain at Hawarden to form a small holding unit within the OTU, known as 3 Tactical Exercise Unit. The syllabus was divided up between advanced gunnery, navigation, photography and army support and there were to be three separate squadrons, two of them at Poulton. Mustangs were to be restricted to Hawarden and Hurricanes and Harvards to the satellite so that some degree of standardisation could be achieved in each airfield's procedures. The TEU closed in March 1944 and 41 OTU resumed its normal programme which had been interrupted for several months.

The final re-organisation took place in March 1945 when 41 OTU moved to Chilbolton in Hampshire and retained its number, whilst the day fighter wing which was by now located at Poulton was to move to Hawarden and became 58 OTU. This new OTU, too, was divided into three squadrons, Nos 1 and 2 at the parent and No 3 at the satellite for advanced training. Each pupil would spend six months at the main station and then move to Poulton for the final two weeks of his course. During the latter period, each pilot would drop a total of 16 bombs on the Fenns Moss Range near Whitchurch and carry out air-to-ground firing at the Prestatyn Ranges on the North Wales coast. Emphasis was placed on observation and each navigation flight had to

Poulton tower in 1973, now demolished along with most other buildings at this airfield (B.H. Abraham).

be followed by a report on convoys and train movements and any other aircraft seen in the air. The object of this was to make the trainee keep a good look-out and further incentive was given by a system of random 'tailing' of aircraft on cross-countries. An instructor would follow a pupil and try to avoid being spotted.

The end of the war in Europe reduced the need for fighter pilots and many of the OTUs were disbanded. No 58 ceased to exist on July 20 1945 and Hawarden and Poulton were taken over totally by 48 MU. Poulton was not used, however, and soon reverted to care and maintenance. The runways have been used since by the Duke of Westminster's Grumman Turbo-Goose G-ASXG and several light aircraft have been based there at intervals. The old airfield is a convenient reporting point for aircraft positioning on final approach to runway 32 at Hawarden and inevitably aircraft have landed here in error. It should be noted that what is left of the aerodrome is on a private estate and casual visitors are not encouraged.

Rednal, Salop

SJ375275. 1½ miles NE of A5 at West Felton

Rednal opened in April 1942, being planned as a fighter OTU with a satellite at Montford Bridge. No 61 OTU was to be its sole user throughout its short life, apart from a brief detachment of Masters from 6 AACU. The OTU moved up from Heston in accordance with the policy of keeping training units away from the operational areas of the south and east. A firing range near Llanbedr was shared with other units in the North-West. The aerodrome was so isolated that the RAF had to persuade the Great Western Railway to run a special train each evening to Shrewsbury and arrange for the Paddington-Birkenhead express to stop at Rednal station so that airmen could get back after a night on the town.

Like several other fighter OTUs, 61 had a 'shadow squadron', numbered 561, so that in the event of an emergency it could rapidly be turned into an operational squadron. The only recorded use of this designation occured on June 27 1943 when four sections of two Spitfires each

were scrambled to intercept a Ju 88 which was reported to be over the Irish Sea but, to their disappointment, no contact was made.

The accident rate on the ageing Spitfires, some of which were Battle of Britain veterans, was very high. Mid-air collisions were common and, in 1977, the Belgian victim of one of these was found in the wreckage of his Spitfire, deep in a Shropshire wood. Pilots of many nationalities attended courses at Rednal, including many who were to become aces, such as Pierre Closterman.

To give pilots some practice in dive bombing with dummy missiles, a target was set up actually on the airfield in 1943 but seems to have been moved to a more suitable location after a collision between two Spitfires over it.

The Thunderbolts from Atcham regarded the Spitfires as their natural prey but the feeling was mutual and many a mock combat took place in the Shropshire skies. Beating up one another's airfield was rife also, until it was forbidden by the Commanding Officers.

A number of military hospitals were established in Shropshire prior to D-Day in preparation for the heavy casualties which were expected. Rednal was one of the stations selected for the receipt of wounded flown direct from the battle front. Personnel from the US Army Medical Service were attached to assist with the evacuation, the first C-47 arriving from a strip in Normandy on July 3 1944. Flights went on throughout July and included wounded German as well as Allied personnel. During August 77 C-47s

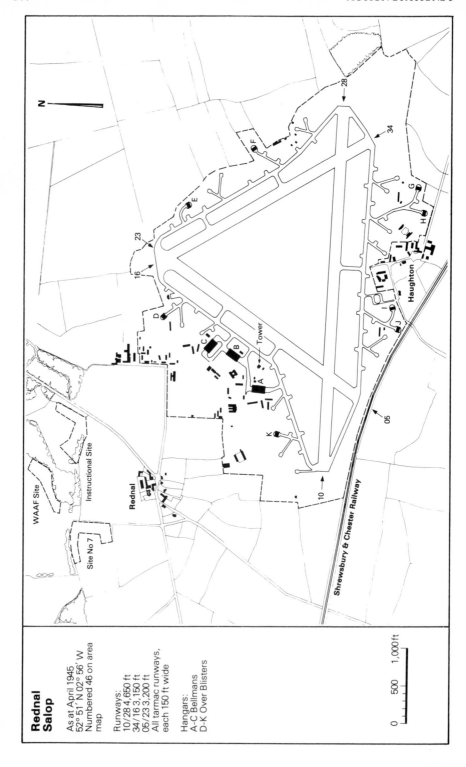

**Rednal
Salop**

As at April 1945
52° 51' N 02° 56' W
Numbered 46 on area
map

Runways:
10/28 4,650 ft
34/16 3,150 ft
05/23 3,200 ft
All tarmac runways,
each 150 ft wide

Hangars:
A-C Bellmans
D-K Over Blisters

0   500   1,000ft

WAAF Site

Instructional Site

Site No 7

Rednal

N

Tower

Haughton

Shrewsbury & Chester Railway

Right *518/40 pattern tower seen at Rednal* (A.S.C. Lumsden).

Below *Huts and concrete floor of Bellman hangar at Rednal.*

flew in about 1,750 men before the evacuation ceased. This was the first war in history in which soldiers could expect to be in a proper hospital within hours of being wounded.

One of the biggest aircraft ever to land here was a Liberator which was diverted in due to bad weather on a flight from Cairo to Prestwick via Lisbon on April 24 1944. Two months later a whole formation of Liberators was successfully intercepted in an elaborate exercise flown by 19 Spitfires from the OTU. Other unusual visitors included a Lockheed Electra, LA621, and Baltimore AG689, the latter belonging to the Empire Central Flying School at Hullavington.

No 61 OTU extended its scope on January 8 1945 when five Mustang IIIs arrived on transfer from 55 OTU. Further Mustangs were received and Harvards replaced the Masters which had been used for dual instruction. An unusual piece of apparatus, a decompression chamber, was in use at this time to give pilots experience of conditions at heights up to 37,000 ft.

On the morning of February 18 1945 an airman found a German prisoner-of-war sitting in the cockpit of a Mustang on one of the remote dispersals. The German, who had escaped from a camp at Oswestry the previous evening, gave himself up without a fight although he was found to have in his possession a bag of black pepper and a sharp knife.

On June 16 1945 the OTU moved to Keevil in Wiltshire. Despite their initial misgivings about its position, the permanent staff had grown to like Rednal and were not impressed with the new base. It had no sports field for a start and Rednal had no less than three by then—cricket,

Spitfire landing at Rednal, circa 1942 (IWM).

rugby and football! Rednal was reduced to care and maintenance soon afterwards, being sold in 1962.

Situated as it is in the heart of the countryside, it has remained almost untouched by vandalism and is now one of the best preserved wartime stations in the county. The dispersed living sites are still largely intact and one gets an idea of how widespread the RAF presence must have been as guard huts and the remains of road blocks peep out from hedgerows some distance from the airfield. The control tower is a cavernous 518/40 type and planning permission was being sought at the time of writing to turn it into a house. The three Bellman and eight Blister hangars have been removed, although the concrete floors remain and the main site huts are used for light industry. A crew building on the perimeter still bears the legend 'A Squadron'. A reinforced concrete structure on the western perimeter was once the Battle HQ from which the defence of the airfield could be directed, in the event of an invasion when it might find itself a rearward line of resistance.

Rhoose, South Glamorgan

ST064674. On B4265, 3 miles W of Barry

Cardiff's modern airport bears little resemblance to the basic wartime satellite aerodrome it once was. Built during 1941/42, as a satellite to Llandow, it was used first by Spitfire K9933 of 53 OTU on October 8 1941. The runways were far from finished and the fighter, which had suffered engine failure, ended up on its belly on the rough ground. The airfield was taken over officially by 53 OTU on

April 7 1942, although it must have been used before this date as one of the OTU's Spitfires had overshot on landing there four days previously. Five more minor accidents occurred in the first week, some of them due to the still incomplete state of part of the aerodrome.

The Spitfires and Masters stayed until May 1943 when 53 OTU moved to Kirton-in-Lindsey. Rhoose was then virtually unused until February 8 1944 when 7 Air Gunnery School operated it as a satellite whilst reconstruction work was done on their base at Stormy Down. The majority of the school, consisting of 23 Ansons, 20 Martinets and 50 pilots, was ferried over to Rhoose and all flying was done from here until August 2 1944. Congestion on the marshalling areas of this rudimentary airfield made it necessary to position an airman at the wingtips of each aircraft in order to prevent taxiing accidents and the only hangarage available was four Enlarged Over Blisters.

The two runways formed an unusual cruciform shape, meeting at right angles and surrounded by a perimeter track which resembled a square. After the departure of 7 AGS, Rhoose reverted to care and maintenance until it was transferred to 40 Group Maintenance Command on November 1 1944 for storage. In the immediate post-war period the airfield became a sub-site of 214 MU at Newport.

Rhoose lay dormant for many years until a replacement for the cramped Cardiff Airport at Pengam Moors began to be sought in 1953. Rhoose was the choice although it was some 14 miles away from the Welsh capital, compared with Pengam's ten minutes from the city centre. All civil flying was officially transferred here on April 1 1954, although the airfield had been used by Aer Lingus since June 1952 for a Dublin-Cardiff service with

Dakotas. By the time the Ministry of Transport and Civil Aviation took over, a terminal building and hangar had been built and it now became the base of Cambrian Airways. In April 1965 the airport passed to the control of Glamorgan County Council who promptly renamed it Glamorgan (Rhoose). This inappropriate name lasted until 1978 when it became, somewhat superfluously, Cardiff (Wales) Airport. In 1970 the main runway (13/31) was extended to 7,000 ft to enable jet transports to use it.

Ringway, Greater Manchester

SJ815845. Southern outskirts of Manchester

Manchester International Airport is one of Britain's busiest and has that cosmopolitan air of airports the world over; concrete, glass, the stench of kerosene and people in a hurry. Few give a second glance to a stained glass window in the terminal which commemorates the wartime training of paratroops here. Thirty-five years ago it was a jumble of austere buildings clustered around the original pre-war control tower and hangar.

Because Manchester's original airport at Barton was too small for the new generation of air liners, such as the Douglas DC-2, which was coming into service, a new airport was laid out at Ringway on the Cheshire side of the City and opened officially on June 25 1938. In fact there had been an airfield here already and the Fairey Aviation Co had held their own opening ceremony on June 8 1937 on completion of a hangar for the final assembly of Battles built at their Heaton Chapel factory. The Dutch

airline, KLM, was one of the first to operate a schedule and was soon joined by the Dragon Rapides of Railway Air Services and Isle of Man Air Services.

As well as Fairey, Avro had a small assembly plant at Ringway before and during the war and the prototype of the Manchester bomber flew from here on July 24 1939, to be followed by many Lancasters.

The outbreak of war saw a detachment of 6 AACU move in with an assortment of aircraft which included Lysanders, Battles, Leopard Moths and Dominies. Their task was general co-operation with army and AA units throughout the North-West. The aircraft pouring from the factories in the area needed pilots to deliver them so, in December 1940, a sub-pool of Hawarden's 3 FPP formed at Ringway. It became 14 FPP in July 1941 and stayed until it disbanded in the autumn of 1945.

Ringway was only used by operational squadrons for brief periods in 1940 and these were merely detachments to provide some token form of defence for Manchester. The first to arrive were 253 Squadron from Kirton-in-Lindsey with a few Hurricanes, then Spitfires of 64 Squadron and finally 264 Squadron which had detached its 'A' Flight Defiants from Kirton for night fighter patrols. In addition a few Whitleys from 78 Squadron at Dishforth were detached in the winter of 1940/41. A new Army co-operation squadron, 613 (City of Manchester), had formed here on March 1 1939 with

Gladiator 1 K6136 of No 72 Squadron in front of Ringway control building in September 1938 (Richard T. Riding).

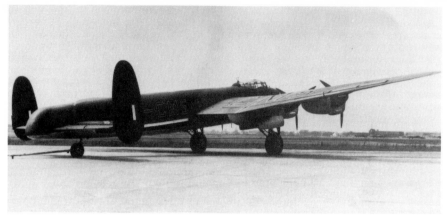

Lancaster mailplane CF-CMS (ex-R5757) at Ringway in 1943 (via Harry Holmes).

Hectors and Lysanders, but had long since left for its war station.

On June 21 1940 the Central Landing School formed here, implementing the Prime Minister's decision to train 5,000 parachute troops as quickly as possible. The success of German airborne troops during the invasion of the Low Countries in May 1940 had focused attention on the lack of similar units in the British forces. Early in July the first draft of 800 men arrived and commenced training. One of the hangars was set aside for instruction in such skills as jump techniques and landing correctly.

The original object had been to turn out 100 trained men per fortnight but this was never achieved owing to delays in receiving equipment and the recruiting of the troops themselves. There was only one Whitley available in July and parachutes only began to arrive towards the end of the month. In September 1940 the CLS was named the Central Landing Establishment and now had the expanded task of training glider pilots as well as paratroops. It was also to be responsible for developing the technique of military parachuting, assisting in the control of the design of gliders and undertaking other similar technical design work such as Rotachute development. (The latter was a small towed gyro-copter carrying one man.) A sub-flight was detached to faraway Christchurch on the south coast for experimental flying with the RDF station at Worth Matravers to determine whether or not wooden gliders reflected radar signals.

The glider training section of CLE moved its Tiger Moths and Kirby Kites to Haddenham in Oxfordshire on December 28 1940 since Ringway was too crowded for glider flying. For the same reason almost all parachute descents were made at Tatton Park. Had there been any choice in the site of the CLE, Ringway would have been one of the last to be chosen because weather conditions were usually unsuitable for parachuting and gliding was unsafe because the local flying area was too congested with aircraft under test. Also, its proximity to the densely populated area of Manchester made any secret training highly insecure.

Nevertheless, some tests were carried out by the Development Unit, including the possibility of towing gliders without the pilot using the controls. A Minimoa sailplane was used but the idea was unsuccessful as the glider tended to gain height and catch up with the towing aircraft. Glider towing at night was also tried out.

A curious collection of aircraft was in use by this branch of CLE, including BA Swallows, Avro 504s, Hectors, Lysanders and an elderly Overstrand, K8176. A four-bladed propeller was fitted to one of the Hectors to make it capable of towing a fully-loaded Hotspur. The latter glider was a new type in July 1941 and one of the first was delivered to Ringway and was soon found to be tail heavy on tow. A Hotspur, BT488, was involved in what was believed to be the first fatal accident resulting from Service gliding when it dived into the ground near the aerodrome, killing all eight occupants. Other work involved trial parachute descents into water using Rostherne Mere and live dropping from a Hudson and Manchester which proved successful.

Meanwhile the training of parachutists had got under way after some early accidents which caused operations to be suspended pending investigations. The first experimental jumps were made from four Whitley IIs using ordinary rip-cord operated parachutes. They were 'pull-offs' from crude platforms which replaced the Whitleys' rear turrets. Thereafter the old dustbin turret apertures were modified for use as paratroop exits and the static line which opened the parachutes automatically became the standard dropping method. As a paratroop aircraft the Whitley was far from ideal as five men were carried forward and five aft of the exit. Those at the back jumped facing the slipstream which often caused somersaulting and 'candles', the dreaded failure of a parachute to develop.

The jumping course was finalised at two weeks with eight parachute descents to qualify for red beret and parachute wings. The first week was devoted to learning how to exit properly from aircraft and balloons. On the Saturday, at the end of the first week, the trainees were taken up in a Whitley for air experience. Then followed three descents, including one in the dark, from a tethered barrage balloon, and then five Whitley jumps. The course failure rate was high and men who decided that parachuting was not for them were returned to their units with no repercussions. After qualifying, things were different as a refusal to jump was a Court Martial offence. Many Allied soldiers attended the courses and General de Gaulle visited on March 3 1941 to inspect Free French troops under training. Churchill also inspected CLE the following month.

Three runways were constructed during the second half of 1941 and in January 1942 the CLE was renamed Airborne Forces Experimental Establishment. Its sub-unit, the Glider Exercise Squadron, became the nucleus of 296 Squadron and moved to Netheravon the same month. The Establishment's subordinate job of training glider pilots was discontinued at the same time. It was indicative of the development of the various aspects of airborne warfare that events had now reached the stage where glider training, parachute training and technical development could be separated. AFEE moved to Sherburn-in-Elmet on July 1 1942 leaving the newly-formed 1 Parachute Training School at Ringway.

The airfield was given a 24-hour trial on March 13 1941 to determine its suitability as a rearward base for fighter aircraft. Five Hurricanes from Church Fenton and 14 Spitfires from 65 Squadron at Kirton-in-Lindsey were flown in but it was found that re-fuelling and re-arming facilities were inadequate and the airfield's surface unsuitable for Spitfires due to extensive waterlogging.

The PTS, which left for Upper Heyford on March 28 1946, became Ringway's main user, first with Whitleys as described, but later with Dakotas. The airfield was shared with aircraft on production test-flights and there were

Lancaster IV PW925 (Lincoln prototype) at Ringway. ATA taxi aircraft, an Albemarle and Albacore, can be seen in the background (via Harry Holmes).

always ATA taxi aircraft coming and going.

Commercial operations were resumed in June 1946, the first service being, significantly, an international one linking Manchester and Paris and flown by Air France. Other overseas airlines soon followed and the airport was established as a major terminal in October 1953 when Sabena started a transatlantic service to New York. During the 1950s Fairey Aviation serviced B-26 Invaders and F-86 Sabres for the USAF and test-flew Fireflies, including the red and yellow U8 target drones. The last Firefly to be built, WP354, was delivered from Ringway in April 1956. No 613 Squadron had re-formed here with Spitfires on November 1 1946. It re-equipped with Vampires and stayed until 1957.

The number of overseas destinations served by the airport has increased by leaps and bounds to the present day when more than 30 major airlines operate scheduled services. Runway 06/24 has been lengthened several times to keep pace with the demands of bigger and heavier aircraft and a project to construct a second parallel runway is meeting with serious local objections. The original control tower and hangar have been swallowed up by the impressive terminal and its piers but some of the wartime dispersals have survived on the eastern perimeter where the approach radar scanner is sited. A Fairey Swordfish airframe survived on these dispersals until

about 1960 and myth has it that its bones now lie beneath one of the new taxi-ways!

Ronaldsway, Isle of Man

SC280685. On A8, 1 mile NE of Castletown

The Isle of Man's modern airport can trace its history back to 1929 when Sir Alan Cobham of Air Circus fame visited the island and flew from a big field adjoining Ronaldsway village in a DH 61 Giant Moth. It is said that landings had been made in this same field since 1926 and, soon after having been listed as an Automobile Association Landing Ground, it was acquired in 1934 by Blackpool and West Coast Air Services to form the nucleus of a proper airport. The firm had previously started a twice-daily Liverpool-Blackpool-Isle of Man service in June 1933 with DH Dragons.

Other schedules were soon started to Dublin, Belfast and Carlisle but competition came on the scene in the form of Railway Air Services. The latter considered Ronaldsway unsuitable for the DH 86, which shows how small it was, but operated Dragons on the Barton-Blackpool-Isle of Man run. Even the smaller twin-engined aircraft had problems as, on July 1 1935, one crashed on take-off in conditions of nil wind. This branch of Railway Air Services was known as Manx Airways and, in 1936, it added Leeds and Glasgow to the destinations available from Ronaldsway.

Dragon G-ACPY at Ronaldsway after its hangar was demolished in a gale. This aircraft was shot down off the Scilly Isles on June 3 1941 (via N.V.F. Doyle).

The private fliers were active too, an annual air race being run from London to Ronaldsway and then twice round the island. The present day Isle of Man Air Rally helps keep this tradition alive in modified form. A rival airport near Ramsey, known as Hall Caine after the Manx author, operated in competition but closed in 1936 after Sir Alan Cobham recommended that Ronaldsway should be the island's official airport. For the record, Hall Caine was not used again by aircraft and was obstructed during the war to prevent landings.

With the beginning of the Second World War a Ground Defence Gunnery School was started at Ronaldsway under Technical Training Command. It was equipped with Lysanders and Westland Wallaces for target-towing and a handful of Gloster Gauntlets for cine-gun practice. A canvas Besonneau hangar and three Blisters were erected to shelter the aircraft. The situation changed little for the next two years and on May 9 1942 a Wellington, two Gauntlets and three Wallaces were to be seen on the airfield.

However, the Admiralty were casting their eyes around for a new air station in the Irish Sea area capable of housing four Torpedo-Bomber-Reconnaissance squadrons by the end of 1943, and the development of Ronaldsway came under active consideration. The first step was the acquisition of 480 acres of land by compulsory purchase, King William's College being deprived of some of its cherished playing fields. Four runways with electric lighting were laid down and a three-storey naval type control tower (still

in use today) was built on the west side near the Castletown road.

As HMS *Urley,* RNAS Ronaldsway was commissioned on June 21 1944 for basic and operational training of torpedo, dive bomber and reconnaissance aircrew, plus anti-submarine training for all three categories. No 713 Squadron reformed for advanced TBR instruction on August 12 1944, followed by 710 Squadron, a torpedo training unit, on October 7 1944. They both flew Barracudas and 710 also had some Swordfish. Derby Haven to the south-east was used for dummy attacks and a couple of Barracudas came to grief in its waters.

A third Barracuda squadron, 705, reformed here for replacement crew training on April 4 1945 but disbanded three months later. Also equipped with this odd-looking aircraft was 747 Squadron which spent most of November 1945 here before moving to Crail and 822 Squadron which disembarked from HMS *Rajah* on November 15 1944 and left for Thorney Island on January 31 1945. Detachments of 776 Squadron, a Fleet Requirements Unit, were here at various times flying Fulmars, Hurricanes, Chesapeakes and other second-line types. Amidst all this naval activity an unusual stranger, on July 4 1944, was a USAAF Liberator short of fuel on a ferry trip from Meeks Field in Iceland to Valley.

The Royal Navy left in 1946, the airfield then reverting to civil use and eventually being purchased by the Isle of Man

Ronaldsway in 1948 (Flight International).

Government in 1948. The narrow runways to the standard Navy width of 90 ft were a handicap to the operation of larger aircraft so, in the winter of 1956/57, the main runway 09/27 was widened to 150 ft, the other strips being improved and lengthened to take Viscount aircraft.

On November 24 1958 the airport proved the salvation of two USAF pilots in a Lockheed T-33 on a flight from Keflavik to Prestwick. The whole of the UK was fog-bound and, as if this were not enough, their radio failed as well. Flying on hopefully with dwindling fuel and contemplating a bale-out, they were rewarded with a miraculous break in the undercast right over the runways and they spiralled down and landed safely.

A modern terminal building has now swallowed up most of the wartime huts but a few survive and these, together with the control tower, betray the airfield's wartime role.

Rudbaxton, Dyfed

SM970205. ½ mile NE of Haverfordwest airfield

In use as 4 SLG from April 1941 by 38 MU at Llandow, Rudbaxton had a very short life because of its unsuitable position. Owing to cloud over the Welsh hills it was never possible to rely on delivering aircraft from here when they were required immediately for operational purposes. A second disadvantage was the airfield at Haverfordwest which was subsequently built one mile south-west of the SLG, the approach to its main runway lying directly over the latter. Any stray

bombs intended for the permanent airfield would probably have hit the satellite and it was therefore hardly the place to store reserve aircraft. Spasmodic use was made of it until September 25 1942 when 38 MU released it to the Ministry of Aircraft Production. It was finally de-requisitioned on July 1 1943.

St Athan, South Glamorgan

ST005685. Beside B4265, 7 miles W of Barry

With a total of 36 large hangars in November 1944, this sprawling MU probably held the record for aircraft accommodation at any airfield in the UK. They comprised no less than 20 Bellmans, two 'D'-type, six 'E'-type, four 'C'-type and four large workshop hangars of unspecified design. There were also about 20 Robin hangars dispersed around the perimeter.

It was and still remains one of the RAF's most important maintenance bases, opening in February 1939 initially as the home of 4 School of Technical Training. No 19 MU formed in March as a civilian-manned Aircraft Storage Unit and, by January 1940, there were 280 aircraft on charge, mainly Battles and Hurricanes. The following summer these aircraft were joined by Blenheims, Lysanders, Defiants and Beaufighters. The School of Air Navigation spent a year at St Athan, having moved west from its vulnerable base at Manston when the war started. Ansons were used until the School was

Row of 'B1's at St Athan (A.J. Ayers).

transferred to Canada in September 1940.

On July 15 1940 a Hurricane on test from the MU encountered an enemy aircraft which was bombing Barry Docks. The pilot of the fighter was somewhat frustrated because his aircraft had no ammunition on board but he was able to drive it away with some dummy attacks. Next month the airfield was bombed probably by chance as the bombs fell at random on the grass and, apart from the craters, caused no damage. It was a different story on April 29 1941 when a dozen aircraft, said to be Ju 87s, dropped incendiaries and high explosive on the hangars. Three Hurricanes were completely destroyed and nine other aircraft suffered varying amounts of damage. The earth covering of the 'E'-type hangars proved its worth when many of the incendiaries burned themselves out harmlessly. A second attack on May 11 caused three fatal casualties and hits on two more hangars. In an effort to disperse some of the numerous aircraft held by the MU, SLGs were opened at St Brides and Chepstow in April and May 1941, respectively.

No 32 MU had also been at St Athan since August 1939 and was mainly concerned with fitting special electronic installations like ASV, IFF and AI to air-craft, which included Catalinas, at Pembroke Dock. An out of the ordinary job was the dismantling of an He 111 at Pontypridd for transport and re-erection at Caernarvon for that town's War Weapons Week in November 1940. In 1941 the MU's work embraced the repair of damaged Whitleys and in 1943 the strengthening of Wellington wing spars after some catastrophic structural failures in flight.

A short-lived unit, 12 Radio School, formed here on September 1 1943 under 27 Signals Group but no aircraft were allocated until December when the Ansons of 'O' Flight 7 OTU were handed over to the School. Ten Oxfords followed direct from Airspeed and five more Ansons from 3 OTU at Haverfordwest. Wireless Operators were trained until May 31 1944 when the School closed down.

A fire in the 'E' hangar at the Picketstone site on February 3 1944 caused far more damage than the Luftwaffe had ever done. Ten Beaufighters and a Mustang were destroyed, the flames being spread by a strong wind. It was assumed that the fire was started when petrol being drained from a fuel tank was ignited by the faulty leads of an electrical lamp.

Beaufighters and Mustangs were the main types which occupied 19 MU at this time. No 32 MU, too, had a Mustang commitment in 1944, the preparation of 60 Mk 1s for the Normandy Invasion. With the war drawing to a close, 32 MU did a lot of conversion work on Lancasters for the Tiger Force intended for use against Japan, but rendered unnecessary by the Atomic bomb. The runways which had been built earlier in the war were lengthened during this period. Beaufighters and Mosquitoes were stored late in 1945 but newer marks of the same types were being prepared for squadron service. At the same time the

'D' Type hangar at St Athan (A.J. Ayers).

first Bristol Buckmasters were being delivered from the manufacturers.

The MUs and the School of Technical Training stayed on after the war and in the early 1950s the latter's courses included a 12-week session for Flight Engineers. The Wales University Air Squadron also operated from here and is still resident with Bulldogs. Major maintenance for the V-bomber force was done and when the Valiants were grounded with fatigue problems most of them were scrapped here.

St Brides, South Glamorgan

SS900735. On B4265, ½ mile S of village

Allotted to 19 MU at St Athan as 6 SLG, St Brides was first inspected by the unit on December 15 1940 but was not ready for use until about April the following year. Hurricanes were the first types to be stored here, succeeded later by Beaufighters and Beauforts. There were, for example, 55 aircraft in store here in June 1943. An unscheduled visitor on June 10 1942 was a Spitfire of 53 OTU which crash-landed on the north-west/south-east runway. By coincidence the MU had already decided that the SLG was unsuitable for Spitfire aircraft. This incident confirmed their suspicions!

Hangarage was not available until May 1944 when a solitary Robin was erected and creature comforts for the airmen had not been provided until October 1943, in the form of a small Nashcrete building to serve as a canteen. In July 1945 all the ground was de-requisitioned except for a small strip on which a few Henley aircraft and 18 Beaufighter 1Fs were being broken up by a working party from the Bristol Aeroplane Company. Closure was completed on September 26 1945.

St Davids, Dyfed

SM790255. 1 mile NW of Solva

The most westerly airfield in Wales, it was built quite late in the war and was planned to house operational squadrons of the US Navy equipped with the PB4Y Liberator. A change of plan soon after it opened in September 1943 resulted in the American units being transferred to Dunkeswell in Devon and RAF Coastal Command squadrons being based instead. It was, however, often used as a diversion airfield by the US Navy and now and again by

USAAF aircraft on the Marrakesh to St Mawgan ferry route.

The first RAF aeroplanes to be based were detachments of Fortresses from 206 and 220 Squadrons at Thorney Island but, in December 1943, the squadrons which were to call the airfield home for nearly a year arrived. The move was so organised that operations could be continued throughout. On December 11 two Halifaxes of 58 Squadron and two from 502 Squadron took off from Holmsley South on an anti-submarine patrol and landed at their new base the following morning. The remaining squadron aircraft soon did the same.

During January 1944 aircraft from St Davids sighted ten U-boats at night and attacked nine of them with no observed results. Retaliation came early in February when Ju 88 intruders destroyed a returning Halifax over St Brides Bay. It exploded and only a wheel was picked up. Another Halifax was warned by Flying Control to orbit clear of base but fuel was running low and it was forced to make a nerve-wracking landing, expecting to be shot down at any moment. Fortunately the raiders had gone and it landed unscathed.

There were now three squadrons at the airfield which made things very crowded. The opening of the satellite at Brawdy in February 1944 resulted in 517 Squadron moving there immediately with its Halifaxes. Paradoxically the satellite had longer runways arranged in a cross shape rather than St Davids' standard triangular pattern. They were also better aligned with the prevailing winds and, if the cross-wind component at St Davids was unacceptable for a full-loaded Halifax, the aircraft were positioned to the satellite with a light fuel load. The tanks were then topped up prior to an operational patrol.

Most of these trips were uneventful but constant vigilance was necessary because the next radar contact could be a fishing boat or an enemy submarine or E-boat. Action, when it came, was short and violent like an incident which happened at three o'clock in the morning on April 26 1944. A radar return was picked up nine miles ahead, flares were dropped at 1½ miles, silhouetting a U-boat and a small ship. They put up a terrific barrage but the Halifax dived through it and dropped four anti-submarine bombs. There was a vivid blue flash and clouds of smoke and a gunner looking through the flare chute saw what might have been the bows of a U-boat sticking up out of the water as if

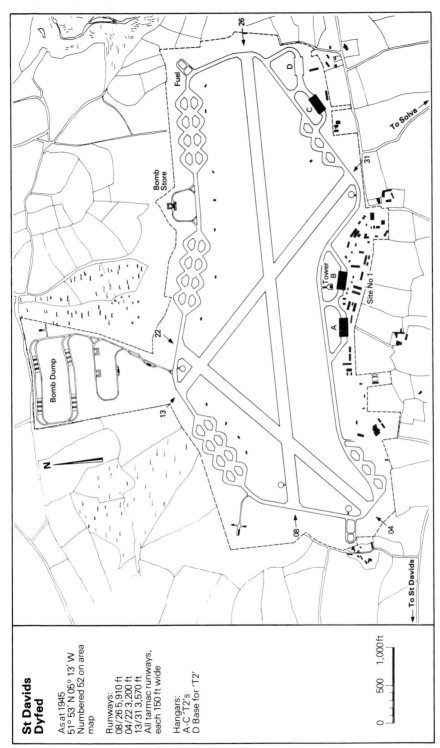

**St Davids
Dyfed**

As at 1945
51° 53′ N 05° 13′ W
Numbered 52 on area
map

Runways:
08/26 5,910 ft
04/22 3,200 ft
13/31 3,570 ft
All tarmac runways,
each 150 ft wide

Hangars:
A–C 'T2's
D Base for 'T2'

N

0   500   1,000 ft

its back were broken. Confirmation of the kill was virtually impossible at night. Radar might show that the target had disappeared but this could mean that it had merely crash-dived. The attacker was hit in the wing leaving a hole two feet across but missing tanks and other vital parts.

D-Day found three aircraft from St Davids flying a box patrol off the French coast between Brest and St Nazaire, one of a series specially planned to provide a constant watch over the enemy's sea forces, expected to interfere with Allied shipping in the Channel. An attack on June 22 was made by 'T' of 58 Squadron on a submarine in Alderney harbour and, on August 20, three surfaced U-boats were sighted off the French coast. The Halifax piloted by Wing Commander Grant, the squadron Commanding Officer, was shot down on the run-in. Five of the crew escaped in the dinghy but two died from injuries during the night and the remaining three were rescued by a Canadian frigate the next day.

A week later 58 Squadron moved to Stornoway and in September No 502 Squadron also left. They were replaced by a detachment of 220 Squadron from the Azores for a two-month conversion course. When the detachment returned to its island base it was intended to move 4 APC from Talbenny but this was dropped and 53 Squadron's Liberators came instead. Mainly uneventful patrols were flown until a move to Merryfield on September 17 1945. There is little of note to record at the station as the war drew to a close, apart from an incident on March 3 when a Mosquito of 8 OTU suffered the failure of its air speed indicator. Another Mosquito led it down safely on to the long runway at St Davids after being delayed by a Halifax with no brake pressure which blocked it temporarily.

The station HQ was moved to Brawdy on November 1 1945 and St Davids was reduced to care and maintenance when both airfields passed to the Royal Navy on January 1 1946. It was used as an RLG for Brawdy and in 1955 by a Fleet Requirements Unit operated by Airwork Ltd and equipped with Sea Hornet NF 21s and Mosquito T 3s. The relief function continues for the RAF units at Brawdy but most of the buildings have been flattened and maintenance restricted to the main runway and associated taxiways.

When it was built it had three 'T2' hangars plus the floor and foundations of one other which was never erected. Thirty diamond-shaped hard-standings were placed in five clusters around the perimeter track and a watch office to pattern 12779/41 was provided. The living sites were dispersed to the south, whilst the bomb dump was in the marshy ground to the north.

Samlesbury, Lancashire
SD630310. On A59, 4 miles E of Preston

Outside the group of people who worked here, this airfield's contribution to the war effort is almost unknown. In the 1930s it was all farm land; flat, wide and remote and ideal for an airfield site. As it was mid-way between Preston and Blackburn both towns collaborated in setting up a joint municipal airport. The government intervened, however, and arranged

Halifax NR134 just off the production line at Samlesbury in August 1944. It served with Nos 434, 426 and 425 Squadrons and was finally scrapped at High Ercall (British Aerospace).

for the construction of a preliminary hangar so that the Preston-based English Electric Co could assemble Hampdens under sub-contract and test them from the new airfield.

December 1939 saw the arrival of the first components for the Hampdens, the initial aircraft, P2062, being flight-tested on February 22 1940 and delivered to the RAF on March 30. By the end of April production was five aircraft per month, a figure which was rapidly increased so that, by the end of the year, 260 Hampdens had been completed. In May 1940 a second hangar was erected in preparation for building the Halifax under sub-contract. The airfield was further improved by a runway extension to cater for the Halifax, the first locally-built example flying in August 1941. At the end of the year a total of 714 Hampdens and seven Halifaxes had been delivered.

In mid-March the last of 770 Hampdens left the factory and total effort was then concentrated on Halifax production, monthly output averaging 36. An order was received during the closing months of 1943 for a further 200 aircraft, this time Mk IIs. More batches followed, the production record being achieved in February 1944 when 81 aircraft were delivered. When Halifax production ceased, a total of 2,145 had been made at this factory.

The wartime team spirit in the plant was incredible. A seven-day week was worked, the hours being 8.00 am to 9.00 pm. The terrible weather of January and February 1940 played havoc with deliveries because in those early days there was only one runway and no perimeter track so the aircraft had to be towed across the grass. When the thaw came, the first Hampden to be towed out became stuck up to the axles.

Quite a number of aircraft came back to the factory for modification and, because of the general shortage of aircraft and the need to get the machine back into service, certain items were sometimes overlooked. On one occasion a bomber was found to have flares still in the flare chute and on another a round was left in the breech of the front gun. The inspector, who was checking the aircraft for acceptance, inadvertently pressed the firing button and sent the missile through the hangar doors and harmlessly across the airfield.

The airfield was used jointly by 9 Group Communications Flight with a mixed fleet of aircraft which included Hurricanes, Masters, Oxfords and a Miles Mentor. No 9 Group's HQ was at Barton Hall (destined to become Preston Air Traffic Control Centre many years later), about six miles away, and this was the nearest airfield for visitors.

Samlesbury emerged almost unscathed from the war, only one attack being made on it when a few incendiaries were dropped on the aerodrome and the village of Balderstone. Today it looks very much the same as it did then, minus the camouflage paint. The air-raid shelters are still there along with the two pillboxes which stand on each side of the main runway.

English Electric built many Vampires in the immediate post-war years but the company acquired Warton on the other side of Preston where there was more room for runway extension and most of the test flying of the Canberra and Lightning was done from there. The Samlesbury factory currently has 2,700 employees engaged in the assembly of major sections of the Tornado and Jaguar, refurbishing Canberras and supplying spares to customers all over the world.

Sealand, Clwyd

SJ330700. On A550, 1 mile NE of Queensferry

In the summer of 1942 the casual onlooker on the edge of the Dee Marshes might have seen a curious aeroplane. It resembled a Hurricane but had an extra wing mounted above the fuselage. Suddenly, this wing broke away and fluttered down like a falling leaf to land on the firing range on the marshes. Instead of plunging to the ground out of control, the aircraft flew on happily and landed at nearby Sealand. This was an ingenious scheme to provide extra fuel tankage to increase the range but allow the Hurricane to revert to its fighting configuration very quickly. F. Hills & Sons did the conversion work on the slip-wing Hurricane, as it was known, and 30 MU did most of the flight trials from Sealand. The idea was dropped, however, when the jettisonable drop tank was perfected, a much less expensive method of achieving the same result.

The airfield from which it flew could trace its origins back to the First World War, being one of the few stations where two airfields were sited side-by-side, divided by a railway line. The southernmost site at Queensferry was planned as

Fairey III F S1862 at Sealand (via J. Molyneux).

an Acceptance Park for American aircraft but was still unfinished when the war ended. The other camp, known as Shotwick, was occupied by 95 and 96 Squadrons in October 1917. Hindered by the fact that the airfield was still under construction, they tried to work up to operational standards on a mixed bag of Sopwith Pups, Camels, Dolphins, Sala-manders, Martinsydes and Avro 504s. No 90 Squadron joined them from Shawbury in November 1917.

As soon as the regular squadrons had moved to France it was intended that they would be replaced at Sealand by training squadrons. However, they were still present when 61 Squadron moved in from Shawbury on April 1 1918 with Camels, Pups and Avro 504s. Another change of policy saw the disbandment of 95 and 96 Squadrons and the dispersal of their pilots and aircraft to other units. No 90 Squadron was sent to Brockworth but it, too, was disbanded soon afterwards. This left room for another Training Squadron, 55, but this was joined by 67 TS to form 51 Training Depot Station on July 15 1918.

At last some standardisation could be achieved, the types now being restricted to Sopwith Dolphins and Avro 504s. The shrinking of the RAF after the war resulted in brief periods when four operational squadrons were based, some in cadre form only, before disbandment. In April 1920 No 51 TDS was absorbed into 5 Flying Training School with an establishment of Avro 504s, flying training now taking place in a very leisurely way as the requirement for pilots was small.

The station was renamed Sealand in 1924 to avoid confusion with RAF Scopwick in Lincolnshire. The popular story had it that the Workshops Officer at Scopwick ordered some equipment for servicing aircraft and, despite reminders, had still not received it months later. Meanwhile, at Shotwick the puzzled Workshops Officer was trying to find out why he had been sent a load of machinery for which he had no use. The other version is that the local Welsh population resented the fact that an airfield in Wales was named after a village which, although it was adjacent, happened to be over the border in England.

A Sealand airman, Pilot Officer Eric Pentland, had the dubious distinction of being the first RAF flyer to escape from an aeroplane by parachute. Whilst on a local flight over the Wirral on June 17 1926 he was practising spins and his 504 got out of control. Prior to 1926 only RAF balloonists had been equipped with parachutes and the Air Ministry in a remarkable piece of short-sightedness had refused to issue them to the rest of its airmen. In fairness, however, it should be admitted that the parachutes of the First

World War were generally too bulky to be carried in aircraft cockpits and were very unreliable.

The RAF Packing Depot arrived from Ascot on May 23 1929, being responsible for the crating of all aircraft which were to be sent overseas and a role in which Sealand was to specialise in the coming war. An amusing story is told about the Depot; one day the Air Officer Commanding arrived unannounced and was taken to the Mess. When he returned two hours later he found his aircraft minus wings. The Depot were expecting a similar type of aircraft and had started to dismantle it for packing. Never has a set of wings been reassembled and re-rigged in so short a space of time! The Depot was also responsible for the design and construction of packing cases for the aircraft, a more difficult task than one might imagine when insulation against sea water, corrosion and tropical climate has to be taken into account.

On June 24 1931 two Americans, Harold Gatty and Wiley Post, made a short refuelling stop here in their Lockheed Vega. They were attempting to fly around the world in ten days and ultimately made it in nine. Five years later, on November 24 1936, another famous personality, Colonel Charles C. Lindbergh, was forced to land at Sealand because of fog which persisted for four days. He was a guest of the Officers' Mess until he could resume his world trip.

Pilot training was affected by the RAF Expansion Scheme in that *ab initio* training was to be carried out by civilian schools for two months, followed by nine months at an FTS where intermediate and advanced training would be given. The Avro Tutors used for primary instruction were now given up in favour of the Hart, Audax and Fury with a total establishment of 65 aircraft.

Expansion resulted also in the formation of 3 Aircraft Storage Unit on December 2 1935, joining the Packing Unit on the South Camp site. New buildings were put up to the east of the A550 road but Sealand was somewhat different from the usual pattern of pre-war stations. Some of the buildings were standard RAF design but many others were one-offs peculiar to this airfield. For example, the barrack blocks were built to three storeys instead of the usual two so as to house the unusually large number of men. The nine Belfast hangars on the South Camp were joined by two 'C'-types and two 'L'-types and a third 'C'-type was built on North Camp. All can be seen today but 18 Blisters, erected around the airfield perimeter during the war, have now gone.

The war was looming ever nearer and it was obvious that there was going to be a serious shortfall in the supply of pilots. Plans to improve this situation were made, but war broke out before they could be implemented. Courses had to be cut down to 16 weeks in duration with 100 flying hours per pupil. Bomber Command soon complained about the standard of the graduates who had neither instrument nor night flying experience. The course length was therefore increased by four

Hart trainer K4941 of 5 FTS flying from Sealand in February 1937 (J.W.G. Wellham via R.C.B. Ashworth).

weeks, but output was reduced by bad weather which water-logged the low-lying airfield.

The introduction of OTUs in the summer of 1940 solved the problem as now the specialised training necessary before a posting to an operational squadron could be done by a separate unit. Some Oxfords had been on strength for twin-conversion but all these had gone by September 1940, the unit's main equipment now being Miles Masters. A few of the Masters were the six-gun variety built as a stop-gap fighter until more Spitfires were available. No 5 FTS kept a few of these armed and at readiness as the fighter defences of the North-West were almost non-existent while the Battle of Britain was raging.

On the evening of August 14 1940 an He 111 made a surprise attack on the airfield, dropping bombs on the barrack blocks and killing several airmen. There was no time to get the Masters airborne but the Spitfire Battle Flight at nearby Hawarden arrived on the scene and attacked the Heinkel. The bomber pilot crash-landed the crippled aircraft in a field and he and his crew set fire to the wreck before giving themselves up to the local Home Guard.

Many American volunteer pilots passed through Sealand and later formed the nucleus of the Eagle Squadrons. However, more hangar space was needed by the rapidly expanding 30 MU which had formed here on July 28 1939 and 5 SFTS was forced to move to Tern Hill in December 1940. Amongst the important work being caried out by the MU at this

Hurricane I GG-L of 151 Squadron at Sealand in August 1939 (H.A.G. Smith via R.C.B. Ashworth).

time was the fitting of AI radar to Beaufighters as soon as they were delivered from the manufacturers. They also converted 70 Havocs into Turbinlite aircraft. This involved the installation of a high-intensity floodlight with which enemy raiders could be illuminated, after an interception at night with radar, and shot down by an accompanying Hurricane fighter. This promising idea proved disappointing and the Turbinlite squadrons were disbanded in January 1943. The pre-war packing depot had become 36 MU, and finally 47 MU, and was extremely busy with, for example, nearly 700 aircraft being crated and dispatched overseas in February 1941, including a staggering total of 329 Fairey Battles to Canada.

Flying training started again on January 21 1941 in the form of 19 EFTS. The Tiger Moths of this short-lived school were worked hard, some 740 pupils being taught to fly before it disbanded on December 31 1941. From March 1941 there was also a detachment of the ubiquitous 6 AACU operating a collection of Lysanders, Leopard Moths, Dragons and Dominies to help train the numerous army and navy units in the North-West. Another EFTS, 24, arrived from Luton in February 1942 and was engaged mainly in teaching future Royal Navy pilots.

The grass surface of the aerodrome was very much the worse for wear and the Air Ministry's overstretched building programme managed to fit in the construction of a single concrete runway. No 30 MU's work was still increasing with repairs to Mosquito, Wellington and Lancaster aircraft so the hard runway was very necessary. The packing unit, too, was so short of space that it had to store packed aircraft all around the airfield perimeter and along the verges of the main road. A request by the Royal Navy to use Sealand for disembarking squadrons from aircraft carriers in the Mersey was swiftly refused, but they were able to acquire Stretton instead.

There were a large number of Polish airmen working in the MUs and most of the pilots of the 6 AACU detachment were also Poles. When the AACU disbanded on December 1 1943 and formed a new squadron, 577, at Castle Bromwich, the detachment remained at Sealand. By now it was equipped with six Oxfords and three Hurricanes, the latter offering more realistic high-speed co-operation for guns, searchlights and radar. The Flight stayed here until November 19 1944 when it repositioned to Woodvale where there was far less congestion—it even had a dispersal to itself!

No 24 EFTS ceased to train Royal Navy pilots in August 1943 and thereafter concentrated on RAF trainees, plus some refresher flying for pilots returning after a ground tour. In March 1945 the school left for Rochester and the airfield suddenly fell almost silent compared to the bustle of the last few years. The only flights were deliveries to 47 MU or test flights and occasional movements into 30 MU. As its other units disbanded, Sealand once more found itself the home of the

Master Is of No 5 SFTS flying from Sealand in 1940 (Neville Duke).

only packing unit in the RAF, although the numbers of aircraft sent out were now small.

Post-war, the station was loaned to the USAF to augment the huge complex at Burtonwood and the RAF MUs went elsewhere. The hangars were used for storage until the USAF left in August 1957, 30 MU reforming on February 1 1959 for radio and radar maintenance. There had been very little flying at Sealand since the war but this was rectified when 631 Gliding School arrived from Hawarden in March 1963. Every weekend, the Sedberghs and Cadets can be seen operating from the south airfield, whilst the north runway is obstructed by a line of telegraph poles and was last used in October 1963 when Gnat XR536 from Valley crash-landed after a flame-out. Sealand is still an important station specialising in the electronic gadgetry of modern war-planes but the hundreds of aircraft which once graced its boundaries are but a memory.

Seighford, Staffordshire

SJ865255. On B5405, 1½ miles SW of Great Bridgeford

A satellite station amongst the leafy lanes of North Staffordshire, one of Seighford's busiest days came on November 16 1944 when 35 B-17s were diverted here on the return from attacking tactical targets near Aachen, in support of the ground offensive. The perimeter track and hardstandings were jammed with bombers and the resident Albemarles of 23 Heavy Glider Conversion Unit were grounded until the airfield could be cleared the next day. Almost as soon as the B-17s had left for their bases, fog descended again and 25 more Fortresses landed. The last one in

became bogged down at the end of the runway and stopped any further flying that day. Things got worse next morning when an Albemarle was stuck on the other runway with a flat tyre. Since there was no spare wheel available on the unit it was hours before the airfield could be used again.

Events usually ran much more smoothly at Seighford (pronounced Sy-ford) which had been a satellite to Hixon at the outset, and was used by the Wellingtons of 30 OTU. It opened in January 1943 and soon received 26 aircraft and crews. By June 1943 it was dispatching *Nickel* sorties over France. Hurried construction resulted in repair work having to be done to the runway almost immediately. Round-the-clock flying could not be interrupted so the job could be dangerous. On August 26 1943 Wellington BK359 was taking off but swung on to the grass straight at some workmen on the other runway. To avoid them, the pilot attempted to take off but a wing hit the front of a lorry and the aircraft finished up in a heap on the centre of No 5 runway. Amazingly the only casualty was the civilian lorry driver who suffered a grazed leg.

Seighford had a longer main runway than Hixon and any emergencies were usually sent here, which also avoided the possibility of the runways at the parent station becoming blocked. On September 1 1943 Wellington HE202 was coming back on one engine at night. The crew were ordered to bale out, with the exception of the pilot and wireless operator who were to try a landing on the satellite's long runway. Nothing more was heard and another aircraft reported a fire on the ground near Eccleshall, yet another

training accident although, for a change, there were survivors.

No 30 OTU lost its satellite on October 28 1944 when the latter was transferred to Peplow's control for use by 23 HGCU. This unit was just beginning to form to train replacements for the serious losses of glider pilots suffered at Arnhem. Seighford was often the scene of mass landing practices by Horsa gliders released from Albemarles after take-off from Peplow. Some were held at night and there was quite a pile-up on December 1 when a Horsa, landing without flaps, ran into two other aircraft which had stopped ahead of it. Luckily there were no injuries and the sturdy wooden machines could easily be repaired. The HGCU moved out in January 1944 and the next residents were Oxfords from 21 (P) AFU at Wheaton Aston on January 26.

Seighford, like Hixon, was near to the American replacement depot at Stone and heavy bombers belonging to the VIIIth Air Force were frequent visitors when new crews were collected. The bright fin colours of almost every group were visible at some time during 1944/45. Marauders of the IXth Air Force were less common and some bore evidence of hard use. 42-96787 had 122 mission symbols on her nose and 42-96195, 'Mary Ann', had 140. An early aircraft, 41-18209, was called 'Little Rita' and was a veteran of 117 missions. A large '89' in red with a black outline decorated the fin. Odd examples of the C-46 Commando made visits, along with a rare C-87 Liberator transport.

For many hundreds of Allied prisoners-of-war Seighford was the first step on English soil for a long time. It became one of several reception points for them and

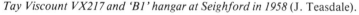

Tay Viscount VX217 and 'B1' hangar at Seighford in 1958 (J. Teasdale).

Bar and rod tracking in use as fencing at Seighford.

processing and medical examination was carried out in a Nissen hut which still stands near the control tower. One of the highest ranking returnees was Wing Commander J.R.D. Braham, DSO, DFC, a top-scoring night fighter pilot whose Mosquito had been shot down over Denmark in June 1944. The first big ferry flight came on May 10 when 917 men disemplaned from 41 Lancasters. At one time there were 33 bombers on the perimeter track together. Men of all Services and nationalities were represented, including Indian soldiers and Chinese merchant navy seamen.

No 21 (P) AFU's enormous establishment of Oxfords was slowly reduced, resulting in the satellite being employed less intensively. On August 23 1946 permission was given to the Royal Automobile Club to hold a practice run to test the facilities of the aerodrome for racing. Nothing seems to have come of this, but flying ceased in December 1946 when 21 (P) AFU moved to Moreton-in-Marsh. Scheduled to be abandoned in 1947, it was re-designated a surplus inactive station and lay dormant until 1956 when Boulton Paul at Wolverhampton Airport were looking for a more suitable airfield for test-flying jets.

The company extended the main runway to 2,000 yards in 1959 and fenced it off, together with part of a taxi-way to the hangars, the rest of the airfield being returned to the plough. Many Canberras were overhauled under contract to English Electric, a visit in July 1959 revealing at least seven of them including an Indian Air Force example, IF897. The prize item, however, was the Tay-Viscount, VX217, a unique twin-jet test-bed conversion of the well-known airliner. Many test flights were made from Seighford and Defford to experiment with electrical impulses to move the control surfaces instead of the conventional mechanical linkages. The aircraft was finally scrapped here in the early 1960s.

The cancellation of TSR 2 resulted in English Electric searching for more work to fill the gap. Canberra maintenance was part of the solution and when the contract with Boulton Paul was not renewed, the latter had no further use for Seighford and closed it in January 1966. By this time they had also done work on a few Lightnings here.

In 1969 planning permission for its re-use as an airfield was refused to Stoke-on-Trent City Council and the fast-crumbling runway is now used only by the odd light aircraft. The winding road from Seighford village is the best approach as it runs between the hangar site to the west of the road and the airfield to the east. A 'T2' and 'B1' hangar stand side-by-side, making a unique comparison. The 'B1' is not original, however, having been erected by Boulton Paul during their occupation. It replaced the wartime 'B1' on the same site which had deteriorated beyond repair. The tower, a 13079/41 type, is reached through a succession of gates in the fencing which is partly made of bar and rod tracking from the dispersal points. The old airfield makes a peaceful scene in summer with its grazing cattle and singing skylarks.

Shawbury, Salop

SJ550220. On B5063 adjacent to Shaw-bury village

One of the oldest military airfields in the North-West, Shawbury dates back to 1917 when the RFC expanded its training programme so that new pilots posted to France would have a little more experience and therefore a better chance of survival. No 29 (Training) Wing formed on September 1 1917 with three squadrons, 10, 29 and 67, plus three more at nearby Tern Hill. Several different types of aircraft were available which was hardly conducive to good training and caused the maintenance staff many a headache. Two of the squadrons combined to form 9 TDS on March 1 1918, the other moving away to Gloucestershire. Training continued on a more organised basis until the end of the war and the airfield closed in May 1920 when RAF strength was drastically reduced.

The hangars and most of the buildings were demolished and the remnants soon fell into disrepair. In 1935, however, the political climate had changed and the Air Ministry was looking for new airfield sites in the relatively safe areas of western England. Shawbury was found suitable for the construction of a much larger permanent station intended for an FTS and MU. Six dispersed sites were provided each with two of the low-profile Lamella or 'L'-type hangars and two of the massive 'D'-types, were built on the western perimeter, as well as four 'C'-types on the main site.

The airfield was still not completed when 27 MU formed on February 1 1938 with a staff consisting mainly of civilians. The types stored and overhauled represented most of the RAF's contemporary combat aircraft, such as Blenheims, Hurricanes, Whitleys and Battles. A month after the war began a total of 324 aircraft was on charge.

The training side of Shawbury's activities was started when 11 SFTS came from Wittering on May 14 1938 with Hart Trainers, Audaxes, and a few Gauntlets, Furies and Tutors. More modern aircraft arrived just as the war started but the biplanes stayed until mid-1940 alongside the Blenheims and Oxfords used for multi-engine conversion.

There were no runways and the grass surface soon got in a bad state under all this traffic. Bridleway Gate and Bratton were taken on as RLGs but they, too, were grass and soon became muddy and useless. Airfields as far apart as Chipping Norton, Lindholme, Llandwrog and Fulbeck had to be used in an attempt to maintain the output of fully trained pilots.

A further complication was that Shawbury was right on the track of enemy bombers on their way to Merseyside. Dummy flarepaths were laid in an attempt to mislead but, on the night of April 27 1941, bombs were dropped on the airfield which was lit up for night flying. Fortunately no damage was inflicted.

Meanwhile 27 MU had expanded steadily and on the last day of 1941, for example, 220 aircraft of 13 different types were held. Runway construction was started at last in September 1941 and finally completed the following summer. The FTS which was re-named 11 (P) AFU on April 1 1942 now had to provide further training for pilots who had gained their wings overseas and now required familiarisation with the harsh realities of flying in wartime Britain.

No 1534 BAT Flight was added on January 16 1943 and another small unit was a detachment of 6 AACU equipped with Lysanders and later Masters. Its duties were transferred to 7 AACU in 1941 but it returned briefly in 1942 before moving to Rednal.

A turning point came on January 31 1944 when 11 (P) AFU moved its 132 Oxfords, four Ansons and one Tutor to Calveley to make room for the Central Navigation School which was due to move to Cranage. The CNS had a mixture of aircraft, mainly Wellingtons and Stirlings, but also a Proctor, Magister, Hudson V and Lancaster PD328 named 'Aries'. The School held courses for post-graduate navigators and trained navigation instructors, also researching into navigation techniques. Many long-range flights were made, the best known being late in 1944 when 'Aries' became the first British aircraft to fly round the world.

The war's end had the usual effect on an MU airfield of turning it and the

Opposite page, top to bottom *Jet Provost T2 prototype in the Storage field at Shawbury, August 1960; derelict Anson C19 VV981 at Shawbury in summer 1963; the sole survivor of Shawbury's many wartime Robin hangars. Note dummy chimney and faded 'half-timbered' paint scheme to match houses in village.*

surrounding fields into a graveyard of unwanted aircraft. In Shawbury's case they were mainly Mosquitoes but Wellingtons, Lancasters and Spitfires were also scrapped. The CNS was by now known as the Empire Air Navigation School and its Wellingtons and Halifaxes were replaced by Lancaster VIIs. However some Wellingtons were taken on strength again when it merged with the School of Air Traffic Control from Watchfield to form the Central Navigation and Control School on February 10 1950.

Ansons were introduced and more Lincolns joined the Lancasters but both types were replaced by the purpose-built Varsity in 1953. The ATC side of the training was reinforced by the arrival of the Ground Controlled Approach School in 1953 and a Vampire Flight was formed to give practice with high-speed aircraft. The airfield also had a secondary function as a Master Diversion Station and was open round the clock. The main runway was extended to 6,000 ft in 1958 to accommodate all the types then in service.

The Chipmunks of Birmingham UAS began to operate from here in March 1958 when Castle Bromwich closed and the navigation element of CNCS was transferred to Manby in 1963 and the unit re-titled Central Air Traffic Control School. No 27 MU succumbed to the defence cuts in 1972 after scrapping many Javelins, Vampires and Provosts in the 1960s.

CATCS's Provosts were retired in 1968 and its Vampires were replaced by the Jet Provosts which are still in service. The UAS re-equipped with Bulldogs, leaving only four Chipmunks with 8 Air Experience Flight. When Tern Hill closed, the Central Flying School (Helicopters) moved over with Whirlwinds and Sioux and Shawbury's future looks secure.

Many of the wartime hangars can still be seen but the vast network of dispersals stretched over a mile from the airfield have been broken up and the fields long since returned to cultivation. A solitary Robin hangar survives on the edge of Preston Brockhurst, cleverly painted to match the half-timbered houses in the village and still sporting its dummy chimney pot.

Shobdon, Hereford and Worcester

SO395605. On the minor road from B4362 at Shobdon village

The evening of September 16 1943 was a

disastrous one for the VIIIth Air Force groups raiding western France. Bad weather on the return trip had scattered the bomber force all over South-West England and the Darkie frequency (an emergency homing system) was alive with calls for assistance. Three Fortresses crashed into the high ground in Devon and South Wales but most of the others managed to put down at any RAF field they could find. One Fort crew flying on three engines was relieved to find a long runway out in the middle of nowhere and landed on it with almost dry tanks after ten and a half hours in the air. A month later an American Thunderbolt pilot did the same thing when he got completely lost on the way back from a mission.

The airfield they found was built in a very isolated area which made it ideal for glider training as there were no other aerodromes near enough to interfere with local flying. The site had been used for flying since 1940 under the name of Pembridge Landing Ground, after another neighbouring village. Fairey Battles and Lysanders belonging to 8 AACU operated from here in support of Army manoeuvres and it was decided to develop it as a proper airfield. During the construction the aircraft moved elsewhere but returned in June 1942, dividing their time between here and Madley until at least the middle of 1944. By this time the detachment had become part of 577 Squadron and was now equipped with Martinets and Oxfords.

The first visitor after the new airfield opened, on May 28 1942, was a Grumman Martlet which force-landed whilst on a flight from Yeovilton to Donibristle on June 20. A few days later two Canadian Spitfires landed after getting lost on a cross-country flight. On July 14 the first aircraft to be based—a Lysander—was delivered by an ATA pilot, followed by two dismantled Hotspur gliders brought by road. The rest of 5 Glider Training School had arrived by July 30 from Kidlington and training was resumed almost immediately. The local people soon became used to the novel sight of labouring Miles Masters towing Hotspurs overhead the airfield, clawing for a little height before casting them off. Tractors were in short supply but they were augmented by cart-horses which dragged the gliders back to the end of the runway so they could be hitched up to the tow-planes again. A runway three times wider than normal helped immensely because a

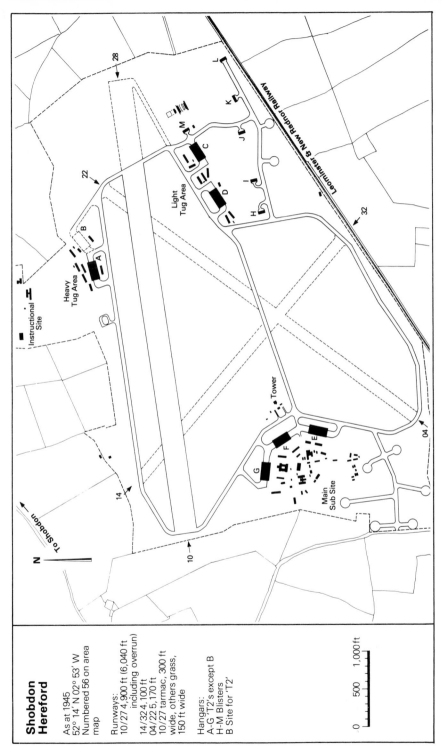

Shobdon
Hereford

As at 1945
52° 14' N 02° 53' W
Numbered 56 on area
map

Runways:
10/27 4,900 ft (6,040 ft
    including overrun)
14/32 4,100 ft
04/22 5,170 ft
10/27 tarmac, 300 ft
wide, others grass,
150 ft wide

Hangars:
A–G 'T2's except B
H–M Blisters
B Site for 'T2'

0   500   1,000 ft

518/40 pattern tower at Shobdon. Note unusual pillars supporting first floor balcony (P. Francis).

glider/tug combination could be marshalled to one side whilst traffic landed on the other half.

A detachment of Bostons from 88 Squadron was based in July 1943 for smoke-laying demonstrations, and December of the same year saw a call for an accelerated output of glider pilots in preparation for the coming invasion of Europe. Unfortunately Shobdon's grass surfaces on which the gliders usually landed were muddy and unserviceable and half the runway width was unusable because of re-surfacing work. The Glider Instructor Flight was therefore detached to operate from the RLG at Hockley Heath near Solihull in Warwickshire. The RLG was promoted to a full satellite of Shobdon on May 22 1944 but difficulties were experienced there with rough ground, particularly when landing at night.

Accidents were relatively few but one, on the night of February 25 1944, led to Warrant Officer G. Woodson being awarded the Air Force Cross for his gallantry. Woodson was the pilot of a Hotspur whose Master tug suffered engine failure, released the tow rope and crashed. He force-landed in the dark near the burning Master and managed to rescue one of its occupants. An unusual incident occurred on October 12 1944 when a tug combination was struck by lightning. The glider got out of control but one of the two occupants baled out in time, the other being killed in the ensuing crash.

Sommerfeld Track was laid to improve the airfield surface and a renewed training effort was made to replace the heavy losses of glider pilots at Arnhem. There was a surplus in the spring of 1945, however, and, by September, 5 GTS was a shadow of its former self although still able to send a Master/Hotspur combination via Croughton for a demonstration at the Hendon Battle of Britain Display. It also sent one to perform at another display at Tilstock in Shropshire.

During November 1945 23 Hotspurs and 23 Masters were flown to Montford Bridge for breaking up by 34 MU and, by the end of the month, the school had disbanded. This peaceful corner of Herefordshire had trained 1,335 glider pilots, 291 gliding instructors and 280 tug pilots. The airfield now became a detached site of 25 MU at Hartlebury, a ground station between Kidderminster and Worcester.

Shobdon was unused by aircraft until the early 1960s when light aircraft began to operate from here as there was no other available aerodrome for miles. The usual lack of capital has prevented it from expanding and the huge runway is only partly usable, as most of it has deteriorated badly. One of the wartime 'T2' hangars is still in use and a small control building has been put up. Many of the original huts remain in varying stages of decay and the old tower, a large 518/40 type, still stands derelict on the south-west boundary where the main site with its three 'T2's was once located. The centre of activity today is in what was known as the Heavy Tug Area on the north-east side of the field. The Light Tug Area was in the south-east corner with two more 'T2's and six Blister hangars on a loop dispersal. The provision of a cannon range and a Battle HQ makes one speculate that the airfield was intended for a more war-like purpose than glider training, but the only operational unit which ever used it was the brief detachment of 88 Squadron mentioned above.

It achieved a certain notoriety among private pilots because there were no navigational aids until 1970 when a Non-Directional Beacon was installed and there are no prominent geographical features to help locate the airfield from the air. Nevertheless there have been many excellent displays and air races staged here. On one occasion a USAF C-123 Provider flew in members of the US Army's Special Forces from Sembach in Germany on a liaison visit to their opposite numbers, the Special Air Service, at Hereford. Another interesting aircraft which has been resident for some time is a Howard 500, a modernised Lockheed Ventura.

Silloth, Cumbria

NY125540. On B5302, 1 mile NE of Silloth town

In September 1940 experiments were conducted by the RAE at Farnborough into a means of illuminating enemy bombers at night. One idea was to fit two one million candle-power flares under the wings of a Hampden. Any aircraft trying this in the south would be a sitting-duck so the aircraft was taken up to Silloth in an area thought to be free from enemy interference. On the first trial, however, an enemy raider was attracted by the light and although the flare-path at Silloth was doused, the airfield and surrounding countryside stood out distinctly in the glare. Bombs were dropped, fortunately with minimal damage, but the RAE were politely told to take their experiments elsewhere.

Silloth was built as a Maintenance Command station, opening on June 5 1939 but its position was ideal for teaching general reconnaissance, so it was transferred to Coastal Command. No 22 MU thus became a lodger unit when the Coastal Command Group Pool formed on November 1 1939 with Ansons, Bothas, Hudsons and Beauforts. The Pool was the fore-runner of the OTUs and served as a bridge between SFTS and operational squadron. No 215 Squadron's Wellingtons were also here for most of November 1939 on air-firing practice.

The MU handled quite a variety of aircraft at first and, after an air raid on July 15 1940 when several bombs were dropped on the aerodrome, more dispersal fields were requisitioned. Camouflage was provided by trees and farm buildings and Robin hangars were erected. Unusual types such as Vigilants and Brewster Bermudas passed through but in May

Bothas of No 1 OTU at Silloth in 1941 (IWM).

Top *Silloth taken from an Anson at 2,000 ft on July 29 1942* (RAF Museum). **Above** *Anson VS595 at Silloth on April 1 1959.*

1943 22 MU began to specialise in Hurricanes and Sea Hurricanes. One of the 'D'-type hangars was used by Cunliffe-Owen for Hudson conversion work and another was loaned to Scottish Aviation early in 1945.

The Hudson was the aircraft chiefly associated with Silloth, so many ditching in the Solway Firth that it was known in the RAF as 'Hudson Bay'. CCGP had been re-designated 1 OTU on April 1 1940 and an Anson defence aircraft was kept bombed-up in case of emergency. On July 15 1940 the Harbour Master at Workington reported a submarine and the Anson made an unsuccessful search.

Silloth had a generally good weather record and became a useful alternative in the rare event of really bad visibility at Prestwick. On December 12 1941 three Liberators landed on diversion and in May 1942 an American officer visited the station to discuss the possibility of American ferry aircraft landing in emergency. The first recorded diversions were 23 B-17s on October 23 1942 and the visits continued spasmodically featuring such aircraft as a C-54 on July 3 1943 and 13 Thunderbolts on October 29 1943 en route from Renfrew to Warton.

No 1 OTU nearly joined the first thousand raid on Cologne but the Coastal Command aircraft and crew due to take part were withdrawn at the last moment. Some 24 of the OTU's Hudsons, each armed with four 250 lb bombs, were flown to Thornaby on May 25 1942 but returned two days later. The Hudsons were

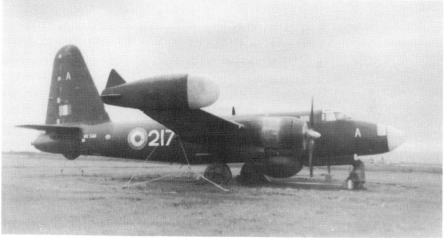

Top *Balliols await scrapping at Silloth on February 27 1960* (J. Huggon). **Above** *Neptune MR 1 WX549 A of 217 Squadron in 1958 awaiting transfer to the Argentinian navy.*

detached to Thornaby again and 24 took part in operations from there on June 25 1942, the night of the Bremen thousand bomber raid. One aircraft failed to return from what were believed to be coastal targets.

When 1 OTU moved out on March 10 1943 its place was taken by 6 OTU with Wellingtons and Ansons. At the same time 1429 COT Flight was absorbed by 6 OTU and was now referred to as the 'Czech Flight'. It was disbanded on August 8 1943 when 311 (Czech) Squadron re-equipped with Liberators. During the summer of 1944 6 OTU aircraft flew anti-submarine patrols from Ballykelly in Northern Ireland.

The OTU left for Kinloss in July 1945 and Silloth was then devoted almost

entirely to scrapping and storage by 22 MU. No 5 FP formed here on October 15 1945 to take over the ferrying from the disbanding ATA. The only other unit here now was 1353 TT Flight with four Vengeances and three Spitfires. It arrived on October 1 1945 and left in January 1946.

Yorks, Dakotas and Lancasters were amongst the aircraft handled by 22 MU after the war and in the late 1950s many Ansons were scrapped. Some scheduled services were operated by Manx Airlines with Bristol 170s in 1956. The airfield closed in 1960 but it is still used for private flying. Like all ASUs it was well equipped with hangars and all except the Robins have survived. There was a large network of frying-pan dispersals on the north side of the airfield and star-shaped multiple standings were constructed on the southern perimeter.

Sleap, Salop

SJ480265. Signposted off A5113, 2 miles N of Harmerhill

A temporary station if ever there was one, Sleap (pronounced Slape) was slow in completion but was destined to outlast most of its contemporaries and is still in use for flying to this day. It was intended as a satellite for Whitchurch Heath (Tilstock) and scheduled to be ready for occupation in August 1942 but this date proved to be optimistic. It opened on January 15 1943 under 93 Group Bomber Command but was still not suitable for flying until the following April when the Whitleys of 'C' Flight 81 OTU were transferred from the parent station. On April 5 two Lancasters returning from operations over Germany were grateful to

find it after widespread fog closed the East Anglian bases. In September a lost Fortress with 19 ferry pilots on board just scraped in with almost empty tanks, but the best days for diversions were to come in the winter of 1944. On November 16, 31 B-17s landed at Sleap on diversion from Molesworth, Grafton Underwood and Great Ashfield.

In the early hours of August 26 1943 a Whitley swung on landing and crashed into the control tower, killing the pilot and air bomber and seriously injuring the rest of the crew and some of the personnel on duty in the building. Temporary repairs were made and Flying Control was soon serviceable again. Unfortunately, a similar accident, two weeks later, involved another Whitley which swung on take-off and the pilot elected to try to climb away at a tangent to the flarepath instead of aborting. This time only the rear gunner survived and three airmen and WAAFs in the tower were killed also. The building

Below left *Sleap tower showing no evidence of damage.* **Bottom left** *Gemini G-AJWG in a Blister hangar at Sleap in 1964.* **Right** *Aztec and hut at Sleap.*

was subsequently repaired and there are no visible signs of these tragedies today.

On January 1 1944 the satellite and parent station were reassigned to 38 Group, Airborne Forces, with a new function to train crews for glider towing. As a Heavy Conversion Unit had just moved into Tilstock it was decided to base all 81 OTU's courses at Sleap and the newly acquired Horsa gliders were towed over here. There were dire warnings of the overheating problems that would occur when the ageing Whitleys began to tow gliders but the ground-crews maintained a relatively high rate of serviceability.

Sufficient expertise had been gained by April 1944 to enable a full-scale exercise to be held. Nine Whitley/Horsa combinations took off at 45-second intervals, made a short cross-country trip and mass-landed at Sleap, the aim of quick concentration on the ground being achieved.

December 1944 saw the OTU re-equipping with Wellingtons and Tilstock being brought into use again. The OTU was re-named 1380 TSCU, 'A' and 'B' Flights remaining at Sleap until the station closed on December 28 1945. It was, however, revived in 1958, after a long period of care and maintenance, as a satellite to Shawbury. The Central Navigation and Control School then used it for the training of RAF air traffic controllers. A GCA caravan was sited at Sleap for this purpose and the aerodrome was refurbished to make it suitable for touch and go landings by Vampires and Provosts.

The RAF finally gave up the airfield in 1964 and it has been used subsequently by the Shropshire Aero Club on a shared basis with a vehicle testing firm. Flying takes place during evenings and weekends, the runways and perimeter track being reserved for lorries on weekdays.

The airfield is very difficult to find, being almost two miles from the nearest main road along its own crumbling concrete roadway. The living sites are currently being bull-dozed and there is not much left on the flying field either, apart from the tower and a fire tender bay. Modern offices have been erected on the site of one of the hangars (there used to be a 'B1' and a 'T2') but one Blister has survived on the far side.

Speke, Merseyside

SJ415835. 7 miles SE of Liverpool city centre

Claimed as the fastest 'kill' of the Second World War but hard to prove, the destruction of a Ju 88 on October 8 1940 was achieved by three Hurricanes of 312 Squadron in less than eight minutes from take-off to touch-down. Its mission was to bomb the Rootes aircraft factory on the edge of Speke Airport but the fighters were scrambled just in time to send it down for a crash-landing at Bromborough on the opposite bank of the Mersey. The pilots were jubilant but sadly one of them, Sergeant O. Hanzlicek, was killed a few days later when he baled out too low after engine failure. The skeleton of his Hurricane, the first production aircraft L1547, can still be seen at low tide in the mud off runway 08.

Speke dates back to 1928 when Liverpool Corporation bought the Speke estate which consisted of about 2,200 acres. Of this, 400 acres were set aside for the development of an airport and in July 1930 it was granted a private civil licence. Imperial Airways began a regular service from Speke to Croydon via Manchester and Birmingham subsidised by the three provincial corporations. This experimental schedule was not a success and was discontinued after three months.

In 1931 Blackpool and West Coast Air Services inaugurated an unsubsidised Liverpool-Blackpool run and later extended it to the Isle of Man. An old farmhouse had become the terminal and control building, a hangar was erected nearby and farm buildings were employed as stores and workshops. Speke was made an airport in the true sense in 1933 when it was given a public-use licence and customs facilities were provided. The opening ceremony on July 1 was indeed a day to remember and the claims of 250 aircraft taking part and that it was the greatest air pageant ever held outside Hendon, were probably no exaggeration. Several of the RAF's display teams so well known at Hendon appeared, including 25 Squadron's 'Tied-Together Drill' with Hawker Furies and the Central Flying School's sustained inverted formation flying in five Avro Tutors.

In 1934 commercial air transport from Liverpool got itself on to a firm footing. KLM flew the first air mail from Speke to Amsterdam on August 13 in a Fokker F XVIII and Aer Lingus started a Dublin service with Dragons. Blackpool and West Coast had by now convinced the Post Office that their Isle of Man service was reliable and the latter agreed that the airline could carry the mail between the city and the island. This led to it becoming the first company to operate the four-engined DH Express airliner to the Isle of Man. Railway Air Services and Hillman Airways were amongst the other operators of this era and 1934 also saw the arrival of the Liverpool and District Aero Club which had flown previously from Hooton, across the Mersey, when this was the official airport for Liverpool.

The RAF came on the scene in May 1936 when 611 (West Lancashire) Squadron, which had formed at Hendon two months before, brought its Hawker Harts and Hinds to Speke. It started life as a light bomber squadron in the Auxiliary Air Force but converted to the fighter role on January 1 1939 and began to receive Spitfires in May, before leaving for its war station in August. Whilst at Speke, one of its aircraft was involved in a tragic accident when it collided on the ground with a Percival Mew Gull. The latter's pilot, who was fatally injured, was Campbell Black, the famous airman who had won the England to Australia MacRobertson Air Race.

Another celebrity who made a brief visit in July 1937 in his Miles Mohawk was Colonel Charles Lindbergh. The same year, two of his fellow countrymen, Richmond and Merill, had chosen Speke as the departure point for one of the first east-to-west transatlantic flights. Unfortunately they had so much fuel on board that the wheels of their single-engined Vultee monoplane sank into the grass and the tanks had to be drained before it could be dug out. It eventually took off light to Southport Sands, refuelled and set off to cross the Atlantic successfully.

Liverpool Corporation pursued a policy of improvement resulting in the airport being levelled and drained. This was done so well that in the extremely wet winter of 1935-36 when almost all the other airports in England were frequently closed, Speke stayed open. Hangar One and the distinctive control tower were built in 1937, the latter standing in solitary spendour until the terminal was finished in 1939, by which time the airport was the second busiest in the country.

War clouds were gathering and Speke now had a major role in aircraft production and, just as important, as a reception centre for combat aircraft from America. Rootes Securities opened a shadow factory in 1938 on the perimeter turning out Blenheims to an eventual total of 2,443. At the same time Lockheed set up a branch to assemble Hudsons shipped to Liverpool Docks. This facility was later to be known as No 1 Aircraft Assembly Unit.

The airport was requisitioned in September 1939 and was occupied by 24 Hampdens of 61 and 144 Squadrons under the Scatter Scheme to protect the bomber force from surprise attack. They did not stay long, however, and another brief detachment was made by seven Hudsons from 1 OTU at Silloth who operated from here for about four days in July 1940 while their base was unserviceable. Bombs were dropped on the night of September 16 resulting in four fatal casualties the next morning when the Royal Engineers were trying to defuse an unexploded one.

On June 17 1940 the Lysanders of 13 Squadron came to Speke from Hooton and, during the stay of about a month, flew regular dawn patrols along the Welsh coast looking out for saboteurs, enemy agents and signs of invasion. The local Liverpudlians made scathing remarks when the aircraft could be seen parked harmlessly on the ground after the air-raid siren had sounded. To help morale, the

Ju 88 of KG 806 lies in a field at Bromborough, Wirral, after a brief combat with Hurricanes of No 312 Squadron from Speke (via J. Molyneux).

pilots took off in formation apparently about to engage the enemy and flew out over the Irish Sea to await a radio recall when things had quietened down! The Lysander was no fighter but it was no use telling this to the long-suffering recipients of enemy bombs.

No 312 was based here soon after 13 Squadron left but, after its initial success described above, it went through a bad patch during which a Blenheim of 29 Squadron was shot down in mistake for a Ju 88. Two days later three pilots got lost and had to bale out before running out of fuel. On December 17 1940 the Czech President Benes inspected the squadron and its aircraft drawn up in front of the terminal building and, a month later, the Duke of Kent visited on one of his many tours of inspection to airfields all over the country.

More Hurricanes, this time from 229 Squadron, used Speke from December 1940 until May 1941 when they were sent to the Middle East. No 312 Squadron left for Valley in March 1941, being replaced by 315, a Polish squadron which had formed at Acklington not long before. It soon became operational and began convoy patrols over Liverpool Bay, its only combat being an indecisive one with a Ju 88 over North Wales. Accommodation was still sparse and the squadron's dispersed flights used aircraft packing cases as temporary offices. After 229 went to Northolt in July 1941, 303 Squadron's Spitfires were posted to Speke for a three-month respite after much action in fighter sweeps over the Channel. No 306 Squadron was the last fighter unit at Speke during the war, its Spitfires being here between October and December 1941.

The airport's proximity to the port of Liverpool was the reason for its selection as the base for one of the most unusual units in the history of the RAF, the Merchant Ship Fighter Unit. Until long-

Halifax BV DG249 ground-running outside Rootes, Speke, early in 1943 (via P. Summerton).

range aircraft like the Liberator were available to combat the menace of the prowling Focke-Wulf Condors, a stop-gap solution was required to protect the convoys. The answer was to catapult launch Hurricane aircraft from suitably-equipped merchant ships and after shooting down or driving off the attacker, the pilot would bale out and hopefully be picked up at once.

MSFU formed on May 5 1941 with an establishment of 56 Hurricanes, most being operational but some were to be retained for training. A catapult was positioned in front of Hangar Two and aimed towards the river, the first rocket launch taking place on July 6. By the time the unit disbanded on September 7 1943, 401 catapult launches had been made at Speke. Although some victories were achieved against the Condors, the unit's main function was one of deterrence, as the enemy could never be sure when a fighter might appear on their tail.

Another nautical connection was the use of the airport from October 1942 by a detachment of 776 Squadron, a Fleet Requirements Unit, which operated a mixed bunch of aircraft such as Chesa-peakes, Rocs, Skuas and Sea Hurricanes until the end of the war. A Seafire squadron, 736B, formed here on March 1 1945 but moved to Woodvale in July. For a brief period, too, the RAF had a few Blenheims and Lysanders based for searchlight and gunnery co-operation. This was the 9 Group AAC Flight which

formed on May 20 1941 and left in November to form the nucleus of 285 Squadron at Wrexham.

Rootes' first Halifax took to the air on March 15 1942, forerunner of 1,070 built at this factory. The firm went on to overhaul 2,690 USAAF fighters under contract to Lockheed. The latter was now assembling P-38 Lightnings which would soon be joined by P-47s and P-51s in large numbers. P-61 Black Widows were received in 1944, the first being issued direct to the IXth Air Force's 422nd Night Fighter Squadron at Scorton late in May. There were other less common types too; a peep through the railings on one occasion revealing a Sikorsky Kingfisher amphibian parked amongst hordes of Mustangs and Thunderbolts. One of the latter was involved in a collision over the Mersey with a Mosquito of 60 OTU. Eight feet of the Mosquito's wing was torn away but both aircraft managed to make emergency landings at Speke.

Control of the airport was transferred to the Directorate General of Civil Aviation on July 10 1944 and on November 13 the London-Liverpool air link which had been abandoned at the beginning of the war was revived by Railway Air Services with Dragon Rapides, government officials having priority for the available seats. The company had kept up services to the Isle of Man and Aer Lingus had done the same to Dublin. When the war ended the flow of new aircraft from the

Halifax BV DG404 just off the line at Speke early in 1943. It was delivered to No 1663 (H) CU on March 31 1943 and was destroyed in an accident on July 12 1943 (via P. Summerton).

Above *Dakotas of Aer Lingus and British European Airways in front of Speke's famous control tower in 1954.* **Below** *Speke before the new runway was built in the left foreground. The former Rootes factory in right foreground shows signs of wartime camouflage* (Liverpool Airport).

USA was reversed as hundreds of fighters passed through for preparation for the return voyage. Rows and rows of Thunderbolts and Mustangs made a fantastic sight in the bright colours of almost every combat group in the VIIIth and IXth Air Forces.

Suddenly all the frenzied activity of the war years was over and Speke was left to the spasmodic services run by British European Airways and Aer Lingus and the Spitfires of 611 Squadron which reformed at its old base on May 10 1946 but soon moved to Woodvale. In the 1950s Airwork had a maintenance base here overhauling Vampires and Sabres for the RAF and NATO, and Starways,

Liverpool's own airline, operated many schedules with DC-3s, DC-4s and Viscounts.

The centre of commercial aviation in the North-west gradually shifted to Manchester's Ringway Airport and, by the time Liverpool Corporation took Speke over from the government in January 1961, the initiative was lost. Attempts were made to improve the situation, the main runway being extended, but the most significant decision was to construct an entirely new runway on land to the south of the existing airfield. The latter may well be used for building development if and when a projected terminal is built beside the new runway.

Squires Gate, Lancashire

SD320315. Southern outskirts of Blackpool

Going back to the early days Squires Gate was the scene of a famous flying meeting in October 1909, organised by Lord Northcliffe of the *Daily Mail,* which gives the airport a longer history than any other in Britain. Several hundred thousand people, an unprecedented number in those days for *any* event, flocked to see a whole week of flying demonstrations and competitions.

The site became a modest airfield immediately after the First World War and in 1933 Blackpool and West Coast Air Services started a Dragon service to the Isle of Man and one with Fox Moths to Liverpool. A couple of DH 86s were purchased in 1936 but the following year the scheduled flights were transferred to Stanley Park, the municipal airport to the north-east of the town. When war came the Air Ministry looked at the coastal location of Squires Gate with its good approaches and flat surrounding country and decided that it would make a good base for a Coastal Command training unit.

Before work commenced detachments of several RAF squadrons used the airfield under the Scatter Scheme. 'C' Flight of 63 Squadron flew some Fairey Battles in during September 1939, 75 Squadron's 'A' Flight brought some Wellingtons the following months, and in November Wellingtons of 215 Squadron

came and stayed until January 1940. After this three runways were built and four Bellmans erected, the airfield becoming operational on December 1 1940.

The MAP built a shadow factory on the edge of the airfield for Wellington production, the first aircraft being rolled-out in September 1940. The plant was a complete duplicate of the parent factory at Weybridge in Surrey which was too vulnerable to air attack. A secondary assembly line was set up at the pre-war Stanley Park aerodrome which now housed a School of Technical Training. By the time production was wound up in October 1945, 2,584 Wellingtons had been built at Blackpool.

No 3 School of General Reconnaissance opened on December 16 1940 equipped with Bothas but, at the same time, the airfield became a major part of Lancashire's air defences. That there were only four aircraft is indicative of how basic these were. No 96 Squadron at Cranage detached four Hurricanes and ground crew on December 21. The next night Flying Officer P.W. Rabone in V6887 was patrolling the coast between Formby and Blackpool at 14,000 ft when he sighted an enemy aircraft. Closing to 50 yards he opened fire, and smoke and flames were seen from the bomber as it dived away. Claimed as a 'probable' this was encouraging and the rest of 'A' Flight were detached to Squires Gate early in January 1941.

No 307 Squadron's Defiants were also based here between January and March

Ceremony held at Squires Gate on October 8 1943 when three Spitfires were 'presented' to the RAF by the Lancashire County Constabulary. MH819 'Red Rose III' in foreground. Note hangar painted to resemble nearby suburban housing (Public Record Office).

Bristol Wayfarer G-AIFM on the apron at Squires Gate, October 29 1960.

1941, their first combat being with an He 111 damaged over North Wales on March 12. They were relieved by 256 Squadron which was just in time to face the height of the Blitz against Merseyside. On April 7 1941 Flight Lieutenant D.R. West shot down a Ju 88 off Southport, but the most successful night was May 7 when three He 111s were destroyed, and two damaged, as well as two Ju 88s damaged.

Enemy retribution was small and probably quite by chance, the airfield being hit by bombs on three occasions in May 1941. The only damage done was to a parked Liberator. Enemy activity decreased in the summer of 1941 and it was October before 256 claimed another victory, a Ju 88. The squadron then converted to Defiant IIs but saw no action with these before it left for Woodvale.

The night fighters had all the glory at this time but Squires Gate was occupied also by a Flight of Hurricanes from 312 Squadron which had formed at Speke in September 1940. A Polish Squadron, 308, had formed here on September 9 1940 but was still waiting for its Hurricanes when it moved to Speke a few weeks later. Also here, but not for very long, was 'R' Flight of 1 AACU equipped with Henleys and Defiants. It moved to Millom on September 13 1941.

Squires Gate had a fleeting contact with two famous personalities. One was Amy Mollison, better known as Amy Johnson, who took off from here into a grey sky on January 7 1941. Her destination was Kidlington but somewhere along the way she got lost above cloud and although her Oxford was seen to crash in the Thames Estuary, her body was never recovered. The other was Squadron Leader J.D. Nettleton who diverted here in the early hours of August 18 1942 after leading six Lancasters of 44 Squadron against a target at Augsburg. His aircraft was the sole survivor and Nettleton was later awarded the Victoria Cross for his courage on this daylight raid.

No 3 SGR, which had long since given up its Bothas for Ansons, was joined by more Ansons of the School of ASR, the latter being present in mid-1944. The airfield was shared between these units and Wellington test flying until the summer of 1945. The following year the airfield was taken over by the MTCA and later passed to Blackpool Corporation.

Having been used for storage since the end of Wellington production, the aircraft factory was reopened in 1951 for the building of Hawker Hunters. A new 2,000 yard runway was constructed and a labour force of over 5,000 was recruited. Hawker Sea Furies were also refurbished including some for the West German Government as target tugs.

Blackpool Airport, as it is now known, is certainly the busiest general aviation airfield in the North of England. Scheduled air services have also been run through here for many years, the most popular being the Isle of Man route. The buildings have not changed much since the war and the original control tower is still in use, although heavily modified.

Stormy Down, South Glamorgan

SS840795, 2 miles NE of Porthcawl

Day after day people living on the coast of South Wales got used to the rattle of gunfire as young air-gunners learned their trade. The targets were sleeves towed by Miles Martinets, the aggressors were Ansons. They flew from a small grass airfield with a dramatic name by the side of the main road to Porthcawl.

It was the home of 7 Bombing and Gunnery School, later becoming 7 Air Gunners School, which started off with Whitleys and Fairey Battles in 1939 but replaced both in 1942 with Ansons, Defiants and Lysanders because of difficulties in obtaining spare parts. It was intended to use the Ansons for familiarising air-gunners with night flying as well but the airfield needed some improvements first. The surface was subject to subsidence owing to broken rock beneath it which allowed water to collect and overflow after heavy rain. Soil was washed out which created hidden cavities causing the surface to cave in when a heavy weight passed over it. Several aircraft, including a Lysander, were damaged in this way.

Unlike most aerodromes in South Wales it was built before the war as 9 Armament Training Station, being renamed 7 Air Observers School on September 1 1939 and then 7 B & GS, two months later. Its original name, Porthcawl, was dropped in favour of Stormy Down early in 1940.

During the opening stages of the Battle of Britain no fighters could be spared to defend South Wales and raids on the area were virtually unopposed. On one occasion the Officer Commanding Flying at Stormy Down, the redoubtable First World War ace Wing Commander Ira 'Taffy' Jones, chased a Ju 88 over Swansea in an unarmed Hawker Henley. Diving out of the sun to within a hundred yards of the raider he fired his only weapon, a Very pistol, and frightened the German pilot into running for cloud cover. Jones pursued him past Mumbles Head but the gunner fired back and holed the Henley's wing. Jones decided it was prudent to return to base at this point but was pleased with his performance in the defence of his native land.

The dull routine of target-towing was occasionally brightened by flying displays over South Wales towns in aid of their Wings For Victory Weeks. On April 3 1943 nine Lysanders performed over Mountain Ash and on May 15 four Martinets showed themselves to the Rhondda. One of the few remaining Whitleys on strength by this time was loaned with a pilot to Fairwood Common to give air experience to ATC cadets.

The war seemed far away and the only threat came from one of our own barrage balloons which broke away from its moorings at Port Talbot and landed partly-deflated on the airfield boundary.

Wallace K3907 of No 9 ATS at Stormy Down (Neville Franklin Collection).

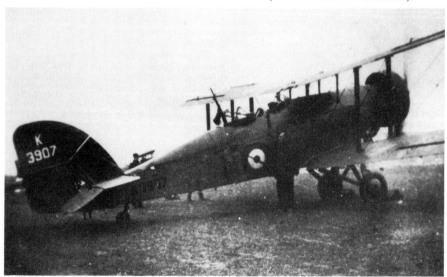

'VR' hangar at Stormy Down (A.J. Ayers).

A moment of drama occurred on May 30 1943 when the Royal Navy at Cardiff passed on a sighting report of an enemy submarine six miles west of the Scarweather Lightship. An Anson searched the area methodically for an hour but failed to locate anything. Perhaps it was just as well as its only armament was a couple of .303 machine-guns.

In November 1943 a cine-gun flight was formed with Martinets so that the correct method of carrying out curve-of-pursuit attacks on the Ansons could be learned. At the same time two Piper Cubs of the US Army were attached to the station for hangarage and maintenance whilst operating from a landing ground at Porthcawl where a US Infantry Brigade had its HQ. The following month Stormy Down fell into line with the new flying control standardisation which required a runway caravan equipped with r/t. Owing to the convex surface of the aerodrome, it was also necessary to position a look-out on the watch tower in r/t contact to report traffic not visible from the vehicle.

In January 1944 a Wellington Flight of two aircraft was posted in for a five-week trial to ascertain whether this type was more efficient than the Anson for air-gunner training. Unfortunately the airfield became unserviceable and the Wellingtons were sent to the runway aerodrome at Llandow accompanied by a Martinet Flight from 7 AGS.

Flying was seriously affected by the state of the ground so the construction of a permanent east-west runway was suggested. On February 8 1944, 7 AGS took over RAF Rhoose as a satellite for a period of three months so that the training commitment could be fulfilled. Rhoose was soon occupied by 23 Ansons, 20 Martinets and 50 pilots, leaving Stormy Down open only to essential visitors and unit aircraft returning for major and minor inspections. The request for a concrete runway was refused but the field was levelled and drained and a PSP strip was laid instead, as well as some new hard-standings. Landing was tricky with all this work in progress and a USAAF Cessna Crane 43-31816 was damaged when it overshot into a mound of earth. Shortly afterwards a Beaufighter crash-landed after undershooting a slow approach into the small field in a gusty wind.

On August 2 1944 all the aircraft were ferried back from Rhoose but 7 AGS had barely settled in again when it was disbanded on August 21 1944. Air-gunner courses to a total of 140 had passed through its life span but there was now a surplus of trained men. The vacant accommodation was filled by 40 Initial Training Wing which moved from Newton in Nottinghamshire on September 1 1944. It was a ground organisation specialising in the training of French airmen but it too stood-down on November 27 1944. The airfield closed in the summer of 1945 but it has been used since for civilian gliding. The buildings are now used as a Rehabilitation Centre by the local employment office.

Stretton, Cheshire

SJ650835. 1 mile W of M6/M56 intersection

Sunday mornings on Merseyside in the mid-1950s were often livened up by a sound which was straight out of the Pacific War—the drone of Grumman Avenger torpedo-bombers in formation. I once saw five of them together and the noise was most impressive, aeroplanes just do not sound like that any more! They came from 1841 Squadron at Stretton which was also the base for the Attackers, Sea Furies, Sea Hawks and Fireflies which were a common sight at that time.

It was a naval air station throughout its career but this thought was farthest from the planners' minds when they selected the site. A runway airfield was needed for fighters defending Manchester and Liverpool, the grass aerodrome at Cranage being only a temporary stop-gap. After the May Blitz of 1941 most of the German bomber units went east to support the invasion of Russia and the new airfield was loaned to the Admiralty as soon as it was completed.

Commissioned on June 1 1942 as HMS *Blackcap* it was conveniently near to the port of Liverpool so that aircraft could be flown directly from carrier to shore station and vice versa for re-equipment or working-up. About 40 squadrons were

here for short periods, the first being 897 which formed on August 1 1942 with six Seafires.

Stretton acted also as an Air Yard, roughly the equivalent of an RAF MU, in that new aircraft were delivered from the manufacturer, modified where necessary and allocated to operational squadrons whose pilots came to collect them. No 827 Squadron for example flew its Albacores in from Macrihanish on January 10 1943 and re-armed with 12 Barracudas. No 897 exchanged its Fulmars for Seafires in the spring of 1943 and 810 gave up its Swordfish in favour of Barracudas before re-embarking on HMS *Illustrious* on June 8 1943.

One arrival late in 1943 was 1833 Squadron, FAA, immortalised in the late Norman Hanson's moving wartime autobiography *Carrier Pilot* (also published by Patrick Stephens). After training on Corsairs at Quonset Point, Rhode Island, Hanson's squadron shipped aboard HMS *Trumpeter* to Belfast, whence they flew to Stretton. Or some of them did. One pilot made a forced landing on the beach outside the Royal Liverpool Golf Course at Hoylake. But Sub-Lieutenant Reggie Shaw simply got lost. 'At long last he saw an airfield and promptly landed. He taxied over to the tower where a young RAF airman ran down the outside stairs to greet him.

"Where am I?" Shaw from the cockpit.

"Weer are yer?" said the boy, fairly open-mouthed. He came from Manchester and had never heard of anyone being lost within ten miles of that northern metropolis. "Yer at Ringway, of course!"

'Reg was a South London boy and Ringway might just as well have been in enemy territory.

"Where's Ringway?" he retorted, rather testily.

"Weer's *Ringway?*" What on earth was going on? "It's Manchester, of course, that's weer!"

"Then where's Stretton?"

"Weer's Stretton? Stretton's ower

Left *Wildcats and a Callender-Hamilton hangar at Stretton in April 1945, with the air yard in the background (FAA Museum).* **Above right** *Wildcats at Stretton on April 18 1945 (FAA Museum).* **Right** *Stretton on April 18 1945 again with Harvards, Corsairs, Ansons, Barracudas and others lined up (FAA Museum).*

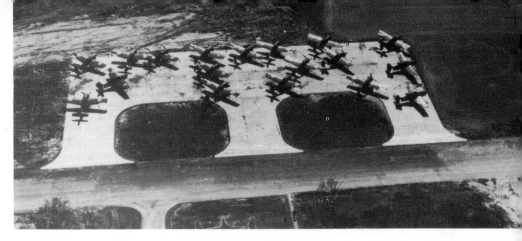

theer!'' said the lad, holding out his arm at full stretch and pointing.

"Good lad," said Reg. "Now, get off the wing, keep pointing towards Stretton and don't move until I fly over you!"

'So Shaw brought his Corsair to Stretton.'

The Fairey Aviation Company had an out-station on the north-east corner of the airfield for Barracuda preparation, consisting of two 'A1' hangars which can still be seen today. The Navy's own facilities were improved in the autumn of 1944 when an Aircraft Repair Yard was completed half a mile to the north and connected to the airfield by a taxi-way. The Yard had four Pentads and seven of the small Admiralty 'S' Sheds, the latter designed to house aircraft with folded wings. A practice bombing range was now available at Budworth Mere near Northwich. Amidst all this activity Air Training Corps gliding was done, the aircraft being kept in a Blister hangar.

The airfield was by now an odd mixture of RAF and Royal Navy style buildings because of its Air Ministry origins. The Air Force ancestry showed in the three runways rather than the narrower four which the Navy would no doubt have laid down, the five double dispersal pens, the two-storey control tower and the Callender-Hamilton hangar on the western perimeter. All the other hangars were Pentads, 'S' Types and the curious Fromsons which doubled as gun testing butts.

Photographs taken in April 1945 show the variety of aircraft to be seen at Stretton in those days. There was, of course, no

Stretton tower betrays the airfield's RAF origins (A.P. Ferguson).

attempt at dispersal that late in the war and they are parked in rows or just untidy conglomerations all over the airfield. Eighteen Wildcats rub shoulders on one parking apron, 19 Corsairs decorate the southern hedge, 14 Harvards line up beside the runway, a neat row of Barracudas with folded wings, the list is almost endless. In all, about 150 aeroplanes can be made out, and there were many more in 1946 when surplus aircraft were flown in for storage or breaking up. A unit known as Ferry Squadron 2 was in residence then and handled most of the deliveries.

Early in 1947 807 Squadron arrived with Seafire 17s, embarked on HMS *Theseus* on June 27 and then returned to Stretton on July 17 1947. Re-equipment with Sea Furies followed before it went back aboard the *Theseus* in August. A Firebrand squadron, 813, disembarked from HMS *Indomitable* on July 25 1951, flying to Lee-on-Solent a few days later. Carrying on the wartime use of Stretton for converting squadrons into new types of aircraft, 767 Squadron re-formed on September 20 1954 with Vampire 22s and Sea Hawks and stayed for nearly a year.

Post-war Stretton is remembered chiefly for its reserve squadrons which made up the Northern Air Division of the Royal Navy Volunteer Reserve. The first was 1831 Squadron which formed officially on June 1 1947 with six Seafire 17s and one Harvard for dual instruction. Sea Furies replaced the Seafires in August 1951 and were themselves ousted by Supermarine Attackers in the summer of

1955. I well remember watching six of these jets practising peel-offs in true World War 2 style over the Dee Estuary as the squadron became acquainted with its new aeroplanes.

A new reserve anti-submarine squadron, 1841, formed at Stretton in July 1952 with Firefly AS 6s. The Fireflies were phased out late in 1955 in favour of Avengers, another obsolescent aircraft but still potent nevertheless. The NAD was disbanded on March 10 1957, a victim of defence economies which plague us to this day, and the 'ST' tail codes were seen no more.

The airfield remained active, having carried on its original function as a holding station with large storage capacity. It was responsible for the disposal of many hundreds of Royal Navy aircraft of all types and in the mid-1950s rows of cocooned Seafires could be seen. It served also as an Engine Holding Unit with storage facilities at RNAS Burscough and as a Receipt and Dispatch Unit handling about one-third of all aircraft required by the Navy. A Mobile Aircraft Repair Unit was also based here. The last aircraft was flown out in August 1958 and earlier in the year the station's last squadron, 728B, had re-formed with Firefly and Meteor target drones prior to a move to Malta on February 26.

The airfield was used spasmodically by private aircraft in the 1960s but it is now bisected by the M56 motorway which approximately follows the line of the east-west runway which had been lengthened to take jets. One of the last visitors was a

Sea Hornet at Stretton Navy Day display in 1955 (via S.G. Jones).

US Army Otter whose pilot thought erroneously that he had landed at Burtonwood!

Talbenny, Dyfed

SM835110. Off B4327, 4 miles NW of Milford Haven

Talbenny was a bleak airfield overlooking St Bride's Bay, having three runways with a central intersection, two 'T2' hangars and 36 frying-pan hard-standings. Its radio call-sign was, appropriately, 'Blue Sea'. Later in the war when it became a Transport Command base some concrete aprons were added to accommodate an additional 22 aircraft.

It started life on May 1 1942 as a Coastal Command station in 19 Group using Dale as a satellite. The Wellingtons

of 311 (Czech) Squadron arrived on June 12 and the satellite was occupied simultaneously by 304 (Polish) Squadron. Both units were intended for anti-submarine patrols in the Bay of Biscay but it was not until August 6 1942 that a Talbenny aircraft, 'P' of 311 Squadron, sighted and attacked a U-boat, although its destruction was unconfirmed. Late in August the second anniversary of the formation of 311 Squadron was marked with an inspection by the Czech Minister of National Defence Mr Masaryk, the Foreign Minister and the Czech Deputy Prime Minister.

A high-level attack was mounted against an *Altmark*-type tanker in La Pallice

Talbenny in June 1945.

harbour on August 25 by all available aircraft of 304 and 311 Squadrons, all of which returned safely. In September 'A' of 311 Squadron was engaged by two Arado 196 floatplanes and limped back to Talbenny with a wounded rear gunner. Some fighter cover was obviously desirable and detachments of 235 and 248 Squadrons equipped with Beaufighters were based to escort the Wellingtons whose further exploits included a shipping strike off the Gironde Estuary in November. At the end of March 1943 the Wellington squadrons left Talbenny and Dale, being replaced by 303 Ferry Training Unit which flew its Wellingtons down from Stornoway. This unit's task was the preparation of aircraft for overseas ferrying and the briefing of the crews on the routes. Courses were brief and there was a fast turn-over of aircraft, the Wellingtons being joined by Warwicks and Venturas as time went on.

On October 11 1943 the airfield was transferred from Coastal to Transport Command but 4 Armament Practice Camp stayed on as a lodger unit. The APC was controlled by 19 Group and gave training in anti-submarine bombing, air-to-air and air-to-sea firing. As well as Hudson and Halifax squadrons, practice was given to Liberators of the US Navy's Fleet Air Wing 7 based at Dunkeswell in Devon. Talbenny had a secondary role as a weather diversion owing to its favourable position out on the south-western tip of Wales. Notable visitors included some USAAF Liberators on January 17 1943, a C-47, 42-100514, from Marrakesh on December 12 1943, BOAC

Huts on the skyline at Talbenny (A.J. Ayers).

Liberator G-AGFO on January 15 1944 and on the following day a B-17 from a US weather squadron based at Watton in Norfolk.

No 303 FTU dispatched 101 Wellingtons in March 1944 and was joined by 3 OADU which moved in from Hurn on July 26 1944. The latter's function was taken over by 11 Ferry Unit on September 8 1944, formed to collect replacement aircraft from Aircraft Preparation Units and send them overseas. It also made sure that the crews were conversant with the demands of ferrying and converted them to other types of aircraft where necessary. Wellingtons and Warwicks were still the major types passing through with Ansons and Spitfires being added later. In August 1945, 11 FU was sent to Dunkeswell and Talbenny was reduced to care and maintenance under Pembroke Dock, only to be abandoned on December 23 1946. Like many of the aerodromes in South Wales it has been cleared of all buildings and presents a picture of flat desolation. Indeed an airfield as transitory as the crews who once used it.

Tatenhill, Staffordshire

SK160240. On B5234, 4 miles W of Burton-on-Trent

Best described as the aerodrome no one wanted, its war was spent as RLG for a number of Midlands training units. Tatenhill had the last laugh though because it continued to operate aeroplanes long after its contemporaries were ploughed-up and still does now. Being the nearest airfield to Burton-on-Trent, centre of the English brewing industry, it was the obvious choice from which to operate a succession of business aircraft,

the latest of which is the Beech Super King-Air G-BCUZ. A Cessna Citation executive jet visited recently and crop-spraying aircraft are often seen here too.

These modern aircraft look very out of place amidst the fenced-off runways and crumbling wartime buildings. The King-Air is kept at one end of the east-west runway in a post-war hangar which resembles a cut-down 'T2' and there is a small control tower attached. The original hangars, a 'T2' and two Blisters, have gone but the old watch tower still stands in good condition a few hundred yards from its modern replacement. It is one of the small satellite types with four windows at the front, all very small to facilitate blacking-out. The upstairs control room retains its wooden floor and some of the internal doors are left, although all the inscriptions are now illegible. A small concrete block-house with no windows stands just behind it, once the 'speech broadcasting station'.

Built in 1941 in picturesque rolling countryside, it was intended as a satellite for 27 OTU who flew Wellingtons from Lichfield on night-bomber training. This it became on November 2 1941, one of the OTU's Flights being detached here. There is also some evidence that it was used by 16 EFTS as an RLG for Burnaston during 1941, until Abbots Bromley became available, although this seems doubtful if construction was in progress.

The airfield was provided with a bomb dump on the south-east side and a number of frying pan dispersals were built on land to the north of the B5234 road, the hangars being situated in this area too. However, Tatenhill was found wanting and considered unsuitable for Wellingtons. It was only used until the larger aerodrome at Church Broughton was completed in October 1942 and was then left under a care and maintenance party. All flying facilities were retained and were used again on November 7 1942 when the station was loaned to Flying Training Command for 15 (P) AFU. This was an Oxford-equipped unit which was forced to use satellites literally all over the country after being displaced from its HQ at Leconfield to Andover for operational reasons.

Tatenhill was next allocated to 5 (P) AFU at Tern Hill as a satellite for single-engined training. The Oxfords of the 15 (P) AFU detachment were to go to Grove in Berkshire. Indicative of the 'musical chairs' situation often prevailing in wartime airfield allocations, it was necessary to move the Heavy Glider Conversion Unit operating from Grove to Brize Norton as soon as possible. When the former station was vacated Tatenhill's Oxfords could go there, leaving room for the Miles Masters. This complicated re-shuffle was achieved by May 4 1943 and 'E' Flight of 5 (P) AFU started flying from Tatenhill, specialising in navigation and night training. This went on until January 28 1944 when the airfield was transferred to the control of 21 (P) AFU and Oxfords reappeared in the circuit.

One of these Oxfords was destroyed in a spectacular crash on August 17 when EB731's trainee pilot failed to notice an aircraft below him on the approach. The runway controller fired a red Very light to warn him, whereupon he turned steeply to starboard and lost control. A wingtip struck the ground rolling the aircraft over and the pilot was very lucky to escape with minor injuries.

On November 22 1944 the surrounding countryside was split by a mighty explosion, said to have been the biggest blast ever heard in the British Isles. The underground bomb-store used by 21 MU at Fauld, only three miles to the north of Tatenhill, had blown up with much loss of life and the huge overgrown crater can still be seen. No 21 MU now had to find a new base and eventually took over Tatenhill, the 21 (P) AFU aircraft moving to Seighford on January 26 1945.

The RAF School of Explosives was also here from October 1945 until January 1947. The airfield was sold in the 1950s and the land between the runways has been cultivated. Many of the buildings near the tower have been converted into chicken houses but the dome-shaped astro trainer on this site has been demolished.

Tatton Park, Cheshire

SJ755825. 1 mile N of Knutsford

From September 1940 to March 27 1946 a total of 425,636 live parachute jumps were made here. Nearby Ringway was too busy so, with the permission of Lord Egerton, a Dropping Zone was established in the park. The aircraft took off and landed at Ringway but occasionally the park itself was used by the Whitleys of the Parachute Training School.

The first experiment took place on July 11 1940 when six dummies were dropped from a Whitley. Human descents then started but a parachute failed on July 25, resulting in the first fatality and training was temporarily suspended. As well as Servicemen the School trained Special Operations Executive agents in the art of dropping at night, the mode of arrival they would use in Occupied Europe. Another more minor job was to give pilots of the Merchant Ship Fighter Unit at Speke the experience of a parachute jump to prepare them for when they might have to abandon a Hurricane over the sea. More details of the PTS syllabus can be found in the section on Ringway.

Tatton Park became 13 SLG on August 6 1941 on which date a few Lysanders were dispersed here from the parent 48 MU at Hawarden. Progress by the contractors in opening up the SLG to take its full capacity of aircraft was slow and it was to be March of the following year before adequate space was available. Bothas and Wellingtons were the most numerous types to be seen here, 35 of the latter being present in May 1942. From October 1942 51 MU at Lichfield also used the park for aircraft dispersal.

The landing ground was in the northern portion of the park to the north-east of Tatton Hall and covered about one-sixth of the total area of the grounds. The joint use as a DZ for the PTS was undesirable and 48 MU had to give up the SLG in May 1943 after which it was used solely to cope with the great increase in parachuting. No 1 PTS moved to Upper Heyford on March 28 1946 on a note of disappointment. The instructional staff had intended to make a final descent on March 14 in front of the

Wartime taxiway at Tatton Park connecting landing ground and dispersal park (B.H. Abraham).

press and Gaumont-British News cameras but the drop had to be cancelled owing to bad weather.

Some wartime buildings remain in the park which is open to the public. The aircraft were dispersed to the south of the Hall and a stream had to be bridged so that they could be towed across it from the runway. There are also traces of a small taxi-way still to be seen.

Teddesley Park, Staffordshire

SJ945160. On unclassified road, 2 miles NE of Penkridge

This was another of the SLGs laid out in parkland to the dismay of the owner of the adjacent stately home. Compensation was paid for the trees which had to be cut down to make room for the usual pair of 800-yard runways, but the pruning was kept to a minimum so as to preserve the natural camouflage.

Opening as 48 SLG in July 1941, it was parented by 29 MU at High Ercall and was used for the storage of the many types for which this unit was responsible. In 1944 a visit revealed many old warriors picketed amongst the trees. Twelve Venturas quietly dripped oil including YH-G: AE736 of 21 Squadron with 15 bombing raids recorded on her nose and YH-J: AE699 which is believed to have flown the record number of sorties for the type—39. Her first took place on November 6 1942 and the last on September 9 1943 against Boulogne. Three early Hudsons with 'P' and 'T' prefixed serial numbers were in evidence alongside some later marks such as AM585 which had the silhouettes of two sinking U-boats painted on her nose. A rare Brewster Bermuda, FF580, was to

be seen near the pair of Grumman Avengers.

Many Hotspur gliders were held in 1945, the last remaining 24 being offered for sale in December of that year. It is not known if any were disposed of in this way, most probably they were broken up and burned. After this the site was closed and restored to something approaching its original condition. Many sections of SMT from the runways were sold to the landowner and some pieces can still be seen fencing the neighbouring fields. The line of the landing strips is just discernible but a few yards of wartime brick wall is all that is left of the SLG.

Templeton, Dyfed

SN100110. On A4115, 1 mile W of Templeton village

Now entirely cleared apart from sections of the old runways, this station's history was not outstanding. It was built in 1942/43 as a satellite to Haverfordwest, and was first occupied on January 7 1943 when 306 Ferry Training Unit formed here. This FTU was intended to train Beaufort crews in long distance flying but it was February 24 before the first aircraft arrived, an early Beaufort Mk 1 for hack duty. In March the unit began to receive new Beauforts direct from 2 Overseas Aircraft Preparation Unit at Filton and, on April 13, the first two aircraft and complete crews left for Portreath and the trip overseas. The FTU was just beginning to function smoothly when it was transferred to Maghaberry in Northern Ireland, leaving Templeton on June 15 1943.

It was replaced by 'O' Flight's Ansons

from 3 OTU at Haverfordwest. This was a Coastal Command unit training crews on the heavier types of aircraft, including Wellingtons and Whitleys. On December 8 1943 the Ansons were transferred to 12 Radio School at St Athan and, in January 1944, the satellite was given up when 3 OTU disbanded and was absorbed by 6 OTU at Silloth.

The airfield was idle for some months until 595 Squadron, which was based at Aberporth, received permission to tow the new winged glider targets from its runways. On August 17 1944 the first target was towed off by a Martinet but crashed on landing. Spitfires were found to be much more suitable for the job than the slower Miles type and most of the subsequent sorties from here were done by them.

The landing procedure necessitated a 'talk down' by an experienced pilot positioned to one side of the runway with a radio set. The tug aircraft approached at 115 knots down to 400 ft over the runway threshold, the pilot, of course, not being able to see the glider behind him which would now be at about 70 ft. When told it was down to about 30 ft he would start increasing power and, with the target at about ten ft, go into a steep climb without gaining speed. The glider should then touch down and the tug pilot would immediately release his cable when instructed from the ground.

When 8 OTU moved into Haverfordwest during the first week of January 1945, with its Spitfires and Mosquitoes, 'A' Flight was detached to Templeton but

Butts at Templeton (A.J. Ayers).

only stayed until February 27 when the bigger airfield at Brawdy became available. Templeton was now occupied solely by a small engineering section which repaired aircraft for the OTU in the single 'T2' hangar. When 8 OTU left Haverfordwest for Benson in June 1945, Templeton was closed and there is little to show that it was once an airfield, apart from a few huts and the old firing butts.

Tern Hill, Salop

SJ645310. On A41, 1 mile S of junction with A53

With its main buildings perched on a wooded hillside overlooking the aerodrome, this is one of the most picturesque of all RAF stations and also one of the oldest. It owes its situation to Major Atcherley, father of the famous brothers who were to play such a prominent part in the history of the RAF. Major Atcherley force-landed at Tern Hill in a hot-air balloon in 1906 and suggested its potential to the War Office.

Many other airfields originated in the same haphazard way and, when war came, some of the sites were requisitioned and developed. This is what happened here and from late 1916 Training Squadrons with Avro 504s and Sopwith Camels became established. Tern Hill was 13 Training Depot Station by the time the war ended, but soon disbanded. It was intended to be kept as a permanent station

in 1919 but the RAF could find no further use for it and it was sold off in 1922 for use as a race horse stable.

The Expansion plans of 1934 resulted in the survey of many former First World War aerodromes for redevelopment. Tern Hill was one which met the requirements, being free of power cables and obstructions and still in the ownership of one man, so it was requisitioned in 1935 and reconstruction was started. Hundreds of rabbit warrens were removed in record time, the ground levelled, drained and re-seeded for the official opening on January 1 1936 for use by 10 FTS. The school's initial equipment comprised Hart, Audax and Tutor aircraft for the advanced training of pilots who had gained their wings at an E & RFTS. Flying training began on February 3 1936 and was destined to continue unbroken in various forms until 1976.

There was room, too, for an MU and the contractors built two 'D'-type and one 'C'-type hangars on the south-east side of the airfield, as well as the three 'C'-types on the main site. Three dispersal sites were provided with two Lamella hangars on each. Conditions were chaotic for the first year with all this building work going on and men had to sleep in hangars until their accommodation was available.

No 4 ASU opened on the still unfinished MU site on June 1 1937 for the handling and storage of Lysanders, Wellingtons and Swordfish. By September

Test pilots and officers of No 24 MU Tern Hill in front of Lancaster I R5491, the first local rebuild of this type. It was destined to be written off on May 28 1943 whilst in use by No 1656 (H) CU (A.S.C. Lumsden).

1939 it had been renamed 24 MU and had 354 aircraft of 26 different types on charge. Congestion was increased by the temporary dispersal of the Whitleys of 10 and 78 Squadrons under the Scatter Scheme.

No 10 FTS, meanwhile, had replaced its biplanes with Oxfords and Harvards, many of which were destroyed on October 16 1940 when a single Ju 88 attacked the station. Four 250 kg bombs and several containers of incendiaries were dropped, hitting one of the 'C' hangars. Two Blenheims and 20 training aircraft were written off and the building was so badly damaged that it had to be demolished. The offices originally along the sides were retained and it has been known ever since as the 'Sunshine Hangar'. A Bellman was erected alongside as a replacement and still stands today.

Things were not all one-sided, however, as a 9 Group Sector Station had been opened at Tern Hill in August 1940 to cover the gap in the defences of the industrial North-West. No 29 Squadron at Digby sent over two, and later four, Blenheims each night for defence and, at the same time, 611 Squadron detached a flight of Spitfires here for daylight patrols.

The first success against the Luftwaffe was scored on the night of August 18 1940 when Pilot Officer R.A. Rhodes and Sergeant Gregory patrolling in a Blenheim spotted a He 111 south-west of Chester and stalked it for two hours. About 25 miles off Spurn Head they managed to get within range and shot it down into the sea. Further results came on November 11 when 611 Squadron shot down two Do

17s and claimed two 'probables' and one damaged during an interception over North Wales. The Spitfires were withdrawn to Digby and replaced by 306 Squadron from Church Fenton with Hurricanes.

During November 1940 No 10 FTS moved to make way for 5 FTS which brought its Masters from Sealand, but the bad weather flooded the grass airfield for weeks on end. A partial solution was to detach Flights to airfields with runways, but it was October 1941 before runway construction was started at Tern Hill.

A succession of fighter squadrons were based in 1941 and all flew many sector patrols but never made contact with the enemy. One of them, 403, arrived from Baginton in May with Tomahawks and Spitfires but soon gave up the American type before going to Hornchurch in August. The last fighter squadron to be based was 131 which moved to Atcham in September.

On April 13 1942 No 5 FTS was re-designated 5 (P) AFU and Hurricanes were received to supplement the Masters. By mid-1943 the former had gone but the unit had an enormous establishment of 145 Masters divided into ten Flights. These were detached to the various temporary satellites, Tatenhill, Condover, Bratton and Calveley being employed when available, in addition to the permanent satellite at Chetwynd. Also

Spitfire AD137, the first to be rebuilt at No 24 MU, Tern Hill, early in 1943 (A.S.C. Lumsden).

Meteor WF791 of the CFS in front of a 'C' Type hangar at Tern Hill.

housed were the taxi aircraft of 25 Group Communications Flight.

April 1942 saw 24 MU transferred to 43 Group with its new task being the repair of Lancasters and Spitfires. At the end of the year the MU was turning out ten of each type per month and its workshops were capable of replacing almost any component and of overhauling all the equipment installed in both types. Spitfire repair was transferred elsewhere in the middle of 1944 and 24 MU then concentrated on Lancasters until November 1945 when Wellingtons began to arrive for the same purpose.

No 5 (P) AFU had added Harvards, Oxfords and Hurricanes to its fleet and was now virtually a finishing school for fighter pilots prior to OTU. However, in May 1945 orders were received that the unit would disband in June and be replaced by 9 (P) AFU from Errol. This unit was to move into Tern Hill using Atcham as a satellite and be renumbered 5 (P) AFU. The new unit disbanded in April 1946 and was immediately replaced by 6 SFTS from Little Rissington equipped with Harvards and Tiger Moths.

No 24 MU was still very much occupied with storing aircraft and refurbishing spare parts and was joined in March 1951 by 30 MU from Sealand. The two units amalgamated as 30 MU on February 1 1959 and returned to Sealand. No 6 FTS now had the station to itself and still retained the wartime satellite at Chetwynd. The new policy of all-through

training on Jet Provosts forced a move to Acklington because of the short runways and 6 FTS left on August 4 1961.

Its place was taken by the helicopter element of CFS from South Cerney equipped with Sycamores, Whirlwinds and Sioux. The helicopters were transferred to Shawbury in September 1976, thus ending 40 uninterrupted years of training at Tern Hill.

The airfield is still in good condition and an excellent view of the hangars and control tower can be had from the A41. The Lamellas on the MU site are used for storage by civilian firms and one of the huge 'D'-type hangars is now a sports centre.

Tilstock (Whitchurch Heath), Salop

SJ560375. Bisected by A41, 3 miles S of Whitchurch

Three miles south of Whitchurch, the A41 trunk road runs straight as an arrow across a crumbling old airfield whose derelict watch tower gazes over it with sightless eyes. My father, who had been in Italy when it was active, thought it was a bomber base and it was many years before I found that this was partly true. The missiles, however, consisted of bundles of leaflets dropped from Whitleys and later Wellingtons over French towns. This was known as *Nickelling* and was part of the course at all night bomber OTUs. It could be dangerous and many an aircraft limped home with flak damage and, every now and then, one failed to return.

The airfield was built by Sir Alfred McAlpine Ltd and originally named Whitchurch Heath when it opened on August 1 1942. Its first aircraft were the Wellingtons of 81 OTU which arrived from Ashbourne a month later. No 81 was a three-quarter OTU but was brought up to full status in February 1943 with an establishment of 54 Whitleys, the Wellingtons being given up. The name was changed to Tilstock after a neighbouring village on June 1 1943, in order to avoid confusion with Whitchurch Airport at Bristol. Its function, too, changed on January 1 1944 when it was transferred from 92 Group to 38 (Airborne Forces) Group with a new task to train crews for the towing of gliders for airborne troops. A second unit arrived on January 22 1944, 1665 Conversion Unit from Woolfox Lodge in Rutland and, to avoid congestion, 81's airborne courses were transferred to the satellite at Sleap.

Mr M.D. Stimson, then a wireless-operator, was at Tilstock during this transition period and describes his experiences thus: 'I arrived at 81 OTU on October 25 1943 with a bunch of aircrew who were mainly from Canada and Australia. We were assembled in a large room, told to sort ourselves into crews and then left alone to do just that. Three days later our crew emerged and we started to fly Whitley Vs, a twin-engined antiquated bomber which had too much bomber and too little engine, resulting in over-heating and many single-engined landings. We did circuits and landings for a few days followed by bombing exercises, dropping 11 lb practice bombs from 10,000 ft on the Fenns Moss Range. Our bomb-aimer succeeded in knocking the centre light out at the range, for which he was congratulated for accuracy but chewed off for the inconvenience whilst repairs were effected.

'This was followed by six-hour day and night cross-country flights which involved running the gauntlet of our own defences because we were routed in and out of our coastline unannounced. In one case on a daylight trip we were fired at over West Wales and over Eire which we entered above cloud by accident. Our instructors were delighted as they considered such an experience worth its weight in gold.

'In January 1944 the RAF, in a sudden change of policy, decided that our whole course and its successors should be committed to Special Operations and Airborne Support so we were posted to the satellite at Sleap. We commenced low-level cross-country flights usually to the Cheltenham area where the navigation team had to find and photograph certain bridges and other small features. We also dropped one container in a designated field to simulate a delivery of supplies or agents to the Resistance, which is what we ultimately did.

'Our short stay at Sleap was a dismal affair due to a fatal crash and the loss of the Bombing Leader who accidentally opened the front escape hatch and fell parachute-less to his death. The site we

Tower and hangars at Tilstock.

lived on was criss-crossed with four feet deep trenches awaiting the laying of drain pipes, there was the black-out and we had little or no spare food. We last flew from Sleap on March 3 1944, went on leave and returned to Tilstock, which was now called 1665 HCU and operating Stirlings.

'We had the distinction of being the first crew to haul a glider into the air with a Stirling and, although scared to death at the time, I can now only wonder how it was done. Our instructor, a New Zealander, took the controls whilst my pilot read the instructions 'suggested' for towing over the intercom to him as we went along. The only completely happy and competent people were the glider pilots. On the next trip our pilots changed seats and on the third take-off we were on our own.

'The course was completed on April 21 1944 and, after a short spell with 1665 HCU Pool Flight, we were posted to a squadron. Life at Tilstock had its humorous side; for example after one night's circuits and bumps it was found that someone had overshot the runway, rolled through the barbed wire fence, turned left along the road to Shrewsbury and then taxied about 600 yards along it, passed the two hangars which are still standing, and then turned left to flatten some more fencing to regain the perimeter track. No one would admit liability and no aircraft had any signs of damage,

Stirling III as flown at Tilstock (via M.D. Stimson).

which was hardly surprising considering the size of the tyres and the fact that the fuselage was 22 ft above the ground at the front end. Another aircraft landing on the same runway touched down too far along it at night, crossed the A49 and finished up in the garden of a house which is still there.'

Four US Army General Hospitals had been set up within a few miles of the airfield in anticipation of heavy casualties in the imminent invasion. Mercifully, the number of wounded turned out to be much less than feared and the USAAF C-47s from France were only occasional visitors. Many other Americans landed, however, mainly Thunderbolts and Harvards from Atcham, either lost or with malfunctions. Four Piper Cubs came in from Worcester one day low on fuel and an A-26 Invader diverted on a flight from Warton with one engine stopped. During December 1944, on two occasions, Liberators from the 44th Bomb Group at Bungay diverted due to fog at their base. A total of 34 and 31, respectively, landed from operational missions to the Continent. Ground crew from Bungay had their Jeep stolen on Christmas Eve, later to be found abandoned in Shrewsbury!

Courses were held in July 1944 to convert Albemarle crews to Stirlings and the following month 1665 CU received six Halifaxes to form a Conversion Flight. No 1665 detached four Stirling IVs to Fairford and Keevil to help with supply dropping at Arnhem in September, two of

them being slightly damaged by enemy fire. Many Stirlings had been wrecked in accidents, usually because an uncontrolled swing on take-off often led to undercarriage collapse and a bent Stirling straddling the Whitchurch-Shrewsbury road was a common sight. The attrition rate was so high that the old Mk IIIs were replaced by IVs in January 1945. As late as March 20 1945, a Tilstock Halifax was shot down by an enemy intruder near Peterborough. The CU moved to Saltby in Leicestershire on March 26 1945 and was replaced by 42 OTU from Ashbourne. The latter had been Albemarle-equipped but was now to merge with 81 OTU and receive Wellingtons up to an establishment of 51.

The war in Europe was now almost at an end and efforts were to be concentrated against the Japanese in the Far East. The distances involved in this theatre were so vast that an efficient transport force was a necessity. Like Bomber Command before it, Transport Command now needed Conversion Units so that crews could make a smooth transition from OTU to front line squadron. No 1380 Transport Support Conversion Unit was therefore formed out of 81 OTU on August 10 1945 and continued to use Wellingtons and a few Ansons. The long runway at Tilstock was being resurfaced at this time, so most of the flying was done from the Sleap satellite. A popular part of the course was a trip over the Ruhr Valley in daylight to see the effects of wartime bombing. No 1380 TSCU disbanded on January 21 1946 but flying had been winding down for some time. When air gunners were deleted from the crews under training, the handful of Spitfires remaining for fighter affiliation were disposed of. Tilstock itself followed into oblivion in March 1946 when it was reduced to care and maintenance under Tern Hill. In the 1950s, it was used occasionally for Territorial Army exercises with support by reserve aircraft of the Royal Navy and Auxiliary Air Force. On one of these Avenger XB323 crashed on the edge of the aerodrome.

Many of the buildings remain today, some still in use. The three 'T2' and one 'B1' hangar were employed by the Home Office for many years for the storage of fire appliances. Sky-diving, usually with a Cessna 172, is done from an 800-metre section of the old 02/20 runway, the rest of the strips having been broken up. This was chiefly to prevent unauthorised motor cycle racing as most of the huge chunks of concrete are still there. The runway configuration runs counter to the normal wartime triangular pattern which was designed, amongst other things, to reduce the concentration of target, and guard against the possibility of a single bomb or crashed aircraft blocking all three at a central intersection. Also, the 07/25 runway was too short to be of much use to a heavy aircraft in anything but the strongest wind. Frying pan hardstands to a total of 31 were provided, together with an extensive bomb storage area to the north-east. A small concrete building on a hillock overlooking the airfield from the north was once the Battle HQ in the event of the staff having to withdraw from the main operations block, which can still be seen in the woodland adjoining the A41. The farmhouse which stands out on the aerodrome was used as a Navigation Flight Office during the war.

Towyn, Gwynedd

SH575015. On small peninsula just N of town

For the crew of a USAAF B-17 on July 8 1944 this tiny airfield was a life-saver. They were unsure of their position on a flight from North Africa, fuel was running low and the weather was closing in. They flew on up the Welsh coast until Towyn appeared. It was hardly big enough for a four-engined bomber but there was no choice. They almost made it but the Fortress trundled across the railway line and hit an air raid shelter, which caused a fire in the wing root. All 15 on board were unhurt and scrambled clear while the station fire party tackled the blaze with the help of the town Fire Brigade. The aircraft was 42-31321 CC-M of the 390th Bomb Group and had probably been one of those detached to Russia to fly shuttle missions between there and Italy during June 1944.

Towyn was established as a base for air co-operation with the Royal Artillery AA Practice Camp at Ton Fanau. The station was still in the process of opening up on September 8 1940 when a Magister flew down from Penrhos to warn of an Invasion Alert. Secret and confidential documents were prepared for immediate destruction by fire if necessary, but, as we know, it never happened. For some time it remained the only airfield on the Welsh coast between Penrhos and Aberporth and, on November 11 1940, a Beaufort of

217 Squadron on a flight from St Eval to Abbotsinch landed with engine trouble.

'U' Flight of 1 AACU equipped with Queen Bee target aircraft arrived in the autumn and 'C' Flight of the same unit brought its Henleys in from Penrhos. 'C' Flight became 1605 Flight on October 1 1942 and joined with 1628 Flight on December 1 1943 to form 631 Squadron. This unit was still using a few Henley target tugs long after similar squadrons had replaced them with Martinets, and only retired the last one in February 1945.

The low-lying aerodrome suffered badly from flooding and when 12 P-38 Lightnings of the USAAF's 97th Fighter Squadron force-landed on December 16 1942 one of them skidded into a gun post on the boundary. The fighters left for St Eval two days later leaving the damaged one waiting for a repair party. The squadron had been based in Northern Ireland and its final destination was North Africa where it was to join the XIIth Air Force. The poor aerodrome surface in the winter cut down on the number of sorties that could be flown and Llanbedr was often used instead.

No 631 Squadron went to Llanbedr for good in May 1945 and, on May 14, Towyn was transferred to 22 Group Technical Training Command but closed on July 25 1945. It became an army camp and Outward Bound School and the landing ground is now a sports field. It has, however, been used infrequently by Army Air Corps Beavers. The wartime hangarage consisted of two Bellmans, two Blisters and two canvas Besonneaus.

Valley, Anglesey

SH305755. Take unclassified road off A5, 1 mile S of Valley village

Valley's station badge, granted in February 1951, incorporates the Welsh Dragon holding a portcullis, the latter indicating the ever-open gates which it may claim to have maintained during its long period as a Master Diversion Airfield. Appropriately too, its motto *'In adversis perfugium'* translates as 'Refuge in Adversity'.

A more war-like role was envisaged when it opened on February 1 1941 as a Fighter Sector Station under 9 Group whose task was to provide cover for Liverpool, the Industrial North-West and shipping in the Irish Sea. Built amidst the sand dunes of north-west Anglesey, it was bleak and uninviting at first as there was little accommodation for the staff and even less for the aircraft. The original name of Rhosneigr was dropped in favour of Valley on April 5 1941. The first aircraft had arrived on March 3 in the shape of a Flight of Hurricanes detached from 312 Squadron at Speke.

At the time Valley opened, enemy air activity over this part of the country was still being conducted on a considerable scale and Valley Sector was served by a number of radar reporting stations strategically placed in the vicinity to give the widest possible coverage. In addition, there was a GCI station at Trewan Sands for which it was responsible.

The Hurricanes left for Jurby on April 18 1941 and were replaced by similar machines belonging to 615 Squadron. This squadron took part in four combats during its five months of convoy patrols. On May 4 a Ju 88 was damaged off Holyhead but got away and, three days later, another was hit over Snowdonia. Two Hurricanes fired on a Ju 88 west of Holyhead on June 27 but it was August 26 before the squadron could claim a bomber destroyed. This was a Ju 88 which force-landed in Eire after being crippled in a fight over Cardigan Bay.

Valley was also putting up night fighter patrols with a detachment of Beaufighters from 219 Squadron at High Ercall. On June 1 one of these sent an unidentified enemy aircraft into the sea off Aberystwyth. The night fighter squadron associated longest with Valley, 456, formed here on June 30 1941 as a Royal Australian Air Force Squadron with Defiants. It did not become operational until September 5 owing to a shortage of aircrew and all except a few were British at first, rather than Australian.

As a result of many accidents in the Irish Sea owing to the number of training aircraft now active in the area, 275 Squadron formed at Valley in October 1941 for ASR duties with Lysanders. The latter were joined later by Walrus amphibians, Defiants and Ansons.

No 68 Squadron, although nominally based at High Ercall, used Valley as an advanced base for many of its night patrols. In November 1941 one of its Beaufighters shot down an He 111 near Gwalchmai with one short cannon burst.

As early as September 1941 the airfield's good weather record had not escaped notice and it was requested that the 1,000 yard runway be lengthened for a future transatlantic ferry commitment. On January 11 1942 ground mist closed all the 9 Group airfields except Valley. This enabled a Beaufighter to take off and pursue a Do 217 all the way to Nuneaton before shooting it down. It was 456 Squadron's first kill after converting to Beaufighter IIs.

The day fighters were not having much success, however. No 242 Squadron left for the Far East in December 1941 after three months here and 350 Squadron formed on November 13 1941 with Spitfires. It was manned by Belgian pilots who hitherto had been serving in two Flights of 131 Squadron, reinforced by more Belgians who had escaped from the Continent. As most of its members were experienced it was soon operational on convoy escort but no action was seen until after the squadron moved to Debden in April 1942.

No 131 Squadron, now somewhat depleted, took time off for training but almost as soon as it had moved over to Valley from Llanbedr, Flight Lieutenant R.H. Harris and Sergeant Vilboux sighted a Ju 88 flying at 50 ft about 30 miles

Above left *Fortress 42-31321 after over-shooting Towyn on July 8 1944* (Public Record Office).

Right *Valley today* (RAF Valley).

south-west of Holyhead. The combat was over within minutes; the bomber pulled up sharply with its port engine burning, stalled and dived straight into the sea.

The ASR Squadron was now out almost every day looking for ditched aircraft. On one occasion an Anson crew were picked up from their sinking aircraft by an RAF launch. A Walrus landed alongside but the airmen had temporarily had enough of aeroplanes and preferred to place their trust in a surface craft!

On July 25 1942 a Lysander of 275 Squadron got lost on a flight to Andreas and had to force-land on a beach in Eire. Having satisfied the Irish authorities that they were on a humanitarian flight they were allowed to continue. By this slight distortion of the truth the CO of 1486 Fighter Gunnery Flight, then based at Valley, managed to escape internment!

As a result of this and other incidents RAF aircrew were briefed to have a suitable story to tell should they be forced down in Eire. Coastal Command crews should claim they were on ASR duties and, to emphasise the humanitarian aspect, state that they were looking for an enemy aircraft believed to have crashed in such-and-such a position! Bomber crews should be briefed to report that they had got lost on a training cross-country flight. The Irish were not this gullible, of course, but were remarkably liberal in their interpretation of neutrality, particularly if the German Ambassador in Dublin had not come to hear of an incident!

No 131 Squadron was having great difficulty in maintaining serviceability owing to the ever-present sand getting into engines and guns. For this reason its Spitfires returned to Llanbedr in April 1942, leaving only 456 Squadron in residence. In May its Beaufighters started a regular daylight patrol off Carnsore Point in Eire with a view to intercepting low-flying raiders. On May 18, whilst escorting a convoy in this area, a Beaufighter attacked a Ju 88 and claimed it as damaged. Two days later the survivors were picked up by a trawler and the kill was confirmed. A night victory was scored on July 30 when Wing Commander Wolfe sent an He 111 down to destruction on Pwllheli beach. No 456 Squadron was to stay at Valley until the following March, converting to Mosquito IIs here but not taking part in any further combats.

On August 23 1942 a Ju 88 was intercepted by a section of 315 Squadron temporarily stationed at Valley. Contact was made near Dublin and in the ensuing combat one of the Spitfires was hit and crash landed, the Polish pilot later dying from his wounds. The Ju 88 also force-landed with a dead gunner near Wexford.

Towards the end of 1942 Valley was selected to receive some of the heavy bombers due to be sent over from the USA. It was to remain under 9 Group's control but Ferry Command would use it as a lodger. To accommodate the anticipated increase in transatlantic movements in 1943 the runways were extended, new taxiways were added and 50 hard-standings were constructed. An American Radio Range for homing and instrument let-down was installed in March 1943, one of the few in the UK.

The Anglesey weather came into its own again on March 22 when six Lancasters returning from a raid over France diverted here when fog covered most of England. The USAAF's 414th Night Fighter Squadron brought its Beaufighters to Valley and stayed for some weeks to gain the benefit of 406 Squadron's experience. The latter flew Beaufighter VIfs but failed to add to its considerable score whilst at Valley. It moved to Exeter and more action in November 1943 after an eight months' stay.

From June 19 1943 the USAAF Ferry Terminal became operational and the first B-17 arrived on July 28 after a routine trip. The first Liberators appeared on August 17 in the form of 11 US Navy aircraft direct from Iceland. Medium bombers and transports were also handled, such as the two B-25s and three C-47s which arrived from Stornoway on September 12 and flew on to St Mawgan the following day.

The Valley Beaufighters were often called upon to act as shepherds to lost aircraft and lead them to the airfield. No 125 Squadron, which had just been posted here to replace 456, scrambled a Beaufighter on November 18 1943 to intercept a damaged Liberator which had been attacked by a Ju 88 over the Bay of Biscay. Inbound from Africa it landed safely at Valley. No less than 38 aircraft found a haven here on December 19, including such diverse types as an Airacobra, four Lightnings and six Thunderbolts from Maghaberry in Northern Ireland, a C-54 from Stephenville in Newfoundland and a Hudson from Wick.

With all this traffic and further runway extensions, the Fighter Sector Station closed on November 1 1943 and operations were transferred to Woodvale. This left only 275 Squadron which continued its ASR work until the following April and 125 Squadron's Beaufighters (replaced by Mosquito XVIs in January 1944) for air defence duties. After 125 Squadron left for Hurn on January 21 1944 the Station's efforts during the war were devoted almost entirely to receiving incoming aircraft from the USA and sending them to the bases in East Anglia. The USAAF Movement Section under their Air Transport Command handled the American aircraft whilst the RAF element took care of diverted British aircraft, but many joint facilities were provided and the two services worked in complete harmony for more than two years.

During the winter of 1943/44 the deliveries were switched to the southern ferry route via the Azores and Marrakesh to avoid the wintry North Atlantic. On February 18 62 C-47s flew in from North Africa but most of the arriving aircraft were B-17s and B-24s. Marauders were now becoming more common and the occasional C-87, the transport version of the Liberator, passed through. On one of these flights two British Army stowaways were discovered.

Their exploit was nothing compared with the bizarre happening on June 30 1944. A UC-64 Norseman appeared in the

Hunter F 6 XF384 of No 4 FTS (A.W. Evans).

circuit and then touched down on the grass across one of the runways and finally stopped. This unusual arrival was reported to US Operations and on investigation it was found that the aircraft was being flown by an American private who had stolen it from Warton and was heading for France when he ran into bad weather. The only glory this would-be pilot achieved was to be placed in the guardroom by the US Provost Marshal!

In the middle of 1944 there was a daily transatlantic C-54 service via Stephenville into Valley. On June 9 it brought in the Chiefs of Staff of the US Army, Navy and Air Force, all of whom travelled to London in the Irish Mail train from Holyhead. One of Valley's busiest days was September 17 1944 when 99 B-17s and B-24s were ferried in from Iceland.

On November 1 1944 No 1528 BAT Flight re-formed here with Oxfords. The Flight moved to Blakehill Farm on December 17 1945 by which time it had been re-named 1528 Radio Aids (Range) Training Flight because it was now teaching American Radio Range let-down techniques to Transport Command pilots.

The station's ferry role was reversed as soon as the European War ended and over 2,600 USAAF bombers passed through on the way back to the States for re-deployment, each carrying 20 passengers and crew. With the departure of the USAAF Movement Section in September 1945, Valley's activities were reduced to a minimum and consisted only of providing accommodation for the RAT Flight and facilities for night flying training for units

based at more congested stations else-where.

In June 1947 it was put on a care and maintenance basis but providing limited diversion capability. Many improvements were made to its buildings, thereby ensuring its permanence in the post-war RAF. From March 1951, when 202 AFS formed here with Vampires, it became one of Flying Training Command's most important stations and remains so to this day. No 7 FTS, and later 4 FTS, also used Vampires, the latter replacing them with Gnats and, more recently, Hawks.

Another unit at Valley was the Guided Weapons Development Squadron with Swifts and Javelins which formed on June 1 1957 being re-designated Guided Weapon Training Squadron on January 1 1959. The latter was re-named Fighter Command Missile Practice Camp on June 1 1962. ASR duties are in the capable hands of a 22 Squadron detachment with Wessex helicopters. A wide variety of modern combat types can be seen here as well as the jet trainers and a good view of the flying can be obtained from the public road.

Walney Island (Barrow), Cumbria

See Barrow

Warton, Lancashire

SD415280. On A584, 4 miles E of Lytham-St-Annes

In 1944 Base Air Depot No 2, as Warton was known, was so crammed with aircraft that two of the three runways had to be used for parking. The ground-crew dreaded a change of wind direction as it

meant that scores of aircraft had to be towed or manhandled to a new position.

The airfield was built originally as a satellite to Squires Gate but, as early as October 1941, before the USA had even entered the war, it was suggested by an American commission as a site for one of the depots required to fill the probable needs of their air force. It was near to Liverpool and well away from the vulnerable areas of East Anglia and the South East and in March 1942 detailed agreement was reached between the USAAF and the Air Ministry for its development as planned.

The first US soldiers arrived at Warton in August 1942 although it was not expected to be fully operational until January 1943. This target fell behind and in June 1943 the depot was only operating at ten per cent of its planned capacity. To meet the need for trained personnel VIIIth AFSC had suggested that it be run by Lockheed Overseas Corporation with American civilians, but USAAF HQ rejected the proposal as it planned eventually to man all depots with military personnel.

On July 17 1943 the airfield was handed over to VIIIth AFSC as Station 582. A shortage of the heavy equipment needed for fourth echelon repair limited output at first but things improved during the autumn even though Warton was still overshadowed by its neighbour at

Below *Warton today* (British Aerospace). **Above right** *Fortress 43-38190 landing at Warton in 1945* (G. Gosney). **Below right** *Bobcats, Norseman, Cub and Mustang on Warton flight-line in 1945* (G. Gosney).

Burtonwood. The overhaul of in-line engines became Warton's speciality in December 1943 and in January 1944 it really began to make its presence felt when over 800 aircraft were modified, more than half of them fighters.

BAD 2 reached its peak during the summer of 1944 when about 10,000 men were working round the clock on every type of maintenance, repair and modification. During two years of operation it handled nearly 10,000 aircraft, including 4,372 P-51s and 2,894 B-24s, and over-hauled over 6,000 aero engines. The 310th Ferry Squadron was on hand to help with the endless deliveries.

There is a sombre memorial to the USAAF occupation of Warton in nearby Freckleton where a Liberator crashed in a storm on August 23 1944. In this appalling tragedy 53 persons, including 35 children in the village school, were killed on the ground as well as the three crew of the bomber. The accident still ranks as one of the world's worst in terms of fatalities on the ground.

The airfield was handed back to the RAF on November 19 1945 and 90 MU became a lodger unit for storage until at least February 1951. English Electric acquired the base for Canberra test flying and it also saw the early flights of the P 1A, later to become the Lightning. Today the Jaguar and Tornado fly from here,

just one aircraft having equal destructive power to all those thousands of World War 2 bombers which passed through here.

The blocks of hangars are original but a modern control tower has replaced the wartime building which now serves as offices. The tall USAAF tower on its stilts was dismantled about 1949 and the main runway has been extended to nearly 8,000 ft.

Wath Head, Cumbria

NY295480. On A495, 7 miles SW of Carlisle

As 10 SLG this site was prepared early in 1941 to disperse some of the aircraft from 12 MU at Kirkbride. One of this unit's test pilots made two trial landings in an Anson on March 23 1941 and pronounced it fit for use. The first aircraft to be stored, a few Hampdens, were delivered on April 7 and a total of 36 machines were received by the end of the month. The SLG was used successfully throughout the summer, machine gun posts being built for defence against airborne attack. The autumn rains, however, showed up a defect in the drainage system which temporarily closed the landing ground until repairs could be effected.

In February 1942 a Halifax made an uneventful test landing in anticipation that large quantities of this type would be stored, and the following month some huts were erected to house a maintenance party. Also in March a team from Air Ministry investigated an allegation of sabotage at Wath Head but nothing was proved. The site was full of Wellingtons at this time and since it was the only SLG of those available to Kirkbride big enough to

accept Halifaxes, it was arranged that another SLG at Hornby Hall should take the Wellingtons. There was now space for Halis and the first landed on May 12 1942, fire-fighting facilities being laid on, an unusual refinement for an SLG, the local brigade normally being called upon in the event of an accident. One did happen on May 19 when Botha W5051 crashed on take-off, the pilot sustaining minor injuries.

No 12 MU began to handle Mitchells in June 1942 but it was decided that Wath Head was not suitable for aircraft with tricycle undercarriages. It was intended to close it down for the winter for extensions to the landing strips but it had to reopen in November 1942 because a sister SLG at Brayton became water-logged and unusable. Coastal Command aircraft were being received by now and it was pointed out that the white fuselage side finish was visible for miles from the air. This was a problem throughout the country and these aircraft had to be covered with camouflage netting to avoid giving away the positions of the secret dispersal fields.

Wath Head was improved and on March 4 1943 the first Mitchell was successfully landed here and many were prepared for squadron use during the rest of 1943. On January 12 1944 control of the SLG was transferred to 18 MU at Dumfries for Wellington storage and scrapping until its closure in September 1945. Little is left today apart from a few huts and there is no trace of the Robin hangar which once stood here.

Weston Park, Salop

SJ810085. Off A41, 1 mile E of Tong Norton

On the south-west fringe of the park which surrounds the stately home is a level area of fields divided by wire fences. The

Watch office bungalow at Wath Head SLG (J. Huggon).

only buildings left to show where the airfield stood are the small watch office, now converted into a cottage, and the former tractor shed. Others are now no more than heaps of brick rubble beside the lane.

The site was selected in October 1940 and was to be known as 33 SLG. Preparation took a long time and it was June 1941 before Spitfires were dispersed here from 9 MU at Cosford. At the same time a Wellington made a successful test landing and, by the end of July, 35 Spitfires were in store, probably taking advantage of the natural camouflage offered by the adjoining parkland which had been laid out by Capability Brown so many years before. No 27 MU at Shawbury were allowed joint use of the SLG from October 1942 but it seems doubtful if it was actually used by them. No 29 MU at High Ercall certainly did employ it in 1943/44 when this unit was trying to disperse up to 700 aircraft as widely as possible.

From early 1944 the SLG had a dual role as a satellite to RNAS Hinstock who referred to it as HMS *Godwit II*. The Oxfords of 780 Squadron were its main users. Weston Park closed in the summer of 1945 but air displays and balloon meetings have been held regularly in the last decade, although over the park proper rather than the former airfield. Apart from helicopters and hot-air balloons, no aircraft have actually landed.

Wheaton Aston, Staffordshire

SJ840150. 1 mile N of Wheaton Aston village

How are the mighty fallen! Pigs roam the control tower from which the operations of one of the RAF's busiest training units were once directed. By the old guard-room a trough of disinfectant is let into the roadway to deter the spread of swine diseases on car tyres. The airfield is now occupied by a very large pig farm and visitors are not welcome, particularly during the outbreaks of swine fever which occur from time to time in various parts of the country. Apart from the tower, however, with its 'VISITING PILOTS REPORT HERE' sign in faded letters, there are only a few original buildings to be seen and a single 'T1' hangar which stands across the road from the main gate is now used for storage. Where they have not been employed as foundations for the

pig houses, the three runways have been broken up and the perimeter track is a desolation of shattered concrete and rusty barbed wire.

Lying as it does astride the line of an old Roman road miles from the nearest town of any size, Wheaton Aston must have been an unenviable posting, especially in winter. It was built in 1941 intended as a satellite for the bomber OTU to be set up at Hixon but was taken over by Shawbury as an RLG on December 5 of that year. Runway construction at Shawbury had forced 11 SFTS elsewhere to keep up its training programme and courses were detached as far away as Ingham in Lincolnshire and even Dalcross near Inverness. This situation was highly undesirable and as soon as Wheaton Aston was nearing completion it was brought into use so that at least one RLG would be as close to the parent station as possible. The runways at Shawbury were not scheduled to be ready until April 1942 and the temporary occupation of Wheaton Aston by Oxford aircraft was to become permanent.

No 11 Service Flying Training School was re-designated 11 (Pilot) Advanced Flying Unit on April 1 1942 and would receive pilots who had come direct from basic training in the Dominions and USA. The original plan for a four-week course was found too short because of the familiarisation needed to cope with flying procedures and map-reading in Britain, as compared to the wide-open spaces and generally better weather of North America. The course was increased to six weeks in duration and most of the night flying practice was done from Wheaton Aston. Early in 1943 the AFU had grown to an enormous size with three Flights at Shawbury and one each at Condover, Perton and Wheaton Aston. Those at the two last-named aerodromes were by now almost self-contained units accommodating all course pupils, instructors and ground-crews, and aircraft only went to Shawbury for major servicing.

In order to make the school more manageable it was decided that a new AFU should be formed from these two detachments. This was 21 (P) AFU which came into existence on August 1 1943, 120 student pilots being posted from Shawbury during the following two weeks. The initial establishment of aircraft was 71 Oxfords, two Ansons and one Magister and the pilot training syllabus was exactly the same as before. Junior

Pigs guard the tower at Wheaton Aston.

flying was conducted at the Perton satellite, followed by a week with 1511 BAT Flight which arrived on September 28, and a return to Wheaton Aston for senior flying.

The swarms of Oxfords were joined on August 16 1943 by a USAAF Fortress from the 95th Bomb Group at Horham which landed short of fuel returning from a mission over France. The canal on the approach to one of the runways claimed a Thunderbolt on July 4 1944 when its engine cut at 3,000 ft over the aerodrome. The pilot nearly made it but undershot and crashed in the canal, fortunately escaping uninjured. Other unusual visitors included three officers of a Brazilian Mission who inspected the AFU in January 1944.

A second BAT Flight, 1545, formed on February 14 1944 affiliated both to 21 (P) AFU and 3 (O) AFU at Halfpenny Green. It was some weeks before it became operational and, on April 25, moved to Halfpenny Green perhaps because the circuit was slightly less congested there. No 21 (P) AFU was by now so busy that a second satellite at Tatenhill had been taken into use on February 1 1944. The aircraft establishment was 148 Oxfords and the actual strength almost reached this figure despite the inevitable attrition from accidents. When 19 (P) AFU disbanded on February 25 1944 its Oxfords were sent to swell the numbers at Wheaton Aston. The aircraft carried double letter codes to distinguish them and in the summer of 1944 one was noted with an unusual painting on its nose. This consisted of the reflection of a face in a cracked mirror but its significance is obscure.

During May 1944, 7,964 day and 2,873 night hours were flown, a staggering total of 10,837 flying hours. This is roughly equivalent to 15 aircraft permanently in the air for 30 days! In August the intake of pupils was 281, a further 220 being passed out concurrently.

This level of activity was maintained into 1945 but the end of the war in Europe reduced the demand for pilots and the AFU began to run down slowly, although there were still 120 Oxfords available. However, by February 1946, it had become clear that the flying programme's target of 8,000 hours per month was impossible to achieve owing to the demobilisation of ground crew and glued joint failures which grounded the Oxfords from time to time. The goal was reduced to 3,000 hours and aircraft were gradually withdrawn from service until only 71 were on hand in August 1946.

On October 25 1946 Aneurin Bevin, Minister of Health and Housing, flew in from Croydon in an Airspeed Consul en route to Stoke-on-Trent for a conference. This was the last event of any note because the AFU moved to Moreton-in-Marsh on December 1 1946, leaving the station to be declared abandoned on July 31 1947. Some of the accommodation was occupied by Polish families until they were re-housed in Stafford in the early 1950s. It was subsequently returned to the 'inactive surplus' list parented by Tern Hill and then passed to the control of the Ministry of Agriculture and Fisheries on September 22 1953. The Ministry set up premises for poultry progeny testing but the station was later sold to the same company who owned the old aerodromes at Lichfield and Church Broughton. The former was grain-farmed with the corn going to the pig unit at Wheaton Aston. What would the station commanders think of their pride and joy as it is now!

Whitchurch Heath (Tilstock), Salop

See Tilstock

Windermere, Cumbria

NY390005. On A591, 2 miles S of Ambleside

An area of outstanding beauty such as the Lake District is a most unlikely place to find an aircraft factory but, from 1942 onwards, Sunderlands were built on the shores of Lake Windermere. Shorts' main commitment was Stirling production but more Sunderlands were required to protect Britain's vital sea communications with America. The big flying-boat was already in production at Rochester, Belfast and Dumbarton, but more manufacturing capacity was essential.

What was needed was somewhere away from vulnerable towns but not too far so that labour could be recruited and the area chosen would have to be close to a large stretch of water, preferably inland or well sheltered for flight testing. Windermere met all of these requirements and, to ensure that the environment would not be permanently spoiled, it was agreed that the factory would be temporary. As soon after the war as practicable it was to be removed and in fact it was. In August 1940 three Singapores had landed on the lake to test its suitability as a base.

Flying from Windermere dated back to before the First World War and in 1917 and 1918 there are reports that a regular air mail service between here and the Isle of Man was operated by the Royal Naval Air Service to overcome the U-boat danger in the Irish Sea.

The lake was also the scene of some experimental flying by a water-based glider. Gliding had been introduced as an Air Training Corps activity in 1941 and it was suggested that inland waters might be used in areas where there were no airfields. A Slingsby Falcon was modified by the fitting of underwing floats and the addition of a water-tight planing hull below the normal fuselage line. A number of flights were made, the glider being towed off the water behind a motor boat, but the idea was not taken up.

Above *Lakes Waterhen on Windermere in 1912* (via J. Huggon). **Below** *Lakes Seabird over Windermere in 1912* (via J. Huggon).

A total of 35 Sunderland IIIs was built here between September 1942 and May 1944 and other aircraft were repaired and overhauled at the same time. Viewing was difficult because of the trees, as Mike Bowyer found even when he craftily went by on the top deck of a bus but only caught a glimpse of two Sunderlands! Production of the Shetland was also planned until this aircraft was cancelled.

The only trace of the wartime activity now is the name 'White Cross Bay' given to the Sunderland mooring area. It only appears on post-war Ordnance Survey maps and is said to have arisen because of the appearance of the white-painted Sunderlands from the other side of the Lake.

Wolverhampton, West Midlands

SJ900030. On NW outskirts of Wolverhampton

Aviation in the Wolverhampton area dates back to July 1910 when the Midland Aero Club held a flying meeting at Dunstall Park. Many well-known pilots of the day appeared, including Claude Grahame-White who flew a Farman. Boulton Paul opened a factory at Pendeford in 1936, their first product from here being the prototype Defiant turret fighter which flew on August 11 1937. The flight trials continued during 1938 but the second prototype did not fly from Wolverhampton until May 18 1939.

A total of 1,060 Defiants was eventually built at the factory, along with 105 Blackburn Rocs and 692 Barracudas built under sub-contract. The Defiant was successful at first during the Battle of Britain but the Luftwaffe soon found its Achilles heel—the lack of forward armament—and it was relegated to the night fighter role as a useful stop-gap until sufficient purpose-built Beaufighter night fighters became available.

Like everywhere else in the 1930s civic pride demanded an airport and Pendeford was the obvious choice, being already established. A small terminal building and hangars were built and the airport was formally opened on June 24 1938 by Flying Officer A.E. Clouston, a record-breaking pilot of the day. A flying display featured three Gloster Gauntlets of 46 Squadron, Amy Johnson in a Kirby Kite sailplane and Blenheim, Battle and Whitley demonstrations amongst others.

In 1941 the demand for pilots still exceeded the supply and efforts were made to open more EFTSs. Air Schools Limited at Burnaston, who already operated 16 EFTS were asked to open a second School, the site chosen being Wolverhampton. The new School, 28 EFTS, was formed on September 1 1941 under the control of 51 Group Flying Training Command, the first course of pupils arriving ten days later. There were 30 Tiger Moths on charge by the end of the month, a figure which rose steadily. The closure of 17 EFTS at Peterborough added 36 more Tigers in May 1942, bringing the unit up to its planned full strength of 108 aircraft.

They were divided into six Flights of 18 aircraft each and RLGs were essential to cope with all this traffic, so Battlestead Hill and Penkridge were taken over for the purpose. The latter came into use on June 19 1942 and all night flying was concentrated there until October 21 when demand led to night-flying being introduced at the parent station as well. The fact that there were no collisions in Wolverhampton's congested circuit is a tribute to wartime training methods. Things got really interesting around mid-day when dozens of Tigers from the RLGs all came back to base for lunch. There was no radio of course, only an airman with a Very Pistol to ward off any attempts by pilots to land on top of one another.

The endless routine of teaching men to fly was a gruelling task but there was some encouragement when one of the instructors, Flight Lieutenant Muir, was awarded the Air Force Cross on April 2 1942. During 1942, neutral Turkish Air Force Officers were sent for training to Wolverhampton as part of a contract that had been won only after secret negotiations under the noses of the Germans. It also necessitated Winston Churchill's personal intervention just as it seemed certain that Turkey would enter the war on the Axis side.

As the war drew to a close the School reduced in size until, by the time of VJ-Day, it was employed either in refresher flying for pilots whose postings were not yet finalised or in giving instructions to pilots of foreign air forces. The year 1947 saw a review of RAF training needs and it was decided that the remaining EFTSs should be transferred to the Reserve to provide refresher training for both pilots and navigators. Thus, on June 26, 28 EFTS became 25 RFS. Air Schools operated it under a new contract with the instructors and staff reverting to civilian status. The aircraft equipment was 12 Tiger Moths and one Anson.

The civil side of the field was soon active again when the Government lifted the ban on civil flying on January 1 1946, the Wolverhampton Aero Club forming with some ex-RAF Magisters. Many air displays and races were held here in the post-war years. At one during 1947 a rare Grumman Duck, NC5506M, belonging to Goodyear was a visitor. Wolverhampton Aviation, as Miles service agents, acquired a number of uncompleted Geminis and associated spare parts when Miles ceased trading in 1948. Five Geminis were assembled from these parts and sold between 1950 and 1952.

After a review of the whole system of private training, the Air Ministry realised that it was unprofitable to train National Servicemen as pilots because few stayed on in the RAF after their two years' tour and could only be attached to an RFS. It was also decided that all future training would take place at RAF stations and that the Reserve Flying Schools were to close forthwith. No 25 RFS was the first to go on March 31 1953.

To balance this loss, however, a Derby to Jersey (via Wolverhampton) service was begun in July 1953 using Rapides but the Wolverhampton stop was discontinued after the 1956 season. Boulton Paul built and tested Balliol trainers and also did taxiing trails with the BP 111 delta research aircraft but work on jet aircraft led the company to move its test facilities to Seighford in 1956.

Private flying thrived at Pendeford and the hangars were always packed with Austers, Tiger Moths, Proctors and other British types in the days before the invasion of Cessnas and Pipers from across the Atlantic. However, when Halfpenny Green re-opened in the '60s many private owners moved their aircraft there and so began a slow decline.

A tragic accident on April 9 1970 proved the death knell of the airport. Dove G-AVHW belonging to Dowty, who had a factory nearby, crashed into a house killing the two crew and a woman on the ground. There was a wave of local protest and the Council finally made the decision to close the airfield. It did not die quietly though, as aircraft were still using it illicitly until over a year after the official date of closure, a hazardous pursuit as old prams and bedsteads were hidden in the long grass! Pendeford will soon be obliterated as the intention is to build 3,750 dwellings on it to house over 11,000 people.

Woodford, Cheshire
SJ895825. On A5102, 1 mile S of Bramhall

From Avro 504s via Lancasters and Tudors to the mighty Vulcan in less than 30 years; such is the test-flying record of this pleasant airfield which stands right on the eastern extremity of the Cheshire Plain where it rises to meet the moors of the High Peak. It started life as little more than a large pasture, acquired two runways during the war, and ended up as it is now with an extension of the 08/26 runway to over 7,000 feet.

In 1924 the Air Ministry's lease on Alexandra Park aerodrome, one of the original homes of A.V. Roe, expired and the owner, Lord Egerton, sold it to Manchester Corporation on the condition that it would never again be used for flying purposes. A.V. Roe then bought some land at New Hall Farm near Bramhall and re-erected one of the Alexandra Park hangars on it. The newly-formed Lancashire Aero Club were invited to use the aerodrome and, in 1925, one of the first flying displays ever held in the North-West took place. On December 22 1926 a less orthodox event occurred when Avro 585 Gosport G-EBPH took off from Woodford and landed on the summit of Hellvellyn in the Lake District, taking off again successfully and returning to base. It was intended as a publicity stunt for Manchester aviation and a commemorative plaque is still to be seen on the mountain.

The Avro Avian was now being built and an improved model of the famous First World War trainer, known as the 504N, joined it in impressive quantities for the RAF and foreign air services. Final assembly and test flying of aircraft took place at Woodford and many of them were towed on their own wheels behind company lorries from the factory at Newton Heath. In the 1930s expansion of the RAF brought more benefits in the shape of an order for 287 Hawker Audax under sub-contract to Avro. In 1935 the prototype Anson coastal reconnaissance bomber, K4771, made its first flight from Woodford.

Many Blenheims made their first flight from here also, having been built under sub-contract but the aircraft which is chiefly associated with wartime Woodford first flew from here on October 31 1941.

This was the first production Lancaster, L7527, which had been converted on the production line from a Manchester. Avro's main factory was now at Chadderton on the outskirts of Manchester where the main components of the Lancaster were built and then transported to the airfield for final assembly. Metropolitan-Vickers also built them at a new factory at Trafford Park and these too were taken to Woodford for test flying.

A unique list of aircraft visiting Woodford between June 1942 and August 1945 has survived in the Company's archives and represents a fascinating cross-section of aircraft types from lightplanes up to fighters and bombers of the RAF and USAAF. Highlights in 1942 were Mosquito NF II DD627 from Castle Camps on June 30, an early Albemarle P1372 from Boscombe Down on July 24, and the rare Parnall Hendy Heck G-AEMR which called in from Ringway on August 14 (and visited again on April 24 1944).

Three USAAF C-47s, 41-7800, 41-7846 and 41-8347, called on August 24, September 27 and October 1 respectively, all from Aldermaston. They were probably visiting the Ordnance Depot which the Americans had set up at Poynton then just to the north-east of the airfield, but today within its boundaries. In September 1942 Poynton was assigned to Burtonwood in order to assist in the maintenance of aircraft for the ever-increasing numbers of bombardment groups being stationed in England. The following month it was removed from Burtonwood's control and made part of an advanced depot arrangement which would, it was hoped, meet more effectively the expanding maintenance needs. It is believed, however, that it reverted to a storage facility.

The only USAAF bombers recorded as landing at Woodford were Liberator 41-29366 of the 466th Bomb Group on August 16 1944 and a B-17 from A-81 airstrip in France on April 17 1945 and it

was 1944 before any more C-47s landed. Another USAAF aircraft in 1942 was Bell Airacobra 42-4555 from and to Coltishall on December 13. Training and liaison aircraft were common at Woodford throughout the war, the latter on business with the company, the former probably because the pilots felt like 'landing away' at random or giving a lift to someone from the Manchester area going on leave. At Advanced Flying Units in particular pilots were required to fly a fixed number of hours to complete their courses and any spare ones were taken up by cross-country trips. Favoured destinations were US bases in East Anglia where the food was as good as it was plentiful!

On May 13 1943 Lancaster ED906/G (the G signifying Guard as the aircraft was secret or fitted with special equipment) landed from Scampton. Only a privileged few knew that it was one of the aircraft to be used for dam-busting by 617 Squadron. Two nights later it went down in history as the aircraft flown by Flight Lieutenant D.J.H. Maltby which delivered the coup-de-grace to the Möhne Dam. A more mundane, but nevertheless interesting, visitor on September 23 was a Cessna UC-78 from the 482nd Bomb Group at Alconbury.

Moving on to 1944, there was a sudden influx of Grumman fighters from RNAS Stretton on March 21; two Hellcats (JV106 and JV133) and a Wildcat IV landed. Early in May a Cessna UC-78 from King's Cliffe, P-38 Lightning CG-C of the 20th Fighter Group at Wormingford and Stinson L-5 42-99525 from Heston were to be seen on the airfield. On May 5 an early Boston BJ474 originated from Benson and Speke sent another one, AX581, on May 27. Amongst all the RAF Oxfords a solitary USAAF example, T1109, called on May 28 from Scorton in Yorkshire where it was probably used for

Manchester L7287 at Woodford early in 1942 (via Harry Holmes).

C-54 Skymaster 'Aramis' at Woodford in November 1945 (via Harry Holmes).

communications by the P-61 Black Widow squadron working-up there.

American light aircraft called in quite frequently, examples being Piper Cubs 43-30109 and 43-29849 on June 17 and June 22, both from an airstrip at Swanwick in Derbyshire, another Cub 43-30393 from a strip at Abergavenny in South Wales, and a Stinson L-5 from Cranage on June 18. September saw some particularly unusual aeroplanes such as Fortress HB779/G from the RAE at Farnborough on the 8th, Mitchell FW139 from 13 OTU at Finmere and a Marauder from Rennes both on the 10th, Lancaster CF-CMV from Prestwick on the 11th and Mustang PB221 from Matlaske on the 29th.

Lancasters from operational squadrons and MUs throughout the UK made frequent appearances at Woodford but the rival Halifax was not in evidence until October 1944 when NP970 and LW625 landed from Foulsham.

Moving on to 1945, we find that a Stinson L-5 44-16911 from Warton visited on January 9, four Wildcats from Long Kesh on January 19 and Barracuda BV700 from Farnborough the next day. A Whitley called in from Beaulieu on February 20, as did Mustang 44-14367 from Wattisham on March 7, a B-26 from the same airfield on June 14 and Cessna UC-78 43-31966 from Hethel on June 19 and again on July 8. The last few known visitors from this period comprised BOAC Dakotas G-AGKA and G-AGHK from Ringway on July 24, Swordfish LS346 from Boscombe Down on the following day, and Hellcat FN353 from Filton on July 28.

The end of the war resulted in the winding down of Lancaster production to be replaced by the unlucky Tudor airliner which was destined never to realise its potential. The tragic crash of G-AGSU at Woodford on August 27 1947 deprived the nation of one of its greatest aircraft designers, Roy Chadwick, who was responsible amongst others for the Lancaster and the Vulcan which had yet to fly.

No 265 MU took over the Poynton depot in 1946 and used it for several years for storage and today it is still known as the MU site. The prototype Shackleton left the Woodford runway on March 9 1949, the first of many for Coastal Command. The prototype Vulcan flew on August 30 and the type is still Britain's main strategic bomber. Another winner is the HS 748 which is undergoing a sudden upsurge in orders now that fuel for the older piston-engined types is so expensive. Nimrods too can often be seen on the airfield and the factory is hard at work on the Nimrod AEW 3.

Woodvale, Merseyside

SD305100. On A565, 1 mile N of Formby

This pleasantly situated airfield is the RAF's only Lancashire base, which is perhaps why it has survived so many Service cuts over the years and continues to thrive. It owes its existence to the raids on Liverpool in the winter of 1940-41 when fighter aircraft were forced to use boggy grass airfields because there was nothing else available. By the time it was completed, however, the enemy had focused his attentions elsewhere. This was not, of course, envisaged in 1941 when work was started in converting a golf course and farmland into an operational aerodrome. There was great urgency in getting it finished and the first runway was ready by October 1941. When the station opened officially on December 7, the administrative and living accommodation was still incomplete and the first airmen posted in found living conditions extremely primitive. Water and electricity were still not laid on to the sleeping sites to the east of the airfield and many personnel had to be billeted in Southport and Formby until facilities were improved.

Woodvale was just about ready to accept aircraft when No 308 (Polish) Squadron arrived from Northolt with their Spitfires on December 12. It had been in action in the south for many months and was now taking the opportunity to rest and train replacements. This did not prevent them from looking for trouble because, on February 11, they damaged a Ju 88 over Lancaster and chased another without result on the 21st. Most of the sorties were routine convoy patrols protecting shipping in the Mersey Estuary and Irish Sea. No 308 Squadron left for Exeter on April 1 1942, to be replaced by 315 Squadron, another Polish Spitfire unit also from Northolt. During its spell on shipping cover the squadron damaged two Ju 88s and destroyed two others, one on May 3, the other on August 23. A detachment was sent to Valley to expand the area of coverage but no more victories were scored before it returned to Northolt on September 6 1942. No 256 Squadron had brought its Defiants over from Squires Gate on June 4 1942 for the express purpose of converting to Beaufighters at Woodvale. They were intended to supplement the night defence of Merseyside but there was only one serious raid after the May Blitz of 1941 so they were sent south to Ford on April 23 1942. Before they left, some Mosquitoes were received and at Ford the new aircraft totally replaced the Beaufighters before a further spell of one month at Woodvale prior to a posting to Malta.

Day fighters were Woodvale's speciality and, on September 5 1942, yet another Polish squadron, 317, came from Northolt with Spitfires to help with the Irish Sea patrols. This time they were unlucky and no action was seen before a move to Kirton-in-Lindsey on February 13 1943. Other activities during 1942 had included the detachment of part of 285 Squadron from its base at Wrexham. Its duties comprised target towing and anti-aircraft gun calibration over an area from the Point of Air on the North Wales coast to Formby Point and as far inland as Manchester. Oxfords and Defiants were used and from August 1943 the entire squadron was based at Woodvale and stayed there until November 19 1944, by

which time it was also using Martinets and a few Beaufighters and Hurricanes.

'C' Flight of 116 Squadron was also here between November 16 1942 and September 10 1944 with Oxfords for similar work to 285 Squadron but covering the north to Barrow and inland to the north of Manchester. The Royal Navy, too, needed target tugs and aircraft for other general duties so most of 776 Squadron, whose nominal HQ was at Speke, brought a mixed bag of Rocs, Skuas, Chesapeakes, Seafires and Martinets to Woodvale on May 16 1942. An unusual employment of the aerodrome in 1942 was for test flying by B-17 Fortresses after delivery to Burtonwood, which at that time had much shorter runways.

In February 1943 the Lancashire skies were split by a new and dramatic sound, the mighty Sabre engine of the Typhoon. No 195 Squadron was working up on this troublesome new type having first been based at Duxford, then at Hutton Cranswick. The aircraft used the dispersals adjacent to the railway line and an old farmhouse was taken over as a crew room. As at Valley the proximity to the coast accelerated engine wear because of sand ingestion and the Sabre engine had problems enough already. With some of its teething troubles over the squadron moved to Ludham on May 13 1943. Two days later, a second Typhoon squadron, 198, arrived at Woodvale for the express purpose of exchanging its Hurricanes for the new type. After a short working-up period, it returned to the south of England on June 5.

The second half of 1943 was notable for the formation at Woodvale of 322 (Dutch East Indies) Squadron, a Spitfire unit composed mainly of Dutch personnel. During its stay, it acted as part of the day fighter defence of Merseyside, although no contacts were made with enemy aircraft. Most of the scrambles were to intercept what turned out to be stray Allied aircraft, such as a Fortress over Liverpool Bay on July 2. The following day, four Spitfires intercepted 80 USAAF Fortresses off Southport as a pre-arranged exercise. Prince Bernhard of the Netherlands inspected his countrymen on August 7, arriving from Northolt in a Mosquito of 256 Squadron. The Dutch Spitfires went south to Hawkinge on New Year's Eve 1943, and joined the thick of the fighting.

The New Year saw yet another Spitfire squadron, 222, in residence for about six weeks having been withdrawn for a period of rest. Its place was taken by 316 Squadron from Acklington on February 16 1944, again with Spitfires. Another short stay was made by 219 Squadron which had been flying Beaufighters in North Africa. Their aircraft were left out there and new equipment of Mosquito XVIIs were received at Woodvale. The pilots made short work of the conversion and were soon operational, although their first victory on the new type was not made until a couple of weeks after moving to Honiley on March 15.

Although the airfield was already bursting at the seams with aircraft, it was presented with another lodger unit on January 10 1944. This was the so-called 'W' or Woodvale Detachment of 12 (P) AFU equipped with Blenheims. Its base at Spitalgate in Lincolnshire had wire mesh runways which were badly worn and causing tyre damage. The unit's satellite at Harlaxton was too small to accommodate all the aircraft so some were sent north. The initial detachment only lasted a month, the Blenheims going to Poulton, but they were not welcome there either and so returned on March 21. A lot of flying was done during the summer and one Blenheim, BA246, came to grief on the fells near Garstang where its remains can still be seen today.

The ranks of the target towing aircraft were swelled in June 1944 by 'B' Flight of 650 Squadron whose HQ was at Cark. It operated Martinets and a few Hurricanes and later Vultee Vengeances to help with the towing until the flight disbanded on March 26 1945. The ubiquitous 577 Squadron also got in on the act with a detached flight of Hurricanes, Vengeances, Spitfires and Oxfords between November 1944 and October 1945 when it moved to Barrow. The last fighter squadron to be based was 63

during July and August 1944 prior to a move to Lee-on-Solent. The build-up to D-Day resulted in a number of squadrons using Woodvale as a refuelling stop on the way south from stations in Scotland. One of them, 440, lost a Typhoon in a crash on high ground whilst en route from Ayr in March 1944.

As the enemy's threat to Merseyside was now almost non-existent, it was decided that the airfield would no longer accommodate operational squadrons. This had little effect on activity and the American takeover of the Palace Hotel in Southport as a Rest and Recuperation Centre ('Flak House') brought a varied selection of USAAF aircraft, ranging from liaison types like the UC-78 Brasshat to B-17s, B-24s and A-20s. One Liberator crashed on a foggy October day in 1944 whilst circling the airfield, killing five of the 20 occupants. At the end of the war, several hundred American prisoners-of-war were flown direct from the Continent to Southport for a brief rest before shipment back to the USA.

With the war in Europe about to come to an end, the airfield was handed over to the Royal Navy as a tender, or satellite, to RNAS Burscough. The rest of 776 Squadron repositioned from Speke which had become unsuitable for fleet requirements work now it had reverted to civilian control. The detachment of 577 Squadron remained as an RAF lodger unit. The first operational FAA squadron to be based was 889 which had disbanded in Ceylon on June 1 and re-formed the same day at Woodvale with Hellcats. On July 1, No 816 Squadron re-formed with Fireflies but moved to Inskip on August 11 to leave room for 822 Squadron to convert to Fireflies from August 28. Victory over Japan resulted in 889 Squadron being disbanded on September 10 and, shortly before that, 822 Squadron had moved to Burscough.

Blenheim AZ259 '48' of No 12 (P) AFU at Woodvale in 1944 (via R.C.B. Ashworth).

During its stay, a dummy carrier deck was marked out on one of the runways for the training of air and deck crews. The closing of the ground gunners school in the locality removed the need for 776 Squadron and it was disbanded in November 1945. The airfield was handed back to the RAF on January 28 1946 and, after a brief period as a motor transport depot, its next flying unit was 611 Squadron from July 22 1946 with Spitfires and Hurricanes. Early in 1951 the squadron converted to Meteors, which necessitated the main runway being lengthened to 5,600 ft, but it was then sent to join 610 Squadron at Hooton Park on June 9 1951.

The station continued to house several training units, namely 186 Gliding School with Cadets and Sedberghs, Liverpool University Air Squadron, and 19 Reserve Flying School. The Temperature and Humidity (or THUM) Flight operated first Spitfires, then Mosquitoes on a daily weather flight from Woodvale after the unit moved here from Hooton on July 13 1951. This involved a climb to 30,000 ft with repeated temperature readings at different height bands and reports on various other conditions. The aircraft landed at Speke Airport on the way back so that the information could be processed by the Meteorological Office there. Thus, the sound of the Rolls-Royce Merlin was still familiar over Merseyside long after it was a memory elsewhere. The flights went on until May 1 1959, after which radar-tracked balloons were used for the job—efficient but soulless.

The multiplicity of wartime co-operation units had gone long ago, their place taken by several Civilian Anti-Aircraft Co-operation Units. No 5 CAACU brought its Meteors from Llanbedr in December 1957, tasked to provide targets for all three services at the Ty Croes Range in Wales and at Benbecula in Scotland. It disbanded on June 30 1971 and since then only Chipmunks and Bulldogs and the aircraft of the Woodvale Aero Club have used the airfield regularly. They are kept in the two Bellmans near the road, all the original Blister hangars having been taken down long ago. Recently, the concrete rendering on the control tower was removed for renovation and a wartime plan view of the runways was revealed, painted underneath. This has been retained and makes quite an unusual feature. My personal memory of Woodvale is Count Cantacuzene, the renowned (and ancient) aerobatic pilot

performing flick rolls just above the grass in a Jungmeister at an air display in 1957. Against all predictions, he was to die peacefully in his bed many years later!

Worcester, Hereford and Worcester

SO855575. On A38, 2 miles N of the centre of Worcester

It was said that the Battle of Waterloo was won on the playing fields of Eton. The statement had a more literal meaning on the northern outskirts of Worcester where what is now a sports field helped win the Second World War. Hundreds of young men from all Britain and the Commonwealth were moulded into pilots at intensive training courses in the Tiger Moths based here. The small grass airfield hummed with activity morning, noon and night, seven days a week.

Perdiswell, as it is more commonly known locally, came into existence during the airport boom of the 1930s when every large town and city was keen to get itself on the aeronautical map. There is too a record of a flying display having been held here in the summer of 1914 when the site was a public park. It was, however, too small and too close to a growing built-up area, so grandiose plans for airline services were soon dropped. Light aircraft used it and Jean Batten and Jim Mollison were among the personalities who were seen here.

RAF expansion brought a war-like sound when the Fairey Battles arrived in 1938. Dozens of Austin-built aircraft were flown here from the tiny strip at Longbridge for pre-delivery testing and this was to continue for four years.

Perdiswell Hall, adjacent to the aerodrome, became the HQ of 81 Group Fighter Command and its Communications Flight was based here. On June 2 1942 the Tigers arrived when 6 Flying Instructors School became the resident unit. It had previously been known as 2 EFTS and had been at Staverton since August 1940. The airmen sent here had been selected for their above-average flying ability and were taught how to pass these skills on to other pupils as future instructors at EFTSs. No 6 FIS reverted to its original title of 2 EFTS later in the war but remained at Worcester.

In many ways the airfield resembled those in France in the First World War. The aircraft were not much more advanced and the pilots had to swathe

Hangar and huts at Worcester (W. Gibbs).

themselves in leather and sheepskin to achieve a little comfort in the open cockpits. Nissen huts and tents served as offices and 'B' Flight's time-keeper was originally housed in a garden shed. Mud and cold were constant companions and the only redeeming feature was that nearly all the trainees were billeted out in cosy private homes around the city. The Bristol Aeroplane Co operated and maintained the airfield and the mechanics worked with a will to keep the trainers serviceable, knowing that the enthusiastic young pupils would soon be on active service in far worse conditions.

In the summer of 1944 scores of wounded British troops were flown in from Normandy by ATA Argus and Anson aircraft. They were destined for the local Ronkswood Hospital, built by the Americans for just this purpose.

Flying ceased in 1945 and the field was de-requisitioned to the city council for use as a recreation area and has remained so ever since. In spite of the countless rugby and football goal-posts the odd aircraft has slipped in here in an emergency. The old hall was gutted by fire after the war and only a rusty hangar and some decaying Nissen huts betray that there was ever an airfield here.

Wrexham, Clwyd

SJ365525. On A534, 3 miles NE of Wrexham

By a strange twist of fate the contractors who once built this airfield were to take it over many years later for their company aeroplanes. The black shapes of Defiants and Beaufighters are now replaced by a single Beech Super King Air which comes and goes peacefully from the last remaining runway. The other two strips have succumbed to the voracious demands for hardcore for new roads. Almost all the wartime buildings have been levelled and on the north side where the tower once stood only a fire engine shed is left. It is a pity that no official plan of Wrexham seems to have survived but it was probably a typical 1941 fighter station with dispersal pens as at Calveley.

On December 16 1940, work started on the construction of an airfield on a plateau east of Wrexham. The builders were the locally-based firm of Sir Alfred McAlpine Ltd and, although the field was and is known as Borras to its neighbours, the RAF chose to call it Wrexham. The Luftwaffe were using a route which took them over the sparsely populated parts of Wales to attack the industrial towns of the North-West and the new airfield was sited to cover this approach. When it opened in June 1941, however, it was used first by the Blenheims and Lysanders of 9 Group Anti-Aircraft Co-Operation Flight who did not move in from Speke until August. No 96 Squadron had been promised it to replace their base at Cranage with its boggy grass and poor night flying facilities. The squadron had looked forward to the move for months so they could operate from hard runways, as well as the prospect of Wrexham Lager, a local brew which, by some quirk of the law, evaded excise tax until quite recently! Two Hurricanes and 14 Defiants flew in from Cranage on October 21 1941, the airfield now being fully completed. Up to May 1941 the squadron had been very successful in shooting down enemy bombers but the trade was now poor as most were now transferred to Russia.

The respite was taken up with converting the pilots to the Beaufighter, a very different animal from their beloved Defiant. The first step was the acquisition of a few Oxfords for twin conversion and some Blenheims with dual controls to acclimatise them to more powerful aircraft. During this interlude, 96 Squadron scored its only kill at Wrexham when one of the Defiants shot down a broken-away barrage balloon! The first Beaufighter II arrived on the station on May 2 1942 and to the CO's pleasant surprise compared favourably with the Mk I and was by no means the killer that it was reputed to be. The Duke of Kent inspected the squadron and the lodger unit, 285 Squadron, on May 5 and on May 17 a show was put on for the Royal Observer Corps. A Mosquito from Sealand demonstrated, as did a Wellington from Hawarden and Beaufighters, Defiants, Hurricanes, Spitfires and other types were to be seen on the airfield. The transition to the Beau was marred by one accident when T3414 failed to get airborne, ran across the road on the northern boundary and finished up in a pond where it burned out. Fortunately, the crew scrambled out unhurt, a tribute to the aircraft's great strength.

The Defiant, meanwhile, had kept the squadron operational with precautionary patrols in case any enemy aircraft ventured further north and on one occasion a Beaufighter was given a vector towards a 'Bandit' in the Crewe area but failed to make contact. The first proper Beaufighter patrol took place on June 30 1942, followed by many others in July without result. The visit of the King and Queen to High Ercall on July 16 was covered by a standing patrol over Wrexham. Enemy activity was now much farther south and it was decided to reposition 96 Squadron at Honiley for the defence of the West Midlands. The move was accomplished in September at the price of one Beaufighter and its crew in a take-off crash at Wrexham.

Wrexham's other resident at this time was an unglamorous co-operation unit, 285 Squadron, which had formed from the previously-mentioned 9 Group AAC Flight on November 20 1941, equipped with seven Hudsons, four Blenheims and six Lysanders. Some Defiants were allotted for target towing and small detachments were at Woodvale and Honiley from time to time. On October 29 1942, the squadron HQ became Honiley but one Oxford and four Defiants were retained at Wrexham. Apart from these and occasional visitors like a USAAF C-47 which came to investigate the crash of a similar aircraft in the nearby hills, this excellent aerodrome was now denuded of aircraft.

However, plans were afoot and, after a brief occupation in February 1943 by the personnel of 121 Airfield, it was transferred from Fighter Command to Flying Training Command as a satellite of Cranage. Three weeks later it was passed to Tern Hill whose 5 (P) AFU sent some Masters there until May 4 1943 when it was taken over by 17 (P) AFU as a satellite of Calveley. This unit had over 170 Masters on strength and the skies over Cheshire and North Wales were rarely free from the sight and sound of at least one of them. It was not to last, however, because once 17 (P) AFU had performed its task of turning out several hundred embryo pilots, it was disbanded on February 1 1944. Calveley was then occupied by 11 (P) AFU with Wrexham remaining the satellite but this time operating Oxfords of the (P) AFU's 'B' Squadron which was formerly at Condover.

There were now over 130 Oxfords at the two stations and accidents were common, the most dramatic occurring on July 26 1944 when HM748 and ED281 collided in mid-air over Cheshire. The tail of ED281 was struck by the other aircraft which crashed out of control but the pilot of the former, Flight Lieutenant D. Fopp, managed to land his Oxford safely at Wrexham. This was a magnificent feat of airmanship as only a few square feet of the elevators were left and a considerable portion of the tailplane had been torn away as well. He was later awarded the Air Force Cross for saving the aircraft.

A change of policy in December 1944 saw 11 (P) AFU converting to single engine training and Masters returned to Wrexham for a brief period before being replaced by Harvards. 'E', 'F', 'G' and 'H' Flights were at the satellite and the local inhabitants had their first introduction to the unique sound of this American trainer. The AFU disbanded on June 21 1945 and Wrexham was then used by 5355 Airfield Construction Wing to assemble plant and equipment preparatory to shipment overseas. Still flying was a detachment of 577 Squadron (formerly a Flight of 6 AACU) with Oxfords and a few Spitfire XVIs. It had been a lodger unit since early in 1943 and soon after it departed for Atcham the airfield was reduced to care and maintenance.

Wrexham is an amalgamation of many characteristic airfields in the area covered by this book. Built as a fighter base but hardly used in this role before it was taken over for training, it has been almost totally obliterated since the war. The remaining runway, however, is still in use for flying and maintains a link with the past.

Index of units referred to in the text

Royal Air Force

SQUADRON
5 - 128
10 - 191
13 - 45, 92, 101, 174
20 - 114
22 - 200
26 - 120, 127
32 - 35, 61, 127
38 - 141
41 - 92, 114
48 - 60, 101
58 - 46, 154, 156
61 - 174
63 - 47, 178, 211
64 - 147
65 - 149
68 - 77, 92, 197
74 - 38, 114
75 - 60, 178
78 - 147, 191
79 - 47, 76, 126
88 - 168
92 - 126
93 - 33
96 - 67, 213, 178
116 - 102, 210
125 - 76, 198
129 - 114
130 - 34
131 - 38, 114, 191, 197
144 - 174
152 - 35
166 - 105
173 - 89
195 - 114, 210
198 - 210
201 - 130
206 - 101, 154
210 - 129

215 - 105, 169, 178
217 - 60
219 - 197, 211
220 - 154
222 - 210
228 - 120
229 - 120, 175
230 - 129
232 - 39, 114
234 - 34, 47
236 - 61
238 - 61
242 - 197
247 - 92
248 - 61
253 - 147
255 - 92
256 - 127, 179, 210
257 - 92
258 - 105
263 - 34, 35, 90
264 - 77, 147
275 - 34, 197
281 - 77
282 - 77
285 - 176, 210, 214
296 - 149
302 - 105, 114
303 - 175
304 - 73, 185, 186
306 - 92, 175, 191
307 - 77, 105, 178
308 - 179, 210
310 - 34
311 - 73, 185, 186
312 - 35, 76, 105, 114, 173, 179, 196
315 - 175, 198, 210
316 - 127, 211
317 - 76, 210
320 - 60

321 - 60
322 - 210
350 - 38, 197
403 - 191
406 - 198
421 - 34, 35
452 - 33
456 - 77, 197, 198
457 - 33, 105
461 - 35, 129, 130
502 - 46, 101, 154, 156
504 - 76
517 - 46, 154
535 - 92
536 - 77
577 - 40, 42, 45, 89, 126, 161, 166, 211, 214
587 - 62, 133
595 - 32, 33, 47, 62, 77, 128
600 - 76
609 - 74
610 - 100, 102
611 - 102, 135, 174, 191, 212
613 - 147, 150
614 - 116, 131
615 - 35, 76, 197
631 - 114, 196
650 - 45, 63, 211
663 - 102, 116

FLIGHTS
3 CP - 99
4 CP - 99
9 Gp AAC - 176, 213, 214
9 Gp Comm - 157
19 Gp Comm - 61
25 Gp Comm - 192
81 Gp Comm - 212
1353 TT - 171
1429 COT - 64, 171
1447 - 62, 102
1456 - 92
1486 FG - 198
1511 BAT - 204
1515 BAT - 138, 142
1521 RAT - 120
1528 BAT - 199
1531 BAT - 69, 70
1534 BAT - 164
1545 BAT - 82, 204
1605 - 196
1606 - 45
1607 - 32
1608 - 32
1609 - 32

1614 - 62
1620 - 45
1628 - 196
THUM - 212

USAAF

GROUPS
1 FG - 92
2 ADG - 56
7 ADG - 56
14 FG - 39
21 ADG - 56
31 FG - 39, 92
495 FTG - 40
2906 OTG - 40

SQUADRONS
14 LS - 69
27 FS - 92
48 FS - 114
49 FS - 114
53 WRS - 54
92 FS - 92
309 FS - 92
310 FS - 57, 201
311 FS - 57
414 NFS - 198

*MISCELLANEOUS
UNITS*
6th Fighter Wing - 39
2025 Gunnery Flt - 114

US Navy
VP-63 - 129

*MISCELLANEOUS
UNITS*
1 AACU - 32, 45, 61, 62,
  107, 121, 179, 196
6 AACU - 45, 126, 143, 147,
  160, 164
8 AACU - 120, 132
1 AAU - 174
7 AAU - 101
2 ACHU - 118
3 ACHU - 128
5 ACHU - 59
21 ACHU - 135
5355 ACW - 214
8 AEF - 166
202 AFS - 125, 200
AFEE - 149
10 AFTS - 141
1 AGS - 127, 128
3 AGS - 40, 124

7 AGS - 146, 181
9 AGS - 118
10 AGS - 40
11 AGS - 34, 106
AHBS - 105
5 ANS - 106
6 ANS - 113
3 AONS - 78, 107
6 AONS - 114
2 AOS - 124
3 AOS - 81
5 AOS - 105
6 AOS - 32
9 AOS - 134
4 APC - 62, 156, 186
11 APC - 77
18 APC - 77
3 ASU - 159
4 ASU - 190
5 ATC - 90, 134
5 ATS - 105
9 ATS - 180
3 BFTS - 51
2 B & GS - 123
7 B & GS - 180
9 B & GS - 134
Birmingham UAS - 166
5 CAACU - 114, 212
CCDU - 35, 72, 102, 130
CCGP - 169
CFS - 63, 192
CLE - 148
CLS - 148
CNCS - 166
CNS - 58, 69, 164
EANS - 166
2 EFTS - 212
5 EFTS - 123
15 EFTS - 52, 107
16 EFTS - 32, 43, 50, 51,
  123, 187, 206
19 EFTS - 160
24 EFTS - 114
28 EFTS - 133, 122, 206
30 EFTS - 43, 50
17 E&RFTS - 42
30 E&RFTS - 50
38 E&RFTS - 107
6 FIS - 212
5 FP - 171
2 FPP - 132
3 FPP - 88, 147
4 FPP - 88
9 FPP - 88
12 FPP - 66

14 FPP - 147
16 FPP - 109
1 FPU - 122, 123
4 FTS - 125, 200
5 FTS - 158
6 FTS - 63, 192
7 FTS - 200
10 FTS - 134, 190
303 FTU - 73, 186
306 FTU - 189
1 FU - 141
4 FU - 89
11 FU - 186
93 GIP - 64
186 GS - 212
631 GS - 89, 101
633 GS - 57, 67
5 GTS - 44, 126, 166, 168
1332 HCU - 120
1665 HCU - 193
1674 HCU - 77, 119
23 HGCU - 138, 161, 162
1 ITS - 106
40 ITW - 181
90 ITW - 69
Liverpool UAS - 102
MSFU - 175, 176
Maintenance Units
5 MU - 44
9 MU - 50, 66, 203
12 MU - 47, 108, 202
14 MU - 107
16 MU - 48, 98
18 MU - 202
19 MU - 63, 152, 154
20 MU - 44
21 MU - 32, 187
22 MU - 102, 103, 170
24 MU - 99, 191
25 MU - 82, 168
27 MU - 84, 94, 99, 130,
  164, 203
28 MU - 38
29 MU - 50, 90, 188, 203
30 MU - 157, 160, 161
32 MU - 153
34 MU - 126, 168
36 MU - 160
37 MU - 54, 94, 99, 110
38 MU - 44, 63, 115, 152
43 MU - 131
47 MU - 89, 160
48 MU - 45, 86, 88, 110
51 MU - 98, 110, 112, 188
52 MU - 132

78 MU - 36, 130
82 MU - 113
90 MU - 201
99 MU - 113
214 MU - 146
236 MU - 66
245 MU - 48
249 MU - 78
265 MU - 209
276 MU - 57

3 OADU - 186
2 (O) AFU - 124
3 (O) AFU - 81, 204
8 (O) AFU - 125
9 (O) AFU - 90, 118, 135, 192
3 OAPU - 115
228 OCU - 47
Operational Training Units
1 OTU - 108, 170, 174
3 OTU - 84, 153, 189
6 OTU - 77, 78, 119, 170, 189
7 OTU - 84, 86, 153
8 OTU - 47, 85, 189
9 OTU - 52, 70, 119, 120
23 OTU - 74, 140
27 OTU - 64, 110, 111, 112, 187
30 OTU - 97, 162
41 OTU - 88, 142
42 OTU - 37, 38, 74, 195
53 OTU - 63, 115, 154
55 OTU - 77, 108, 119
57 OTU - 46, 86, 88, 142
58 OTU - 88, 142
59 OTU - 70, 119
60 OTU - 92
61 OTU - 125, 143, 145
81 OTU - 37, 48, 74, 172, 173, 193
83 OTU - 137, 138
109 OTU - 70

5 (P) AFU - 40, 46, 58, 63, 65, 125, 187, 191, 214
11 (P) AFU - 54, 59, 64, 65, 69, 126, 141, 164, 203, 214
12 (P) AFU - 70, 98, 142, 211
15 (P) AFU - 187
17 (P) AFU - 58, 214
21 (P) AFU - 138, 141, 142, 162, 163, 187

PAU - 122
1 PTS - 141, 149, 188, 203, 204
4 RDFS - 62
2 RFS - 43
3 RFS - 133
15 RFS - 107
16 RFS - 51
19 RFS - 102
25 RFS - 206
4 RFU - 85
104 RFU - 113
RRE - 76
3 Radio School - 102
4 RS - 120
10 RS - 62, 102
11 RS - 102
12 RS - 84, 153, 189
2 SAN - 67, 69
S of ASR - 179
5 SFTS - 38, 63, 113, 160, 191
11 SFTS - 46, 137, 141, 164, 203
22 SFTS - 59
3 SGR - 178, 179
1 SPTU - 62
2 STT - 67
3506 SU - 45
4 TDS - 100
9 TDS - 164
13 TDS - 190
51 TDS - 158
3 TEU - 77, 142
4 TEU - 77
TFU - 74
1380 TSCU - 173, 195
1383 TSCU - 72, 120
1 TWU - 47
Wales UAS - 154

Royal Navy

SQUADRONS
701 - 101
702 - 95
705 - 151
707 - 52
710 - 151
713 - 151
728B - 184
734 - 95
735 - 52, 104
736B - 176
737 - 52, 104
739 - 95

747 - 104
758 - 95, 139
760 - 104
762 - 73
763 - 104
764 - 110
766 - 104
767 - 184
772 - 33, 37, 54
772B - 34
776 - 54, 151, 176, 210, 211
780 - 95, 139, 203
784 - 73
790 - 73
794 - 35, 73
798 - 95
801 - 37
806 - 47
807 - 47, 52, 184
808 - 52, 88
809 - 52
810 - 52, 182
813 - 37, 104, 184
816 - 104, 211
822 - 52, 151, 211
827 - 182
835 - 52
838 - 104
846 - 52
860 - 37
861 - 37
879 - 52
885 - 88
887 - 52
888 - 52
889 - 211
894 - 52
896 - 52
897 - 182
898 - 47
1771 - 52
1772 - 52
1791 - 104
1792 - 104
1820 - 52
1831 - 184
1833 - 182
1836 - 52
1840 - 52
1841 - 184

MISCELLANEOUS UNITS
1 ARDU - 36
7582 Flt - 95